Teaching English Online

to Young Learners:

100 FAQs

Dr. Jun Liu
et al.

Teaching English Online to Young Learners: 100 FAQs

by Dr Jun Liu et al.

ISBN: 9781625753168

Library of Congress Control Number: 2020949597

First Edition

First Printing: October 2020

Printed in China

Phoenix Tree Publishing Inc.

5660 N. Jersey Ave · Chicago, IL 60659

Phone: 773.250.0707 · Fax: 773.250.0808

Email: marketing@phoenixtree.com

For information about special discounts for bulk purchases,

please contact the publisher at the address above.

Find out more about Phoenix Tree Publishing at

www.phoenixtree.com

Teaching English Online to Young Learners: 100 FAQs

▶ Introduction

Globalization and technological innovation are redefining the field of English language teaching with regard to teacher preparation, teaching methodology, curricula development, course design, and assessment and evaluation, among others. What was impossible a few years ago is reality today. Teachers do not need to travel to another country to teach English to kids worldwide, nor do they need to leave home to teach English in regular schools or classrooms. Likewise, teachers' living rooms or children's bedrooms are transformed into virtual classrooms. The inevitable change to remote learning has altered the conventional classroom as we know it. It puts extra pressure on language teachers to figure out how we can teach communicatively, interact with students meaningfully, engage students in group activities and collaborative learning, and more importantly, ensure personalized learning.

This change has also created unprecedented opportunities for us to embrace an energizing adoption of new technologies to support online language education; to seek an unavoidable revolution of pedagogical solutions to online language learning; and to align curricula, tasks, and activities with self-paced learning, both synchronously and asynchronously, to maximize language-learning efficacy. Nevertheless, the most crucial factor to ensure effectiveness is English language teachers whose passion towards, knowledge about, and skills in online teaching will directly impact the ultimate learning outcome of language learners.

As such, teacher education or teacher development, fundamental to success in language education, now has new implications for online teaching. English language teachers are essential in providing effective English language instruction and facilitating students' learning. Teacher readiness for online teaching in terms of what they should know, think, believe, and do is critical because it not only involves teachers' mental preparedness, including their underlying rationale for online teaching practices, but also influences how they choose to do what they do to make online learning accountable.

Switching from teaching English in regular classrooms to teaching through an online platform has urged us to actively address the new challenges as well as the potential we face. Expanding the scope of language teacher education to online particularities and characteristics has allowed us to explore the newly emerging framework of language teacher knowledge and skills necessary for success in online language teaching.

This emerging framework of teacher knowledge and skills for successful online language instruction calls for several critical dimensions that are intertwined and interconnected. Knowledge and skills are now blurred and enhanced by technology. For instance, second language acquisition theories are no longer taught and understood in isolation from one another. They will be reflected in teaching principles and methodology that are prompted or facilitated by online teaching technology and further shaped and determined by the learners' cultural and linguistic backgrounds. After seven years of successful online English language education, VIPKid International, a pioneer global education technology company, for example, has connected more than 700,000 young learners in China with approximately 100,000 teachers in North America for real-time online education (about 200,000 online classes daily) and has inspired and empowered children and teachers alike.

Lying at the heart of this innovative enterprise are our teachers, the most passionate and mission-driven teachers, who are active in this global classroom where they connect cultures, spark lifelong and joyful learning experience for the kids, and motivate learners to learn English from early on to aspire to become global citizens.

As someone who has devoted his life to English language education by serving as Professor of Linguistics and Applied Linguistics in universities in the United States, past President of TESOL International, and most recently, Chief Academic Officer at VIPKid International, I had the opportunity to visit many online English teachers. I observed their on-line teaching; watched their interaction with their learners and learners' parents; and interviewed them to learn about their challenges and difficulties, their passion and enthusiasm, their strategies and techniques, and their needs and wants. A question that has remained in my mind is what I can do to help these teachers renew their skills, replenish their knowledge, and recharge their batteries to become successful online English teachers.

The search for an answer to this question has resulted in this book—*Teaching English Online to Young Learners: 100 FAQs.*

This book aims to provide English language teachers with solutions to commonly occurring problems or challenges in online teaching. In order to make this book more useful and practical, we have conducted both teacher surveys and teacher interviews over the years, and we have collected more than several hundred cases with problems and challenges online English teachers often encounter. We have carefully chosen 100 of the most representative cases for analysis based on four themes: namely, second language acquisition theories, teaching principles and methodology, the tools and functions of technology in language teaching, and Chinese children's learning styles and parental and societal expectations. We have carefully selected each case to contextualize the teaching scenario in which we clearly spell out problems, difficulties, or challenges via a key question. We then analyze the situation with explanations, interpretations, justifications, and/or implications before making concrete and practical suggestions or recommendations for our teachers. In addition, we added "Reflection" sections to enable our teachers to reflect on their own learning experiences or those of their learners to make connections, to think differently, and to make inferences to other related or similar problems they have encountered or will encounter. Each case ends with key references for those who want to dig deeper into the issue and become experts themselves as well as keywords for the ease of search.

We hope that all online English teachers can benefit from reading this book. In particular, those who teach English online to Chinese young learners, such as VIPKid teachers, will find it extremely relevant and useful, as the cases are derived from big data through hundreds of thousands of classes taught on this platform. For instance, commonly encountered problems or challenges in the following areas are highlighted in our case analyses: classroom & time management, pronunciation, vocabulary, oral skills, literacy development, error correction, teacher feedback, online teaching and technology, and Chinese culture, among others.

These topics are very relevant to language teaching in general, online language education, online curriculum, and online learners in particular. It is our hope that this book will become a desk copy for online English teachers who can find useful information and recommended solutions to the questions or problems they will encounter while teaching.

This book is the result of a collective effort by my team in the VIPKid Research Institute, the leading thought engine in powering research-based best practices in online education. First of all, I would like to thank Cindy Mi, founder and CEO of VIPKid International, for her inspiring vision and steady support for this project to empower teachers. In particular, I am grateful to Dr. Xiaoqiu Xu, Senior Director of Curriculum and Assessment, VIPKid International and Head of Academics and Research for the VIPKid

Research Institute for her great enthusiasm and direct contribution to this project by serving as a leader, and coordinator for the writing group that consists of Julie McGeorge, Senior Curricular Manager; Brandon Lambert, Curriculum Developer; and Rui Fan, Curriculum Specialist whose thoughtful analysis of cases and deliberations on useful and practical recommendations are commendable. Special thanks go to Wenqi Han, Head of Parent and Teacher Communications in the VIPKid Research Institute for her extraordinary work in exceptional coordination and efficient and effective communication to make this book a reality. I am grateful to Kevyn Klein, Global Director of Teacher Community and Hunter Kubryk, Program Manager, Teacher Experience, for their enthusiasm about the book and proactive planning to link this book with their social media network through the teacher community. Moreover, I would like to give special thanks to Wade O. Nichols, Senior Consultant of VIPKid International, for his contribution and meticulous editing of the book. Last, but not least, I would like to thank Mr. Hao Yun, Chairman of the Board, Beijing Language and Culture University Press, and Tony Shiqi Yuan and his team for their unwavering support in making publishing this book a priority. Without the concerted support and joint effort of this fabulous team, this book would not have been possible.

I hope this book will fill the void by providing food for thought for our online English language teachers in dealing with constant challenges, in solving daily problems, in reflecting on their teaching, and, after all, in making them better teachers.

Jun Liu, Ph.D.
Former President, TESOL, International
Professor of Linguistics
President, VIPKid Research Institute

▶ Lead Author

Jun Liu holds a Ph.D. in Second and Foreign Language Education from The Ohio State University, and has been Professor of English, Applied Linguistics, and Linguistics, respectively, at three major research universities in the United States. A past President of TESOL International, he is Vice President of TIRF (The International Research Foundation of English Education). Having published extensively and spoken widely in English language education, he currently leads the VIPKid Research Institute as its founding President.

▶ Contributing Authors

Xiaoqiu Xu holds an M.S. in TESOL and a Ph.D. in Educational Psychology from Stanford University. She has worked at VIPKid Inc., Pearson Inc., Stanford University, and Nanjing University. She has extensive experience in second language acquisition research, teacher training, language assessment development, and educational technology.

Julie McGeorge has more than 15 years' experience with Chinese learners of all ages and levels, including opening and managing schools in locations throughout China. She has also developed content for major assessment companies and publishers and works as the face-to-face instructor for a 120-hour EFL certification course.

Brandon Lambert is a curriculum designer and educator with a passion for pedagogy. He brings an interdisciplinary background in education, having taught diplomats and designers before developing courses for VIPKid learners. Brandon has an M.A. in TESOL from the Middlebury Institute of International Studies at Monterey.

Wade O. Nichols has worked in children's English teaching and teacher training for three decades. Having worked for Oxford University Press, Pearson Education, Disney English, Nickelodeon Publishing, VIPKid, and others, he is an author of 22 children's English courses. Mr. Nichols holds a Master's degree in Applied Linguistics from Columbia University.

Rui Fan holds a Master's Degree in Curriculum and Instruction. Additionally, she is a certified PreK-12th grade language teacher. With eight years of teaching experience, she focuses on fostering personalized learning of second language learners. Before joining VIPKid, she was a content specialist primarily responsible for curriculum development.

Debbie Dugdale, Senior Assessment & Curriculum Manager at VIPKid Inc, has multiple years of experience developing, validating, and researching language tests. She previously worked at Pearson, creating large scale computer-delivered automated-scoring four-skills language tests. She holds an M.A. in Linguistics with a Specialization in Language Teaching from the University of Oregon.

Amanda Mohan has 18 years of education experience. She began as a K-12 French and ESL teacher. Then she worked at Educational Testing Service in English Language Learning Assessment Development. She played an integral role in the design and development of TOEFL Primary as well as other ELL assessments.

Wenqi Han has more than ten years of experience in management consulting and project management, with a specialization in online English learning. She currently heads the Parent and Teacher Communication and Project Management Offices for the VIPKid Research Institute. She graduated magna cum laude with a B.S. in economics and finance from the University of Hong Kong.

Contents

Part 1
Case Analyses in Second Language Acquisition Theories

► Introduction

"Second language acquisition theories" sounds academic, heavy, and scary sometimes, as theories are usually not well-received by teachers whose primary focus is on effective teaching with approaches, methods, and techniques that can generate the best learning outcome. But whatever we teach and however we teach it, the teaching approaches, methods, and techniques are almost always linked to, guided by, or reflected in language teaching theories. Therefore, the issue is what fundamental theories English language teachers need to be aware of and understand and how these theories are introduced and applied to real practice. Given the particularities and characteristics of online English education to young learners, we have collected and selected a number of cases closely related to online contexts that are believed to be most relevant to basic second language acquisition theories. The analyses of these cases will be linked to one of multiple second language acquisition theories that will give you more justification and reasoning in doing what you should in dealing with challenges or difficulties in online teaching.

In this part of the book, we selected 15 cases that address common problems or challenges online English teachers encounter. The problems or issues in these cases are directly or indirectly related to second language acquisition theories. They relate to concepts such as acquisition vs. learning, first language (**L1**) influence, successful second language (**L2**) learning, **plateauing**, **fossilization**, error correction, recognizing language mistakes, providing **comprehensible input**, **noticing**, background knowledge, classroom language, repeated exposure, **comprehensive output**, **reticence**, and **language functions**.

For example, learning English in China is fundamentally different from learning English in English speaking countries, such as the United States, simply because English is not commonly used in Chinese society. But when Chinese young learners are taught by North American teachers online, and teachers do not understand or use Chinese for the medium of instruction, learners are forced to use English although they struggle sometimes. This creates an indistinct context between acquisition and learning. Therefore, second language acquisition (SLA), as a field of study, is a term that covers both acquisition and learning, as sometimes the two terms are less distinguishable due to interconnectivity in context, resources, international communication, and the role of English as an international language. Therefore, SLA is usually referred to as a systematic study of how learners acquire or learn an L2. When we talk about SLA, there are certain grounding principles we need to know in order to best teach a second (or foreign) language.

We might wonder how English as a second language or an additional language is learned? What goes on in the process that all teachers need to be aware of? There is also an assumption regarding the process of language entering the brain and how it is used to re-produce similar language spoken or written by the learner. While we do not know much about what happens neurologically for language acquisition to happen, there are some core processes we can "observe" or understand by deduction. Theories in SLA provide us such an explanation. There are four core concepts for the flow of information in language acquisition: input, intake, output, and interaction.

- **Input** is the language that is actually available to the learners (the teacher's voice, lessons, experience with other learners, experience outside of the class).
- **Intake** is that which has been taken in by the learner. An analogy is that input is the stuff on the store shelves, and intake is what you actually buy.
- **Output** is the language that the learner is able to produce, demonstrating what was actually taken in.
- **Interaction** refers to communication between the learner and other speakers (e.g., teachers and other learners) speaking the **target language** in real-life situations that facilitate L2 acquisition.

These four foundations of language learning, while stressing the importance of comprehensible input for language acquisition, emphasize that comprehensible input is most effective when learners have to use the target language to interact and communicate. During the interaction, learners must frequently negotiate for meaning. For example, one speaker in a conversation says something that the other does not understand; the other speaker will then use different strategies (e.g.,

rephrasing what they thought they heard or asking for clarification) to continue the interaction.

Another mystery or puzzle many English language instructors face is why our learners do not say anything when we repeatedly teach them English for a long period of time, especially for beginners. What is going on in their mind? SLA theory has an explanation. Teachers must be aware of the possibility of encountering learners who go through a **silent period**, a period of time in which the language learner does not orally produce language. It is quite common in children learning a second language and is especially prevalent among very young learners (VYLs), typically children between the ages of three and seven. It occasionally occurs for a shorter period of time with young learners (YLs) who may be in early primary school. A silent period can last from a couple of weeks to a year into the SLA process, depending on the child and their shyness, lack of confidence, previous exposure to English, and cultural influences. It can also result when a learner is actively processing the language mentally and is actually learning. However, it can be recognized when eye movements, physical actions, etc. indicate the child is mentally processing or has understood. It does not prohibit teachers from encouraging learners to produce the language using patience, friendliness, etc., and to allow them to take production steps when they are ready. It requires teachers to provide ample response time and encourage the learner to take risks and try to respond without fear of punishment. It can be overcome through the use of illustrations, multiple age and level-appropriate examples of new sentence structures with different vocabulary words substituted in, and repetition. It necessitates the teacher using physical actions and supplementary tools. In language acquisition, comprehension precedes production and is learned through exposure.

It is worth noting that parents often do not understand or may not accept the idea of a silent period and may want their child to begin speaking in English as soon as possible. For this reason, it is best to continue to help learners to emerge from their silent period as early as they can and help parents understand the concept of the silent period.

It is understood that teachers care about the learners' learning outcome, while parents are eager to know whether their children have learned what they are supposed to learn. But what is the learning outcome? Simply learning 50 words by heart does not equivocate to learning outcomes if they do not know how these words are used in context. Likewise, a learner answering all test questions correctly does not mean the learner is proficient in English. There is much more to measuring learning outcomes. SLA theories have given us benchmarks to measure communicative competence.

Communicative competence means being able to communicate effectively in a range of different situations. Perfect accuracy is not necessary; the key is how well the other person understands you and responds to your intended meaning. There are four sub-competencies of communicative competence:

- **Linguistic Competence**: This is knowledge of the language itself: grammar, vocabulary, pronunciation, and syntax (sentence structure). This was the main focus of the traditional teaching methods that will be discussed in greater detail in Part 2 (the Grammar Translation, Direct, and Audio-Lingual Methods).
- **Discourse Competence**: is how we combine words and sentences to produce longer, more meaningful spoken utterances (i.e., spoken conversation) or written texts (e.g., poetry and essays). While linguistic competence is focused more on words and sentences, discourse competence concerns how we piece them together meaningfully.

You might find that many of your students can create simple sentences but cannot take those simple sentences and engage in a conversation.

- **Socio-Linguistic Competence**: This is the ability to use language effectively in a contextually appropriate manner. It is a fundamental aspect of a more general communicative competence. Pragmatic or socio-linguistic competence is also reflected in choosing the most appropriate language to use based on the situation and who you are communicating with. For example, you might say to a friend, "Gimme your pen!" but this would be inappropriate to a stranger or your teacher, who would expect to hear, "Could I please borrow your pen for a moment?" A language learner might have perfect grammar, vocabulary, and pronunciation, but selecting the wrong formality level would be a major barrier to effective communication.
- **Strategic Competence**: This competency tends to be the one that people find the most complex. Strategic competence is what the speaker actually does to achieve effective communication, both verbal and non-verbal. Strategies include asking for repetition and clarification, paraphrasing or summarizing what you have understood, and using body language or other visual clues when you don't know a word or do not understand your **interlocutor** (the person with whom you are communicating).

It is important to point out that communicative competence is not only the goal for language learners but also the means for language learning and teaching. Only by understanding this can we look for methods and techniques suitable and effective for our learners.

Perhaps one of the most frequently asked questions by English language teachers is how to give students feedback. When it comes to SLA and corrective feedback, there are many different opinions and views on what it is and how to do it effectively with your learners. First, we need to define what it is for the purposes of this training. **Corrective feedback** is used, either orally or in writing, to correct student errors during a lesson and to reinforce the learning expectations. In later parts of this book, we will look at how to do corrective feedback with your learners. For now we will look briefly at some of the views on corrective feedback based on the theories we looked at earlier.

Early researchers believed that teachers are able to predict learner errors by identifying similarities and differences between the **L1** (first language) and the **L2** (second language). They would then be able to explain those differences and prevent learner errors. As the field of linguistics developed, there was a shift in thinking to the idea that errors showed that learning was taking place. This standpoint was soon pushed aside, as it was not clear if the errors were caused by L1 influence or from the learning process.

As Krashen's Natural Approach grew in popularity, his sequence of hypotheses led teachers through the language acquisition process to the **Affective Filter Hypothesis**. As the affective filter is raised, the assumption is that learning becomes more difficult for the learner. Corrective feedback probably raises the affective filter and so was discouraged. In Krashen's early years, he was not in favor of corrective feedback, but over time, there has been a shift to a more balanced view that included careful corrective feedback.

What does this mean for you, the language teacher? First, we would continue to encourage you to do some research on your own regarding corrective feedback and how to do it well. Second, this means that feedback is important. While most theorists have their positions on corrective feedback, it is fair to say that they all encourage some sort of corrective feedback on the feedback spectrum. Your

learners, the parents of your learners, and your employers expect that feedback is happening. Your personal experience probably tells you that learning happens not only through making mistakes and errors but also through feedback that informs you what you need to do differently next time. As we can see, the SLA learning process, the silent period, and communicative competence are just a few illustrations of SLA theories embedded in the 15 cases in Part I of this book. These theories are also interconnected and complementary to one another from different schools of thought and from various disciplinary vantage points. It is language teachers who will make the ultimate decision as to why you are doing what you are doing to make your learners learn well.

As we can see, the field of SLA has generated much research and theory development over the past 100+ years. There are a number of theories out there. For this book, we have selected a handful to give you a quick overview of a few of the most useful ones. You are encouraged to do more reading on your own using resources available to you, including the references at the end of this part of the book.

Question	Sub-Topic
1. How is learning a child's first language (L1) different from learning an additional language (L2), and how should that influence the way I teach?	**Acquisition and Learning**
2. How does my learner's L1 (Chinese) influence their English language learning, and how can I help?	**L1 Influence**
3. What are the common behaviors and attitudes of a successful L2 learner, and how can I encourage these behaviors in class?	**Successful L2 Learning**
4. How can I help a learner who seems to plateau in their language learning?	**Plateauing**
5. How can I help a learner work against fossilization?	**Fossilization**
6. How and when do I correct my learner in class?	**Error Correction**
7. How can I help my learner recognize their own mistakes?	**Recognizing Language Mistakes**
8. How can I provide comprehensible input in class?	**Providing Comprehensible Input**
9. How can I help my learner notice new language?	**Noticing Language**
10. How can I help my learner connect with background knowledge when reading and listening?	**Connecting Background Knowledge**
11. How can I help my learner better understand classroom language?	**Understanding Classroom Language**
12. How can I help my learner who struggles to remember language despite repeated exposure?	**Repeated Exposure**
13. How can I help my learner produce comprehensible output and avoid L1 interference?	**Producing Comprehensible Output**
14. How can I support a learner who is quiet or is hesitant to respond?	**Supporting a Quiet or Hesitant Learner**
15. How can I help my learner understand and use language functions in my lessons?	**Language Functions**

ACQUISITION AND LEARNING

How is learning a child's first language (L1) different from learning an additional language (L2), and how should that influence the way I teach?

Keywords
#acquisition #active #conscious #engage #language functions #L1 #L2 #learning #passive #subconscious

▶ **The Situation**

I have heard that learning another language involves different processes from learning a first or native language, and younger learners are more likely to pick up on language learning than older learners or learners who start learning an additional language later in life. *How is learning a child's first language (L1) different from learning an additional language (L2), and how should that influence the way I teach?*

Analyzing the Situation

- Some believe that acquiring our first language involves subconscious, passive processes in natural settings that are separate and distinct from the conscious, active learning processes in classrooms. These two processes are termed **acquisition** (subconscious, passive) and **learning** (conscious, active).
- Others acknowledge the difference between these two processes, but emphasize that both can occur in a variety of settings. Subconscious acquisition can take place in classroom settings, and conscious learning can take place in natural ones.
- For teachers, it is important to recognize that both subconscious and conscious processes are at work, and different

environments can help facilitate these processes.

Suggested Strategies

You do not need to get lost in theory. You do need to familiarize yourself and think of ways to help learners benefit from both types of processes. Here's how.

- **Engage with Authentic Materials:** Connect learners to natural settings with authentic materials like advertisements, menus, and cartoons. This can help learners realize that the things they interact with or enjoy in an L1 (first language) context exist in an L2 (second language) context as well. Consider bringing one piece of authentic content into each lesson, no matter how simple: show the date on a newspaper to reinforce days of the week or take a screenshot of a mobile game and use it to practice words like click and drag.
- **Encourage English Outside of Class:** Although there is no way to control whether or how much your learners interact in English outside of class, there are ways of encouraging that interaction. Learn about your learners' lives and activities and use that information to help learners find even more opportunities to practice in natural settings. You can also give your learner a specific list of tasks or interactions to

attempt in English before the next class. This list could include saying "hello" to at least five people, introducing yourself to two people, or asking three questions. After all, there are plenty of coffee shops and retail stores that require their teams to speak in English. It is also helpful to have your learners listen to language-learning songs while eating meals, playing, riding in the car, bathing, or getting ready for bed. (The curriculum you are using likely includes some such songs, and there are many more about all kinds of typical lesson themes available online.) They can also listen to the audio of children's stories or watch videos of them being read online. Even if the learners don't fully understand all the language they hear, regular exposure will help.

- **Focus on Functions:** Natural settings require learners to fulfill certain language functions in order to successfully interact, such as narrating, apologizing, and asking for help. Make sure your instruction includes attention to functions like these that are most relevant for learners as they begin to explore English online and in their communities. If learners' parents, other family members, or family friends speak English well, they could also try to use English in everyday interactions.

- **Self-Access Apps:** Find some of the many online English learning apps designed for kids, many of which use games and activities to help kids practice English on their own, and make your learners' parents aware of them and perhaps which ones you would recommend for your learner's age and level. (It's best to let parents make final decisions on how much time their child spends using such self-access online

apps because many of them do charge fees after a free trial, and some parents are sensitive about their children spending too much of their time online, even if their child is playing an educational game.)

- **First Language Matters:** Depending on a speaker's first language, learning a second language could be more or less challenging, linguistically speaking. For example, if a learner who speaks Chinese as a first language is learning English as a second language, it is very challenging since the whole language system is different from Chinese as a Sino-Tibetan language to English as an alphabetic language. Chinese uses characters, while English uses an alphabet. Some English **phonemes** do not exist in Chinese. Stress and intonation patterns are different. Unlike English, Chinese is a tonal language. That means it uses changes in pitch (falling from high to low, rising from low to high, ect.) of a phoneme to distinguish word meaning. As teachers of English to Chinese young learners, we must be aware of the differences in these two languages and provide input, meaningful repetition, and noticing in our teaching. Also, we should be patient and understand that some mistakes or errors take time to correct. Please see the detailed strategies in the next case.

Reflection

- Consider how you learned your first language as a child. Now, consider how your learner is learning a second language online. How are the experiences similar and different?

02 | L1 INFLUENCE

How does my learner's L1 (Chinese) influence their English language learning, and how can I help?

Keywords
#influence #L1 #L1 influence #L2 #language families

► **The Situation**

I know that Mandarin and English are very different, and I would love to help my learner navigate the differences. I have noticed my learner has a hard time with certain sounds in English, and grammar seems to be a real challenge. *How does my learner's L1 (Chinese) influence their English language learning?*

Analyzing the Situation

- There are significant differences between English and Mandarin because they are from different language families. English is from what is known as the Indo-European language family, and Mandarin is from the Sino-Tibetan language family.
- One of the biggest differences between the two languages is the phonological system although many English sounds do have one-to-one matches in Mandarin.
- Mandarin can also influence learners' grammar in different ways. For example, certain categories of words, like the articles *a*, *an*, and *the* exist in English but not in Mandarin. This means our learners commonly leave these articles out or confuse pronouns.
- The same goes for gendered pronouns like *he*, *she*, and *it*. In Mandarin, the sound for *he*, *she*, and *it* is the same. Naturally, Chinese English learners tend to confuse these pronouns, as they tend to focus on the sound rather than the forms.
- In English, we often use adjective clauses

to modify the key words. For instance, "Yesterday, I went to the hospital, which was very close to my home." But in Mandarin, the adjectives appear before the key words. For instance, the sentence pattern in Mandarin would be: "Yesterday, I went to the very-close-to-my-home hospital." Therefore, Chinese learners tend to make mistakes influenced by processing in Mandarin.
- Certain categories of words are also modified differently. For example, verbs in Mandarin do not get conjugated to express time (e.g., present, future, etc.) as they do in English, so errors involving verb endings are also common.

Suggested Strategies

You do not have to see the gap between English and Mandarin as a barrier. Instead, build bridges to better understand your learners. Here's how.

- **Use Timelines:** Think about specific strategies relevant to the common errors above. For teaching and reinforcing verb tenses, timelines can help learners visualize the differences.
- **Use Visual Cues:** For differences like those related pronouns, consider visuals to prompt learners. For example, simple, brightly colored props with pronoun labels (e.g., "he," "she," "it") could be used during class. When discussing a female character, you could hold up the "she" prop as a reminder,

or use it to help with error correction. Later, you can remove the pronoun label for a less **scaffolded** prop. You could apply this same strategy to articles. Shapes can be used to help make it clear which parts of speech go where. For example, you can draw rectangles around nouns and ovals around verbs.

- **Give Time for Input:** Use the stories that are part of the curriculum and other relevant resources to provide enough **comprehensible input**, especially when introducing new language. Not all input needs to be written text. Also, use audio input like recorded stories, simple thematic songs, etc.
- **Support Noticing and Pattern Recognition:** For younger learners, use rhymes or songs to encourage the repetition of **high frequency words** (**HFWs**) and phrases (e.g., *how* or *you* and *I*). For older learners, encourage them to more independently explore and notice new language by engaging with resources like a digital library
- **Be Mindful:** Always keep in mind that there are marked differences between the two languages, so if your learner regularly

makes a particular mistake or type of mistake, consider the fact that it could be due to **L1** (first language) and **L2** (second language) differences. In such cases, it may be helpful to ask a Chinese-speaking teacher or acquaintance if the habitual mistake could result from such differences. If so, use the above tactics to support the learner to help them understand the differences.

Reflection

- Reflect on your own experiences with other languages. What were some challenging differences between English and the other language(s) you were learning?
- Think back on (or watch if there is a recording) one of your previous lessons. What possible L1 influence do you notice based on what you learned above? Which of the suggested strategies could you use next time to support this learner?

03 | SUCCESSFUL L2 LEARNING

What are the common behaviors and attitudes of a successful L2 learner, and how can I encourage these behaviors in class?

Keywords
#error correction #L2 #language learning #listening

▶ The Situation

I want all my learners to be successful language learners, but I am worried that they do not know how to get there. It seems like I do not have enough time to teach all of the content and language I need to, let alone explain how to be a successful language learner. *What are the common behaviors and attitudes of a successful L2 learner, and how can I encourage these behaviors in class?*

Analyzing the Situation

- Although there is no magic formula for successful language learning, the most successful learners demonstrate similar attitudes and behaviors. Successful language learners regularly
  - engage with listening, taking full advantage of available input;
  - experiment with the new language, making mistakes and learning from them;
  - identify learning strategies that work for them, applying them when needed;
  - ask questions, taking advantage of opportunities to interact with teachers; and
  - accept correction, finding ways to understand, and incorporate feedback.

Suggested Strategies

We want all our learners to be successful. You can help your learner develop behaviors and strategies that will benefit them for years to come. Here's how.

- **Encourage Experimentation:** Set up activities that make experimentation a basic expectation and part of your regular class routine. During certain activities, lower the stakes by reducing the type or amount of error correction and find ways to help the learner integrate new language with previous knowledge. Keep reminders of previous learning present in your classroom or prompt your learner during free talk to discuss a familiar topic with new language.

- **Model It:** Show your learner what some of these behaviors look like. For example, engaged or active listening and reading can be modeled as listening or reading with your learner. Give eye contact, nod along, and ask questions. Praise them for taking risks, even if they make mistakes. Help them to learn from mistakes and to then perform the task successfully. Ask direct questions related to the lesson to your learners and encourage them to ask you similar questions.

- **Introduce Feedback Intentionally:** Make sure that feedback has a clear purpose and value. If an error interferes with meaning or completing a task in class, focus your feedback there. If your learner is frustrated or confused by the feedback that may not be directly relevant to the learning targets at hand, this feedback can discourage rather than encourage positive risk-taking.

- **Bring it Up:** If you notice behaviors that are not consistent with the behaviors described above, take the opportunity to discuss them with your learner (or their other teachers or even parents). For a younger learner, you can demonstrate two responses to an activity—one that relies on what is comfortable and one that involves more risks. For an older learner, explain how risks involve making informed guesses about how to use language. Then, with direct or indirect feedback, your learner can either confirm or reject these guesses. This often results in more autonomous learning that sticks.

Reflection

- Consider one of your learners who has shown a lot of progress in learning English. How would you describe that learner? Can you identify the behaviors and attitudes described above?
- Consider one of your learners who has struggled to make progress in learning English. Which of the suggested strategies could you try to support positive language learning behaviors and attitudes?

04 PLATEAUING

How can I help a learner who seems to plateau in their language learning?

Keywords
#comprehensible output #fossilization #growth #intermediate learner #L1 #plateau #progress #skills

▶ The Situation

My intermediate learner has been studying for a while, but he does not seem to be improving. Feedback that used to be effective no longer seems to work. It used to be so clear to see him make and demonstrate progress, but now it is difficult to see any growth. *How can I help a learner who seems to plateau in their language learning?*

Analyzing the Situation

- There are a number of factors that can affect intermediate learners and their progress with language learning:
  - Learners may have higher receptive or productive skills. Some learners often seem more comfortable reading than speaking.
  - Learners may have become more fluent but have not moved beyond simple grammar.
  - Learners may not have developed a sufficiently large vocabulary to interact with more advanced content.
  - Learners may be able to produce language, but in a way that sounds unnatural. Learners often have difficulty shifting between academic and more informal types of language use.
  - Learner errors may have fossilized.

Suggested Strategies

With a range of issues causing the plateau effect, a range of strategies is necessary. You can still help your intermediate learner demonstrate real growth. Here's how.

- **Try Something New:** If a learner is struggling to use language in contexts provided by the curriculum, consider finding other activities or resources that also include the target language. For example, if a learner struggles to remember the use of articles (*a*, *an*, *the*), write sentences that involve characters or stories the learner loves or even encourage identifying articles within those stories.
- **Raise Awareness:** Your learner needs to understand where they are relative to where they want to be. Encourage your learner to watch class videos and create a log of their own errors and facilitate awareness-raising in writing by teaching learners how to identify errors more independently with self-editing checklists.
- **Help Focus Output:** To help your learner move beyond a current range of structures, provide sentence frames or use substitution drilling. By focusing on a specific topic, set of structures, and **lexical set** of vocabulary, you can often see the same sort of rapid improvement within that focus that you saw when the learner was a beginner. More importantly, your learner can see and feel it, which results in self-satisfaction (and their

parents can see it, reminding them that their child is still just as skilled at learning as they were early on). If you try this sort of focused approach and still don't see good improvement, you may, indeed, be dealing with **fossilization** rather than mere **stabilization** or plateauing.

- **Explain the Phenomenon:** Use a metaphor the learner (and parents) can understand to explain why it may feel as if the learner is not progressing as rapidly as before. Learning a language is rather like trying to fill an inverted cone with sand. In the beginning, at the narrow part of the cone, it seems to fill quickly, but as you get closer and closer to the top of the cone, it takes the input of more sand to see the same sort of perceived fill rate. (Actually, perhaps it's more like filling a funnel, because some items may be "forgotten" so leak out the bottom as you are filling from the top.)

- **Give Them Time:** Reducing the cognitive demands on a learner during a task can help them focus on the target language. Provide planning and rehearsal opportunities such as a brief period of silence before a speaking exercise or teacher-led warm-up.

- **Encourage Deeper Word Knowledge:** A learner's word knowledge can often be shallow because many vocabulary activities only focus on one element of word meaning: definitions. By leveraging the language your learner already knows, vocabulary can be quickly expanded. Consider how to include multiple meanings, word forms, idioms, and **collocations** into your vocabulary instruction.

Reflection

- What is your current approach when dealing with a learner who seems to have plateaued?
- Consider one of your intermediate learners. What issues are they facing, and which suggested strategies could help them transition to more advanced language use?

FOSSILIZATION

How can I help a learner work against fossilization?

Keywords
#awareness #fossilization #interference #noticing #stabilization
#transfer

▶ The Situation

I have had learners who consistently make the same mistake. Sometimes it is as simple as a pronunciation mistake, but it also happens with sentence structures, grammar concepts, or even using the wrong word to express something. ***How can I help a learner work against fossilization?***

Analyzing the Situation

- Even though a learner can be growing in other areas, some errors can become fossilized. This means that certain errors persist and become habits despite other growth.
- **Fossilization** can occur due to **language transfer (interference)**, where a learner applies elements that are correct in their native language to the new language they are learning. When these the new language mistakes are not appropriately corrected early in the learning process, they can fossilize.
- Fossilization is often linked with **stabilization.** Both are correctable as long as we have effective strategies.
- In order to overcome fossilization/ stabilization, a learner must be aware of the mistakes they are making and have the motivation to approach the same content again.

Suggested Strategies

Although challenging for both teachers and learners, fossilized/stabilized mistakes can be overcome with persistence and simple strategies. Here's how.

- **Empathize:** Fossilization can be very frustrating for a learner. You can ease this frustration by sharing examples of certain things even you may struggle yourself with saying correctly or that even many native-speaking politicians or tv news reporters often use mistakenly. A common example would be someone saying something like, "It was so hot today that I was literally melting." Obviously, they weren't literally melting, or they would look like a half-used candle. Rather, they were "figuratively melting," or it "felt like they were melting."
- **Put "Fossils" on Display:** Either when the mistake occurs, or at the end of an activity or lesson, draw your learner's attention to the fossilized language. Use a clear example from their use, then guide your learner to generate an accurate example of their own. This pair of examples will not only highlight the learner's mistake, but will also provide a model for how the learner can self-correct in the future. You can also show a signal to the learner when they are approaching the need to produce language they have made a mistake with in the past due to fossilization.
- **Link to Rewards:** Consider linking rewards in a particular class to performance on the fossilized issue. This can help with

awareness-raising and gives the learner a new reason to pay attention to an "old" issue without feeling frustrated by repetitive content.

- **Use Focused Practice:** It may be necessary to isolate the mistake and provide intensive practice using only the problem structure. However, this isolation does not necessarily mean decontextualized practice. For example, you can find a reading or listening passage with several repetitions of the structure. Then, highlight it for the learner to notice in a text or transcript. Later, remove the highlighted words to allow the learner to produce the **target language** in context. A skilled teacher may even be able to do this through a carefully guided conversation that repeatedly puts the learner into a situation in which they must correctly use the language that had become fossilized.

- **Don't Give Up:** It can take some time to help a learner to overcome a fossilized mistake. Therefore, if you teach the same learner again in subsequent lessons, it is a good idea to use a bit of your lesson time on each meeting to practice correct usage of the problem language. Continue doing so until the fossilized mistake seems to have been overcome and repeat this process if it

occurs again in the future (or with any other fossilized/stabilized mistakes that might pop up). If possible, leave a note in the learner's records to inform any other teachers they may have of the fossilized language and request their help to provide focused practice on it.

- **Use Comparison and Contrast:** Encourage your learners to record their own conversation or reading aloud and listen afterward. While listening to their own recording, encourage your learners to pay special attention to the differences between their own voices with that provided by the teacher or a pre-recorded model (e.g., the audio recording of a reading text). In this way, they will notice the obvious differences such as the pronunciation of a word or intonation of a sentence, then make an effort through imitation and/or correction.

Reflection

- Consider one of your learners who has struggled with learning new grammar. Which of the suggested strategies could you use with this learner in their next lesson?

# ERROR CORRECTION

How and when do I correct my learner in class?

Keywords
#accuracy #confidence #error #error correction #fluency #mistake #slip

► The Situation

Even though I have been teaching online for a while, I am still unsure which errors I should be correcting, how often to correct them, and how to make sure the correction sticks. It feels like there are so many factors and a lot of different approaches. I do not want to hurt my learner's confidence, but I want to make sure they are aware of their errors and know how to correct them. ***How and when do I correct my learner in class?***

Analyzing the Situation

- It is essential to differentiate between **errors**, **mistakes**, and **slips**: an error occurs because a learner does not have the required knowledge; a mistake occurs when a learner has the knowledge but fails to apply it; a slip is when a learner makes a mistake but is easily able to correct it themselves. Based on the type, you can adjust your approach to feedback.
- Mistakes and errors that affect whether a learner can be understood are the most critical to address. Depending on the situation, verb tense issues may be more urgent to correct than articles because they can affect meaning more significantly.
- From a parents' perspective, error correction is an important job for the foreign teacher. Parents are concerned about the **accuracy** of their child's language use and can become concerned if they think errors are being ignored or under-addressed.

Suggested Strategies

Correcting learner errors can be tricky, but with some tips and a bit of practice, you can make sure your learner gets the feedback they need. Here's how.

- **Put Communication First:** Understand that expressing oneself and being understood is always the primary purpose in meaningful communication. Teachers should always encourage their learners to take risks despite possible errors or mistakes.
- **Focus Your Feedback:** Focus your feedback on one or two specific areas instead of attempting to correct every mistake or error. Giving a learner feedback on multiple errors and mistakes after a short oral response could overwhelm a learner's working memory. Avoid correcting issues with articles, verb forms, and pronouns at the same time. Instead, think about the goal of the current activity, and focus your feedback there. If the lesson is introducing a new verb form, provide feedback on verb form errors. You can always correct other errors if they get in the way of communication but put **target language** first.
- **Use Prompts and Recasts:** To prompt an error self-correction, guide and encourage the learner to use their own language resources to rephrase and correct their language. (e.g., S: He went to the store. T: Who went to the store? S: Oh, <u>she</u> went to the store.) To **recast**, provide input in the form of a correct reformulation. (e.g., S: He

went to the store. T: <u>She</u> went to the store. S: Oh, she went to the store.)

- **Use Rewards and Praise:** It is just as important to reward or praise a learner who self-corrects, corrects with the help of a prompt or recasting, or even says something correctly that they may have made a mistake with on a previous attempt as it is to correct mistakes or errors in the first place.

- **Tailor Your Approach:** Work collaboratively with your learner to identify strategies that work best. Everything from a learner's skill level to their personality can affect how error correction is received. Monitor your learner's progress and be responsive to when your learner moves from needing your correction to correcting their own mistakes more independently.

- **Know Your Goal:** When deciding how to approach error correction, keep in mind whether your goal in that activity is improving **accuracy** or **fluency**.

- **Explain to Parents:** Chinese parents are especially notorious for wanting teachers to correct every single mistake or error, so you may need to explain to them that in certain lessons you will be focusing on producing certain language correctly, so will produce errors related to that specific target but that you will avoid correcting every single error so that you do not discourage their child from taking risks and producing language. If the parents do not speak English, and neither do you, you may need help from a Chinese-speaking colleague to communicate this to parents.

Reflection

- How do you currently handle error correction? What's working, and what's not?
- Are there specific errors you find difficult to correct? How can you apply the strategies above to help you with these types of errors?

RECOGNIZING LANGUAGE MISTAKES

How can I help my learner recognize their own mistakes?

Keywords
#mistake #error #recognize #recognizing #notice #noticing
#correction #recasting #overt

▶ The Situation

Sometimes my learner seems to make mistakes without ever really noticing what they have done incorrectly. Because of this, they often keep repeating the same mistake in the future. ***How can I help my learner recognize their own mistakes?***

Analyzing the Situation

- It is important to determine whether a learner has made a **mistake** or simply an **error**. An error occurs when a learner is incorrect simply because they were never taught how to do something correctly. A mistake is when a learner is incorrect even though they have been taught the language needed.
- Making mistakes is actually one of the most effective ways for your learner to improve, but for the learner to learn from a mistake, they must recognize or **notice** the mistake made. This process is referred to as **noticing**.

Suggested Strategies

Getting your learner to recognize their mistakes does not mean that you have to raise a red flag each time you hear something wrong. It does mean that you should have creative options to help a learner become aware of their own mistakes. Here's how.

- **Assess Prior Learning:** Ensure that what the learner is expected to produce is the language that has been addressed earlier in the lesson or in previous lessons. You should not expect your learner to notice errors, but you can help them notice mistakes.
- **Recast with Emphasis:** One effective way to help a learner notice mistakes is by recasting (restating what they likely intended to say using correct grammar and vocabulary). Use a slight pause, slow speech, and voice emphasis to help your learner notice the recast.
- **Try Different Contexts:** If a mistake is made, and you have used emphatic recasting, be sure to put the learner into other situations in which they must use the same language to respond correctly and recast again if the mistake persists.
- **Use Direct Questioning:** If a learner makes a mistake, you can also use direct questioning to help suggest they may have made a mistake, so the learner knows to look for that mistake and correct it themselves. For example, S: "He rided the bike?" T: "What did he do?" S: "Oh, he rode the bike."
- **Use Elicitation:** Repeat the learner's statement back to them up to the point where they made the mistake and encourage them to notice the error and finish the utterance correctly.
- **Repetition:** Repeat exactly what the learner said, including their mistake, possibly putting

some emphasis on the mistaken portion and raise an eyebrow. Learners universally recognize their teacher repeating something back to them as a friendly way of saying, "Think about that one and give it another try." (Think back to your school days when a math teacher walked past your desk, pointed to one of your answers and asked, "Are you sure that's right?" Clearly, the meaning was actually, "That's wrong. Try it again.")

- **Use Overt Correction:** If a learner is still not noticing and self-correcting a mistake, it may be necessary to resort to overt correction. Overt correction refers to singling out a mistake, telling the learner that it is a mistake, and giving them direct instruction on correcting it. It is best not to immediately use overt correction during practice, but to take note of the persistent mistake then dedicate some time at the end of class to review and discuss the issue.

- **Serve a Feedback Sandwich:** If you do need to resort to overt correction, try to do so using what is often called a "feedback sandwich." First, praise them for the part they got right, then point out what they did wrong, and follow it up with additional praise of their subsequent correction or something else they did well.

- **Monitor Over Time:** For a regular learner, keep in mind the mistakes they've made in the past and use future lessons to ensure they are conscious of the issue and trying to self-correct. Also, add a note for other teachers to explain which errors to look out for.

Reflection

- How often do you find yourself recasting or using another error correction technique?
- Which strategies (above or otherwise) have you tried? How could you tweak your approach?

08 PROVIDING COMPREHENSIBLE INPUT

How can I provide comprehensible input in class?

Keywords
#comprehensible input #planning #prepare #simplify

▶ The Situation

Sometimes when I'm teaching my learner, he struggles with new vocabulary or grammar. In some classes, it seems like he doesn't "get" much of what we cover, and he becomes frustrated when he doesn't understand every word. Of course, I don't want to have a learner who is so visibly frustrated in my lessons. **How can I provide comprehensible input in class?**

Analyzing the Situation

- **Comprehensible input** provides learners with a message they can understand. Learners may not understand all of the words and structures provided through comprehensible input (nor do they need to). Generally, comprehensible input is one level above that of the learner, so it can only just be understood.
- Comprehensible input is important because it provides the right kind of exposure to new language that learners need. Input that is too challenging can be demoralizing, while input that is entirely familiar may not provide the right incentive to develop new language.

Suggested Strategies

You do not only have to provide new language for your learner all the time. After all, they still need to practice using it! You should try to think of ways to engage the learner at their level while still covering the lesson content, though. Here's how.

- **Simplify Your Language:** Use simple language or simplify the language presented in the slides. Simple language often involves shorter sentences, fewer verbs, fewer extended noun phrases, and fewer additional clauses (e.g., "Listen to the song." vs. "Now pay attention and try to follow along with the new song that's about colors around your house".) You may also want to try a combination of gestures and miming. Especially for a younger learner, avoid overexplaining or presenting too many variations of the same language.
- **TTT:** Typically, inexperienced children's **EFL (English as a Foreign Language)** teachers talk too much. If the teacher rattles on explaining everything in detail, even activity directions, the learner will become confused and frustrated because they cannot understand it all or discern the **target language**. In the field, we often refer to **TTT (teacher talk time)**. Make it your goal to have each learner in your class (even group classes) speak more English than you do. This is surprisingly achievable by having learners both ask and answer the questions, by having them reading texts, by having them use substitution practice, and (in group lessons) having them talk to one another rather than only to the teacher.
- **TTQ:** Also consider **TTQ (teacher talk quality)** and only say what is essential to help the learner understand the target and how to produce it themselves.
- **Don't Explain:** Of course, some elements need to be explained, but well-designed

language learning activities may require no explanation at all. Rather, simply demonstrate or model once what the learner is expected to do. In many cases, the learner can see what is expected of them simply from how the activity is designed and presented.

- **Plan Supports:** If you are introducing new vocabulary or grammar, be prepared with synonyms, examples, and visuals (pictures, drawings, props) to support comprehension.
- **Build Context:** Be sensitive to your learner's cultural and language background by including materials that draw on their prior knowledge and experiences. Where prior knowledge does not exist, build it. For example, if a reading or listening text involves multiple references to zoos, but a learner has never been to the zoo, introduce relevant vocabulary and phrases to make the input more comprehensible.

- **Break It Down:** If a task includes multiple steps, break down the instructions into multiple, incremental steps. Consider what the learner needs to know in order to do the task—or part of the task—at hand.
- **Be Patient:** Using comprehensible input requires using many examples and plenty of practice so that your learner can use strategies such as guessing words from context and inferring meaning. This means it might take some time for your learner to pick it up.

Reflection

- Think about one of your current learners. Using one of the strategies above, how can you target your language input slightly above their current understanding?

09 | NOTICING LANGUAGE

How can I help my learner notice new language?

Keywords
#attention #awareness #error correction #new language #noticing #skeleton dialogue

► **The Situation**

I want to help my learner remember what they learn, but I have a hard time focusing their attention on new language. Some learners want to rush through content, and others seem to be following along but later cannot really demonstrate what they learned. ***How can I help my learner notice new language?***

Analyzing the Situation

- Teachers and learners can sometimes get too comfortable practicing previously learned language because it is more comfortable than teaching new language. But if we aren't getting through some of the discomfort of presenting and promoting **noticing** opportunities, we aren't teaching our learners anything new (and this can make it hard to get through lesson objectives or gain momentum).
- Noticing involves bringing language into focus. This process of drawing attention to forms and other language features can help learners transform input like a new song into meaningful understanding of how the language works.
- Noticing and awareness-raising can be especially important during the first exposure. Taking the time to ensure noticing can occur will help your learners in later lessons as they are expected to apply what they learned with you.
- With noticing, error correction becomes easier for both you and your learners. When learners have a clear picture of the **target language**, it is easier for you to explain a mistake or error and easier for learners to correct their own.

Suggested Strategies

Since almost every lesson you teach outside of assessments will involve new language, be sure you are prepared to make the language stick. Try these strategies.

- **Enhance New Language:** Provide opportunities for noticing by underlining, circling, or highlighting examples of target language. You can also do this with props or by gesturing to prompt noticing.
- **Focus on One at a Time:** When introducing new language, focus on one thing at a time. If you are introducing the indefinite articles *a* and *an*, those might be the only words that are underlined in a text. This does not mean the learner will not notice other language. In fact, it will help your learner build relationships between these words and the surrounding language. It would be an easy step to next guide your learner to notice that *a* and *an* came before nouns, establishing the grammatical function of articles in English.
- **Name Dropping:** If names or personal pronouns are used in the new structures you are teaching, replace them with the learner's name or a name of a favorite cartoon character or a famous superhero to draw their attention to the structure.

- **Correcting the Teacher:** As the teacher, intentionally make a "mistake" in reading a target structure on the screen and encourage your learners to correct you. If you do this regularly in your lessons, your learners will concentrate on the text trying to catch the teacher making a mistake. By making the "mistake" exactly at the point of the new language, the new language will be the focus of attention.
- **Gamify It:** Get your learner motivated about noticing by setting a time limit and turning a text into a timed scavenger hunt. Your learner gets to search for and notice words, phrases, or structures and have fun doing it.
- **Use Skeleton Dialogues:** Take advantage of existing dialogues or create your own. Enhance the dialogue by highlighting the target language. Next, give the learner a "skeleton" of the dialogue (or even just two lines of dialogue) with the target language removed. At this point, encourage the learner to produce the missing target language. And voila! From noticing to recall in just a few steps.

Reflection

- Consider your current approach. Which of the suggested strategies are common in your toolkit? Which are not?
- Consider a current learner. What specific issues are they struggling with? How can you use the suggested strategies to help leverage noticing to support your learner?

10 CONNECTING BACKGROUND KNOWLEDGE

How can I help my learner connect with background knowledge when reading and listening?

Keywords
#background knowledge #content schemas #elicit #formal schemas #KWL chart #listening #reading #schema

▶ The Situation

My learner often struggles with understanding what they read and listen to, even if they understand individual words and phrases. They seem unsure or hesitant when reading a new text and can get lost quickly. It seems like they have a hard time putting it all together, even when the texts are related to topics I know they are familiar with. *How can I help my learner connect with background knowledge when reading and listening?*

Analyzing the Situation

- The terms background knowledge and **schema** can be used interchangeably to refer to your learner's existing knowledge and the connections they make between this knowledge and a text.
- There are many ways to differentiate between types of background knowledge. Some examples include **formal schemas** (knowledge of the language and its structures) and **content schemas** (knowledge of a topic, including cultural topics).
- Activating background knowledge can significantly impact a learner's ability to interact with a text and make meaning.

Suggested Strategies

While it can be challenging for a language learner to make sense of a text in front of them, you can help your learner connect with background knowledge. Here's how.

- **Avoid Assumptions:** Do not assume background knowledge. Instead, provide your learner the space to demonstrate what they know. You will often be surprised (especially with a learner who is typically less expressive) with how much your learner knows about certain topics.
- **Praise It:** A learner can often experience stress and anxiety when encountering a new text in a foreign language. Give your learner confidence to engage by eliciting (or drawing out) how much they know and praising them when they share. Appreciating what your learner brings to the table themselves can be an effective motivational strategy.
- **Direct Questioning:** Directly ask your learners questions about their possible background knowledge of certain content. You may need to prepare pictures or props for lower-level learners to help them understand what you are asking.
- **Have a Routine:** Make pre-reading/listening part of your routine when asking your learner to work with texts. Background knowledge can be activated or even built in during this phase of your reading/listening

routine. For example, a simple review of relevant vocabulary or a quick brainstorm will help you and your learner identify both prior knowledge and gaps.

- **Incorporate Strategies:** Encourage your learner to activate prior knowledge themselves every time they read. Model the use of strategies like previewing, predicting, and asking and answering questions.

  KWL charts (know, want, learn charts) are graphic organizers that help your learners share what they know, what they want to know, and what they learned. KWL charts are a great way to scaffold this type of strategic reading and listening.

- **Involve Parents:** Ask parents if their child has had certain experiences. Have them talk to their child about having had those experiences or even attending the lesson with photographs or souvenirs on hand that they can share with you.

Reflection

- Consider one of your next lessons. What background knowledge might be needed to engage with the text? Using the suggested strategies, how can you help your learner connect with this knowledge and apply it to the lesson activities?
- Consider a reading or listening activity that seemed especially challenging for your learner. What seemed to make it challenging? Which of the suggested strategies could you use in the future to make this activity more manageable and enjoyable?

11 UNDERSTANDING CLASSROOM LANGUAGE

How can I help my learner better understand classroom language?

Keywords
#feedback #grading language #instructions #praise #Teacher Talk Quality (TTQ) #Teacher Talk Time (TTT)

▶ **The Situation**

I feel like I sometimes talk too much during class time, and I am not sure if my learner understands or benefits from it. I want to be able to mix up the kinds of language I use to present and practice language to interact with my learner and just use it in the classroom and hope she picks up on it over time through exposure. But I am unsure of how she will know the difference between the different kinds of language I use. *How can I help my learner better understand classroom language?*

Analyzing the Situation

- Many language teachers do indeed speak a lot in classrooms, and that is expected. Consider all of the ways we use our **Teacher Talk Time (TTT)**: to manage our classes, to motivate our learners, and to provide feedback. However, what we talk about and how we talk about it can vary widely and can change our relationships with our learners.
- Being aware of the function of your language can help you understand the learning environment you are creating. Is your classroom language primarily focused on classroom management, giving instruction, and testing? Then your relationship with your learner may feel very formal. What if your language is largely used to focus on learner information and to ask thinking questions? What type of relationship does this create?

Suggested Strategies

You do not have to script every word you speak in your classes (though if you're feeling ambitious, go for it!), but you do need to consider the words you use in an intentional way. This includes making sure your learner gets the most out of classroom language. Here's how.

- **Count the Functions:** If you are uncertain about the kinds of language you are using in the classroom, consider counting the different language functions you are using during a class period. List out the functions of different kinds of talk (e.g., giving instructions, feedback, praise, asking for information, giving information, providing models, testing understanding, joking, etc.) then mark how often you use each function. This can help you with your self-audit of TTT and make sure you have high **teacher talk quality (TTQ)**.
- **Use Classroom Rules:** Effectively setting expectations about whose turn it is to talk will help your learners feel more secure in the classroom. When we want our learners to respond, we should have a clear indication that it is the learner's time to talk.

You can accomplish this by using a visual cue like a flashcard or other props such as a two-sided "stoplight" with the red light showing on one side and the green light showing on the other side. (The red light means to listen to the teacher; the green light means the teacher is listening and expecting you to talk.) You could also use physical modeling to get your learner to respond.

- **Be Clear and Leveled:** Be certain you are using language at a level that your learner can understand. This may mean grading your language by using short sentences, slowing down your speech rate, and being certain to enunciate clearly.
- **Demonstrate:** Often, you don't really need to talk at all for your learner to understand what they should do in a certain activity. Rather than talking, consider simply demonstrating what to do once. Sometimes learners will be able to tell what they are expected to do simply based on the design and presentation of the activity, so it may not even be necessary to demonstrate.
- **Be Consistent:** Use a consistent and limited range of classroom language that can be used from lesson to lesson. Very specific

language and explanation that is not likely to be used repeatedly might not offer enough ongoing, receptive exposure to help a learner pick it up. Write this language down for yourself and make it easy to reference during class.

- **Watch Yourself!:** Your company probably keeps recordings of your lessons that you can access. Watch these recordings and notice how much you talk, when you are talking but don't need to be, the quality of your talking, and whether you are using a lot of vocabulary, structures, tenses, etc. that the learner wouldn't know yet. (If your company can't provide access to such videos, get a second camera and record yourself delivering lessons that way.)

Reflection

- Are you able to categorize the types of classroom language you use? Consider what types of functions your teacher talk is providing.
- Consider one of the courses you currently teach. Which strategies above could you apply to improve your learner's understanding of your classroom language?

REPEATED EXPOSURE

How can I help my learner who struggles to remember language despite repeated exposure?

Keywords
#deep processing #exposure #memory #long-term memory #repetition #rote memorization #shallow processing #short-term memory #working memory

▶ The Situation

I have a learner who has been with me for several months. She is a model learner who always listens attentively and participates actively in class. However, she easily forgets the vocabulary and sentences learned in the previous lessons, even with a lot of repetition and practice. This is really frustrating to her and sometimes hurts her motivation to learn. *How can I help my learner who struggles to remember language despite repeated exposure?*

Analyzing the Situation

- **Memory** plays a critical role in language learning and is one factor used to predict language learning outcomes. There are two kinds of memory: **short-term memory** (also known as **working memory**) and **long-term memory**.
- Multiple strategies can help learners enhance their short-term and long-term memories, including stimulation of all senses, meaningful interpretation, **deep processing**, focused attention, **chunking**, and association between items.

Suggested Strategies

You do not need to focus solely on **rote memorization** and have your learner regurgitate words from an associated image or translation on a flashcard. You do need an integrated approach that incorporates techniques to help your learner develop different aspects of their memory. Here's how.

- **Stimulate the Senses:** While you do not have to stimulate all five senses in a single lesson, try for as many as possible. Try to engage your learner's visual and auditory senses and invite them to utilize objects around them. For example, when teaching colors, consider preparing a palette for your learner to visualize real colors and see how, when mixed together, they become a new color. When teaching textures, consider asking your learner to touch the texture of certain clothes or furniture at home.

- **Leverage Different Types of Mental Processing:** Different children tend to mentally process information in different ways. Some are very good at processing ordinary linguistic information. Others may remember it better if it is in the form of a simple song. Maybe they process information visually. Some children learn best if you connect vocabulary or even other elements to physical movements.

- **Think About Context:** Always provide a meaningful context that can engage a learner's emotions. We recall and retain information that is personally meaningful to us. When teaching vocabulary, try to create a fun story or a scenario that is relevant to your learner's life. For example, when teaching the word *embarrassed*, ask your learner to describe a real situation that made them feel embarrassed before.

- **Focus on Target Language:** Direct your learner's attention to the target language. You can circle or highlight the words, phrases, or sentences you think the learner is likely to forget; tell them, "This is a very useful word," and "We are going to see if you remember this word in the next lesson." Towards the end of the lesson, you can draw the learner's attention back to the particular language to reinforce the memory then follow up in the next class.

- **Encourage Deep Processing: Deep processing** enhances both short-term and long-term memory more than **shallow processing**. Instead of rote memorization, have your learner create a story using new words learned in class. This way, your learner has to connect new language together for a story. This practice will help your learner acquire language in a more effective way.

- **Make Associations:** You can help your learner make associations or connections between words, sentences, and scenes to aid with memory. For example, when teaching words related to animals, remind your learner of other animals learned before. When teaching the prefix ex-, group together words that include the same prefix.

- **Use Graduated Interval Recall:** After introducing a new vocabulary word, sentence structure, grammar concept, etc. and practicing it a few times, bring it up again after a couple of minutes. Then bring it up again after ten minutes, then after twenty minutes, in the next lesson, and several lessons later. This will help to ensure that the language target moves from short-term memory to long-term memory.

Reflection

- Which strategies do you currently use in your lessons? Which strategies would be new for you?
- Which strategies from above do you want to try? How could you tweak your approach to fit the needs of your learner?

13 PRODUCING COMPREHENSIBLE OUTPUT

How can I help my learner produce comprehensible output and avoid L1 interference?

Keywords
#comprehensible output #early learner (EL) #gaps #interference #L1 #productive skills #young learner (YL)

▶ The Situation

My learner always seems to struggle with speaking; it looks like they are working so hard! I don't know if they are trying to translate from Mandarin into English or worry about making a mistake, but I want to help them learn to speak without so much trouble. ***How can I help my learner produce comprehensible output and avoid L1 interference?***

Analyzing the Situation

- Through output and production (speaking and writing), learners test guesses they have about language. They think they have a sentence formed correctly, and they give it a try. Based on the response they get, they may modify their language.
- During the process of trial, error, and feedback, learners become specifically aware of gaps in their knowledge. For both teachers and learners, this process can be challenging because it involves "failure" by definition—failing to form a sentence accurately. However, this is not a failure. It is part of the language learning process, and the facilitation of this is a key responsibility of the language teacher.
- Comprehensible output can sometimes be considered as "pushed output" when teachers know that the learner is able to say something already learned though the learner might not realize that or might

not feel ready to do so. It is important for teachers to encourage their learner to practice what has been learned in a timely fashion.

Suggested Strategies

Getting a learner to feel comfortable speaking and writing in another language is tough! However, you can still give your learner a chance at success. Here's how.

- **Praise Partial Responses:** Do not withhold rewards or other praise for partial responses or partially accurate responses. Partial responses could be the first words (e.g., "I like...") or the completion of a sentence frame (e.g., T: I like...., S: ...chocolate cake). Partially accurate responses could be those that include an inaccurate verb form in an otherwise accurate sentence. Your learner needs and deserves credit for "parts" of a response as well as the "whole," especially since it may take a significant amount of time for **early learners** (**ELs**) and **young learners** (**YLs**) to produce "whole" responses.
- **Understand Errors:** By understanding the likely areas of **interference**, you can be prepared with the appropriate strategies to support your learners. If you do not speak Chinese, talk to friends or colleagues who do and ask them about differences between the two languages that are often confusing.

- **Become the Learner:** If you do not speak Chinese, consider studying it. This will help you empathize with your learners and see where linguistic interference may be an issue. If you are already bilingual in Chinese and English, then start learning a new language to keep in mind the challenges of language learning.
- **Model It:** Provide models orally, in writing, or both. Make sure models are clear and without any distracting incidental language. Models of articles (e.g., *a*, *an*, and *the*) in use may be short noun phrases such as "a cat" or "a blue cat." This sort of isolation can help a learner focus on the **target language**.
- **Provide Plenty of Opportunities:** Provide your learner with a range of opportunities to produce the target language. This can be as simple and arbitrary as timed-free talk, where a learner talks about anything they want, without stopping, for 30 seconds. It could also be as specific and **scaffolded** as picture prompts with accompanying sentence frames. For example, you could show your learner a picture of a clothing store and provide sentence frames for "I want_____," and "I don't want _____." After your learner completes the sentences in writing, they can share them with you.

- **Be a Bit Silly:** When using picture prompts as described above, every now and then throw in a picture prompt that is a bit silly, but still grammatically correct. For example, if you are using the frame "I'm hungry. I want a _____." use mostly known food item cards, but every now and then throw in a picture of another word they should know but would make for a rather silly meal like an elephant or a shoe. This will make substitution practice much more fun for both of you.
- **Wait Time:** Sometimes all early learners need is for you to wait for a few moments for them to respond. Once you prompt a learner to speak, count slowly to five in your head to give them a chance to answer before you interrupt their thought process.

Reflection

- Consider one of your current learners. Which of the suggested strategies could you use to support this learner?
- Consider the different courses and levels you teach. How would you apply the suggested strategies differently?

14 SUPPORTING A QUIET OR HESITANT LEARNER

How can I support a learner who is quiet or hesitant to respond?

Keywords
#hesitant #quiet #silent period #Stephen Krashen #teacher talk time (TTT)

▶ The Situation

I have a learner who seems so shy. She rarely repeats any new language and rarely responds to questions. When I encourage her to repeat new vocabulary, she just stares at the screen or looks off at her parents. When I ask a question, I often get a similar response. **How can I support a learner who is quiet or hesitant to respond?**

Analyzing the Situation

- There are a number of reasons a learner may be quiet or hesitant to respond. We must be careful to avoid using labels like "shy" to describe a learner.
- In some cases, the language you are expecting from your learner is beyond their current abilities, causing stress or anxiety. In others, the learner may not understand the instructions or what is expected of them. There could also be some confusion related to the content or an unfamiliar cultural reference. Also, sometimes a learner is introverted, and they tend to focus more on listening rather speaking.
- There is also not necessarily a reason to panic if a new or lower-level learner is still in what Stephen Krashen called the **silent period**. They may be actively processing input even though they are not yet producing much output.

Suggested Strategies

You do not need to feel like you are playing a waiting game with your learner each time you are in class. You do need to have patience and give your learner the best opportunity to participate, even if they seem quiet or hesitant. Here's how.

- **Make Them Laugh:** Use humor to draw out a learner's personality: "Does your teacher have brown hair or blue hair?" or "Do you wear shoes on your hands or your feet?" Show your learners that it is OK to laugh. For a younger learner, use a puppet and a silly voice to repeat words or phrases in the lesson. For an older learner, try tongue twisters and simple jokes.
- **Connect to Their Interests:** Learn about a learner's interests and find ways of incorporating those interests into the lesson. If a learner is a fan of a superhero or celebrity, use that to personalize examples that you provide orally or on a whiteboard. For example, in a lesson on the use of *can* and *can't*, you could give these examples: Can [Superhero] jump? [Superhero] can't fly.
- **Get Physical:** Find opportunities to get the learner up and moving. Use songs and animations as well as simple games by encouraging clapping or other movements. Also, consider zero-prep games like the mirror game, which requires a learner to

mimic your movements like a mirror.

- **Talk Less:** Increase the amount of time you wait for a response and cut down on your **teacher talk time** (**TTT**). It is important to give your learner the space to jump in and respond.
- **Role Play:** Assign your learner a dialogue with you and take turns.
- **Praise Partial Responses:** When a learner does respond, even if only partially, acknowledge that effort with praise or a reward. Do this often. Partial responses could be the first words (e.g., "I like …") or the completion of a sentence frame (e.g., T: I like …, S: … chocolate cake). Partially accurate responses could include an inaccurate verb form in an otherwise accurate sentence.

Reflection

- How do you currently manage situations in which a learner is quiet or hesitant to respond? What's working and what's not?
- Reflect on one of your current learners. How could you use one of the strategies above to support and encourage this learner?

LANGUAGE FUNCTIONS

How can I help a learner understand and use language functions in my lessons?

Keywords
#interaction #language forms #language functions

▶ **The Situation**

I have a regular learner who struggles with almost any interaction in class. From asking questions to sharing opinions, her language is often inconsistent and hard to follow. Sometimes, I am not sure what she is trying to say. In addition, when I do things like give instructions or explain a word, she does not always seem to know what I am doing. *How can I help a learner understand and use language functions in my lessons?*

Analyzing the Situation

- **Language functions** involve how learners use language to communicate and achieve goals, while **language forms** focus on the structure of the language itself. Most language curricula are designed with some focus on language functions in mind.
- A key aspect of language functions is that they are used for relationship-building. Learners who learn to exercise functions appropriately are often more successful at establishing relationships and are often more satisfied with their interactions with others.
- Identifying, describing, giving advice, making invitations, and sharing opinions are examples of language functions. Each function has associated norms and routines that are often fixed, requiring that learners receive sufficient exposure to produce the most idiomatic and polite forms.

Suggested Strategies

Teaching with language functions in mind can be fun and meaningful. Here's how to provide this meaningful experience for your learner.

- **Prepare for Functions:** When focusing on language functions, it is important to pre-teach any vocabulary or phrases that are part of the interactional sequence. Your learner is then able to engage with the task focused on achieving a functional goal, not struggling to pronounce a new word, or understand an unfamiliar idiom.
- **Act Their Age:** Be sure that the functions you ask your learners to perform are age-appropriate for them. Always use functions they do at their age in their everyday lives. For example, very young learners don't place an order in a restaurant. Rather, they might tell a parent or a teacher what they want to eat.
- **Build Visual Associations:** Because language functions occur in particular contexts, it is important to provide visuals that help your learner understand when certain functions occur and build associations between context and language. Use visuals of people, places, objects, and situations and link them to relevant functions. For example, use a photo of someone extending their hand for a handshake to prompt your learner to introduce themselves. For an older learner, you may provide a more general visual, such as a classroom full of learners, then ask your learner to explain the range of

functions that could be needed.

- **Information Gaps:** Information gap activities are an excellent place to start when teaching language functions. Consider the function of giving directions. Provide a simple map to your learner, then give simple directions toward a goal on the map. The learner is filling in the "information gap" of "how to get to the goal" by listening to directions. This type of task can always be flipped to allow the learner to fulfill both roles related to a particular function. Other examples include having your learner explain the layout of their home to you while you try to draw it, explain all the items they have eaten that day, guess what items from a particular set of vocabulary words you have in a box or opaque bag, etc.

- **Do What They Tell You To:** Have the learner explain a process to you and act out doing everything they tell you to. (Kids love telling their teacher what to do for a change!)

- **Make It a Routine:** Some language functions like asking for help and sharing opinions could become a part of every lesson. Take time at the end of a lesson to ask your learner to share their opinions of the text

they read or pause after each exercise to encourage your learner to ask for help with something they did not understand.

- **Plan for Authentic Opportunities:** When working on a particular language function, consider creating authentic or semi-authentic opportunities for the learner to practice the interaction. For example, in a lesson on apologizing, perhaps you "accidentally" skip ahead a few slides then "apologize" to your learner.

Reflection

- Consider a current learner. What are some of the language functions they struggle with the most? Which of the suggested strategies could you use to teach those functions?

- Consider one of your upcoming lessons. What are some of the language functions you might need to teach? Which of the suggested strategies could you use to teach those functions?

References

Aljaafreh, A., & Lantolf, J. (1994). Negative feedback as regulation and second language learning in the zone of proximal development. *The Modern Language Journal, 78*(4), 465-483. doi:10.2307/328585

Cameron, L. (2001). *Teaching languages to young learners*. Cambridge, UK: Cambridge University Press.

Cook, V. (2013). *Second language learning and language teaching*. London: Routledge.

Eberhard, D. M., Simons, G. F., & Fennig, C. D. (Eds.). (2019). *Ethnologue: languages of the world* (22nd ed.). Dallas, Texas: SIL International. Retriered from http://www.ethnologue.com

Erten, I. H. (2018). Activation of prior knowledge. In J. I. Liontas, T. International Association, & M. DelliCarpini (Eds.), *The TESOL encyclopedia of English language teaching*. doi:10.1002/9781118784235.eelt0801

Harmer, J. (1998). *How to teach English: An introduction to the practice of English language teaching*. Harlow: Longman.

Liu, J. (2002). Negotiating silence in American classrooms: Three Chinese cases. *Language and Intercultural Communication, 2*(1), 37-54.

Liu, J., & Zhong, J. (2005). Exploring the nature of silence of Chinese students in American classrooms. *Modern Foreign Languages (Quarterly), 28*(4), 393-402.

Mendelson, M. A. (2018). Understanding functions in learner speech. In J. I. Liontas, T. International Association, & M. DelliCarpini (Eds.), *The TESOL encyclopedia of English language teaching*. doi:10.1002/9781118784235.eelt0719

Mitchell, R., Myles, F., & Marsden, E. (2013). *Second language learning theories*. London: Routledge.

Mokhtari, K. (2018). Prior knowledge fuels the deployment of reading comprehension strategies. In J. I. Liontas, T. International Association, & M. DelliCarpini (Eds.), *The TESOL encyclopedia of English language teaching*. doi:10.1002/9781118784235.eelt0488

Moon, J. (2005) *Children learning english*. Oxford: Macmillan Heinemann.

Nassaji, H. (2018). Errors versus mistakes. In J. I. Liontas, T. International Association, & M. DelliCarpini (Eds.), *The TESOL encyclopedia of English language teaching*. doi:10.1002/9781118784235.eelt0059

Richards, J. C. (2008). *Moving beyond the Plateau*. New York, NY: Cambridge University Press.

Sarandi, H. (2016), Oral corrective feedback: A question of classification and application. *TESOL Quarterly, 50*: 235-246. doi:10.1002/tesq.285

Scrivener, J. (2005). *Learning teaching*. Oxford: Macmillan.

Shehadeh, A. (2001). Self- and other-initiated modified output during task-based interaction. *TESOL Quarterly, 35*(3), 433-457.

Swan, M., & Smith, B. (1987). *Learner English: A teacher's guide to interference and other problems*. Cambridge, UK: Cambridge University Press.

Taguchi, N. (2018). Presenting new language items. In J. I. Liontas, T. International Association, & M. DelliCarpini (Eds.), *The TESOL encyclopedia of English language teaching*, 1–6. doi:10.1002/9781118784235.eelt0193

Van Lier, L. (2014). *Interaction in the language curriculum: Awareness, autonomy and authenticity*. London: Routledge.

Zagorac, A. (2005). *Memory techniques in language learning*. Retrieved from https://ihworld.com/ih-journal/issues/issue-38/memory-techniques-in-language-learning/

Part 2
Case Analyses in Online Language Teaching Principles & Methodology

▶ Introduction

Unlike SLA theories, language teaching methods resonate easily with language teachers as teaching English requires methodology, and sound methodology will guide teachers in their daily practice and ensure positive learning outcomes. However, is there a particular language teaching method or methods that are more effective than others when it comes to teaching English to young learners online?

The 20th century has witnessed the rise and fall of a variety of language teaching methods ranging from the **Grammar-Translation Method** (**GT**), to the **Audiolingual Method** (**ALM**), to **Suggestopedia**, **Total Physical Response** (**TPR**), and **Communicative Language Teaching** (**CLT**). While some have achieved wide recognition and acceptance at different historical times, others faded away soon after they came into existence. Common to each method is the belief that its application is more effective and appealing than previous ones. But after more than a century of proliferation of methods in language teaching, we have reached "the post-methods era" (Brown, 1997; Richards and Rogers, 2001; Liu, 2007). By post-methods era, we mean that we are no longer confined to one particular method in language teaching as we have different learners with different learning objectives defined in curricula

and syllabi (scopes and sequences) and constrained by learning context, language contact, as well as many variables and factors. It is time for us to consider a principled and guided eclectic approach in language teaching (Liu, 2007).

An eclectic approach, by definition, is a compromise solution to the practical demands of teaching, and the specific content varies accordingly (Liu, 2007). For instance, how can we teach grammar without stifling communication and teach communication without ignoring grammar? For another example, how can we correct learners' linguistic mistakes without causing them to be hesitant to express their ideas, and how can we encourage their expressing of ideas without providing **corrective feedback**? These dilemmas in language teaching are not going to be solved with a simple or single solution. What we need is principled eclecticism (Larsen-Freeman, 2000) to meet the diverse demands of learners. There is a fundamental need for language teachers to keep abreast of language teaching principles.

In language teaching today, no one single approach is dominant. All the methods have both strengths and weaknesses. Perhaps more importantly, what benefits one learner in one context will not benefit a different learner in a different context. We are teaching individual people, each with their own experiences, motivation, and learning styles.

Since the late 1990s, individual approaches have been less evident. Instead many teachers use what has become known as **Principled Eclecticism**. This means selecting different activities from different approaches and methods to best meet the needs of the learners—"eclectic" because of the range; "principled" because you should always be able to justify why you have chosen it.

In Principled Eclecticism, **needs analysis** is important. Teachers should find out about what their learners need and want from the course. This can include preferred topics, preferred types of activities (reading, watching videos, discussing), and issues such as how much they want the teacher to correct their mistakes. It is also crucial to know why the learner is taking the course: to prepare for an exam, to travel or study in an English-speaking country, or because their parents are forcing them to!

Once the teacher or the course administrator has this information, they can prepare suitable topics, language goals, and activities to meet the learner's needs. This is particularly suited to one-to-one teaching–the teacher can design a course that should exactly meet that learner's individual needs. In a bigger class, the course content needs to balance the needs of all the learners.

In Part 2: Case Analyses in Online Language Teaching Principles & Methodology, we focus on basic language teaching principles that are reflected in 42 cases related to teaching pronunciation, vocabulary, and grammar to train learners' listening, speaking, reading, and writing skills. We cover both cognitive development and affective factors in learning. Moreover, we zoom into some techniques effective in teaching young learners English online, such as the use of music, songs, and games and how to assess their learning outcome.

Among all teaching principles relevant to language teaching, we highlight the following:

- **Maximize Learning Opportunities** No matter the subject area, teachers who maximize learning opportunities make the best use of the limited time that they have to work with their learners. In your context, you may only have a handful of minutes each time you meet with your learners. In online one-to-one teaching scenarios, for instance, the teacher can adjust the teaching pace based on the learner's reactions and responses. For those who have difficulties in following the instruction or interacting with the teacher, the pace can be slowed down while those who can easily follow and react should be given more challenging tasks by moving a bit faster so the learners will be engaged in learning without feeling bored.

- **Facilitate Negotiated Interaction** Essentially teachers want learners to use what they know to negotiate for meaning or for understanding. As a teacher, you will assist learners as they negotiate the understanding of the unknown information. Other components that would help to facilitate understanding are things such as pictures, video, or role-play, and props designed to facilitate communication in online learning.

- **Minimize Habitual Mistakes** As your learners become more comfortable and more willing to use the English that they know and are learning, teachers will begin to notice the same spoken or written mistakes occurring. As you address your learners' habitual mistakes, keep in mind that the first thing to do is to develop a safe teaching environment that allows learners to make mistakes. When learners feel safe to take risks and use their new language, it also allows them to feel free to make mistakes. It is through corrective feedback and correction of mistakes by way of recasting, prompting to self-correct, asking for clarification, and elicitation and repetition that learners learn and continue to build their confidence in their own language abilities.

- **Fostering Language Awareness** Language awareness means that learners are made aware of multiple-meaning words, the social registers that they will encounter, and the unique variations of the English language and ways to ask learners to engage with the English language. For instance, learners might be able to communicate their ideas without any problem, but the way they express themselves is different from the way native English speakers will do. Therefore, it is important for learners to be aware of the differences in how meaning is communicated and to be more conscious in trying to expand their vocabulary and expressions to maximize their linguistic and sociolinguistic repertoire.

- **Contextualizing Linguistic Input** In teaching English to young children, it is important to provide a context where the new words or sentences appear. It is tempting sometimes for teachers to teach isolated words or phrases for fear that learners might not learn everything if we present more than what we want them to learn. In fact, contextual clues are a great advantage for learners for both comprehension and output. However, in order for learning to take place from input to output through interaction and intake, teachers should always find a way, such as **scaffolding** (providing just enough support so that the learner can complete tasks successfully), to ease the learner in the process.

- **Integrative Teaching of Language Knowledge and Skills** When it comes to being an effective English teacher, it is not possible to teach a single skill or domain without teaching all four domains (listening, speaking, reading, and writing), as they are intertwined. Every lesson should include listening, speaking, reading, and writing though with different foci for each lesson.

While you may not be thinking of all four domains when preparing to teach, if you go back and look at a well-designed lesson, you will find all four domains addressed. For example, when you are asking learners to write, it is usually in response to something that they have read or seen—a story, a dialogue, or a simple picture prompt preceded by spoken instructions. When you then ask them to share what they have written, reading and speaking will come into play. In order to have a conversation, the basic requirements are two people who are willing to listen and respond. There is a reciprocal back-and-forth exchange of thoughts, ideas, or opinions through interaction and communication.

- **Foster Learner Autonomy** As a teacher, one of your goals for your learners is that they become autonomous in their usage of the **target language**. It is important to empower your learners in the understanding that they are competent in and capable of using the English that they are learning by making sure that you are building upon their prior knowledge and skills when engaging them in meaningful tasks and by encouraging them to take risks in using language they know. Also, it is important that you structure activities so that learners are working independently and/or with a partner or a small group. It is also useful as you come to the end of a lesson to have learners reflect on what they learned that day.

- **Provide Student-Centered Learning** The field of education has moved away from using teacher-centered learning methods and toward incorporating student-centered (also called learner-centered) instructional methods. This change in perspective affects the way in which teachers interact with learners and the expectations of how teaching should be done. Keep in mind that the teacher could be teaching in a way that is familiar to them but unfamiliar to their young learners. The potential problem is that neither the learner nor their parents may understand the value or methods of student-centered learning that values the extroverted, talkative language learner and risk-taker over the more introverted and cautious learner. When learner factors must be taken into consideration in the teaching of English as a foreign language, it is useful to have other strategies as options. Indeed, the focus on incorporating student-centered learning into **L2** (second language) education helps to move the field toward teaching through inquiry. The focus is on language use (how learners will use the language) not just on language knowledge (what the learners must know to give the right answers). It helps the learner make connections and learn how to ask questions, investigate, and even to reach their own conclusion.

- **Encourage Spontaneous Interaction**
While online English language classes are usually designed to keep in mind the attention span of learners at different age levels, learners could easily be distracted due to many factors such as a distracting learning environment, a lack of understanding, a lack of interaction, or a lack of direct physical appearance of the teacher to name a few. There needs to be engagement and spontaneous interaction between you and your learners. It might require some spontaneity on your part. When you feel the energy lagging on the part of your learners or in the lesson, create an element of surprise to get an excited or spontaneous response. It is important to have a number of spontaneous energizers to allow for a natural flow of conversation. Rather than staying true to the script of your lesson, allow for more give-and-take kinds of conversations.

In sum, we believe that the above nine teaching principles will guide you in selecting teaching methods and techniques that will best suit your learners. Since different learners have different learning styles, different learner characteristics, and varying language proficiency, it is better not to ask all the teachers to stick to one method or one technique for all. Rather, we hope that teachers will use common sense guided by these teaching principles to figure out how to teach your learners in a way that can ensure better learning outcomes. All the cases in this part will be thoroughly analyzed with recommendations for problem-solving and teaching effectiveness.

Question	Sub-Topic
1. How can I develop my skills as an English language teacher with limited time for professional development?	**Professional Development**
2. How can I focus my instruction on helping my learner meet learning objectives?	**Learning Objectives**
3. How can I make the most of limited planning time to support my learner during class?	**Planning**
4. How can I successfully give instructions so I am confident that my learner knows what to do?	**Giving Instructions**
5. How can I monitor my learner's work without class seeming too quiet?	**Monitoring Work**
6. How can I use rubrics to help my learner understand expectations?	**Using Rubrics**
7. How can I help my learner overcome a fear of testing and see the value of assessment?	**Understanding Assessment**
8. How can I gather real-time feedback about how my learner feels about activities?	**Gathering Feedback**
9. How can I incorporate the principles of the lexical approach in my lessons?	**Using the Lexical Approach**
10. How can I teach vocabulary that is especially difficult or is challenging to explain?	**Teaching Vocabulary**
11. How can I help a learner who struggles with new vocabulary?	**Vocabulary Struggles**
12. How can I use a phonics approach to help my learner become a better reader?	**Understanding Phonics**
13. How can I help my learner move beyond reading the words on the page to comprehending the text they just read?	**Reading Comprehension**
14. How can I incorporate top-down and bottom-up reading strategies into my classes?	**Reading Strategies**
15. How can I help a learner who struggles with reading?	**Reading Struggles**
16. How can I help a learner who struggles with new grammar?	**New Grammar**

17. How can I integrate concept checking questions into my lessons?	**Concept Checking Questions**
18. How can a teacher balance their focus on grammatical forms and meaning?	**Form Versus Meaning**
19. How can I balance my focus on fluency and accuracy?	**Balancing Fluency and Accuracy**
20. How can I help my learner practice spelling?	**Practicing Spelling**
21. How can I encourage my learner to express themselves while writing across the curriculum?	**Expressive Writing**
22. How can I provide appropriate feedback on learner writing?	**Writing Feedback**
23. How can I help my learner make the reading-writing connection?	**Reading-Writing Connection**
24. How can I help a learner who struggles with pronunciation?	**Pronunciation Struggles**
25. How do I encourage my learner to respond to questions instead of just repeating the question back?	**Moving Past Repeating**
26. How can I help my learner ask questions more independently?	**Asking Questions**
27. How can I help my learner who struggles to summarize thoughts or text?	**Summarizing**
28. How can I better help my learner remain on task during listening activities?	**Listening**
29. How can I incorporate top-down and bottom-up listening strategies into my classroom?	**Listening Strategies**
30. How can I help a learner who struggles with listening?	**Listening Struggles**
31. How can I help my learner make the listening-speaking connection?	**Listening-Speaking Connection**
32. How do I facilitate a worthwhile experience for a learner with mismatched skills?	**Mismatched Skills**

33. How do I facilitate a worthwhile experience for a learner who is in the wrong level?	**Wrong-Level Learners**
34. How should I differentiate lessons for a more advanced learner?	**More Advanced Learners**
35. How should I differentiate lessons for a less advanced learner?	**Less Advanced Learners**
36. How do I adapt material for an older learner who is in a lower level?	**Adapting Materials**
37. How can I help a learner who is behind when there are only 25 minutes in class that do not account for "catch-up?"	**Playing Catch-Up**
38. How can I help a learner who tries to rush through tasks?	**Rushing**
39. How can I facilitate role-play activities in a one-to-one classroom environment?	**Using Role Play**
40. How can I use games to help my learner in the classroom?	**Using Games**
41. How can I effectively use music in class?	**Using Music**
42. How can I encourage my learner to be a risk-taker?	**Taking Risks**

PROFESSIONAL DEVELOPMENT

How can I develop my skills as an English language teacher with limited time for professional development?

Keywords
#**communities of practice (CoP)** #**professional development (PD)**
#**standards**

► ## The Situation

II feel like I spend so much time planning, teaching, and writing feedback, that I do not have time to improve as a teacher. I have taken some workshops, but I have a hard time integrating those ideas into my classroom and don't always have time for those workshops in the first place. I want to make sure I'm the best teacher I can be for my learners and make more consistent efforts to improve. *How can I develop my skills as an English language teacher with limited time for professional development?*

Analyzing the Situation

- **Professional development** (**PD**) comes in many shapes and sizes and does not always involve a class, textbook, or scholarly article (although these are sometimes great places to start). Regular reflection and participation in professional **communities of practice** (**CoPs**) that can take place in your schedule can be just as meaningful.
- It is important to understand the range of skills required to be a successful teacher. VIPKid has developed a set of four teaching modules to help you understand the skills and subskills you need to be at your best: Theories and Principles of Second Language Acquisition, Teaching Methods, Teaching English Online, and Teaching Chinese Young Learners. In fact, these

FAQs are organized around these strategies to support your professional growth and development.

Suggested Strategies

You don't have to have hours of free time to improve your teaching. You do need your willingness to examine your own teaching and be intentional in your approach to professional development. Here's how

- **Utilize Existing Resources:** Take advantage of the range of PD opportunities provided by your employer or available to you for free online. Beyond workshops, certification, and mentoring, your company may work to develop resources like these FAQs to make learning accessible for teachers. The company may also facilitate a professional community of practice on social media through its Facebook page and Instagram channels.
- **Make PD Relevant:** The best professional development is targeted PD. Keep track of the challenges you face in the classroom and find learning opportunities and resources that are directly related. This will help you feel like the time you spend on professional development is time well-spent, and you will see your return on investment more clearly. You can also keep track of your successes and share them with your community of fellow teachers; this, too, will

help you to grow as a teacher.

- **Make Reflection Collaborative:** Instead of thinking of reflection as just another task on your own to-do list, consider organizing meetups or sharing a recent experience with your community on Instagram or Facebook. Simply taking the time to speak or write about your challenges and successes can allow you to discover so much about your own teaching and teaching of others. Do this regularly, and you will see your skills and professional network grow.

- **Be Systematic:** Identify areas of your teaching practice that you would like to improve and set a goal to pay close attention to your current approach for a week. Take notes on what worked and what did not. Next, spend 10-15 minutes every day exploring resources or connecting with your community of practice around that area of your teaching. Keep track of any insights you have or new strategies you want to try. Finally, spend a week putting those insights and strategies into practice in your classroom, finding what works for you and your learners. In under a month, you may be able to make noticeable progress that can positively impact how you feel about teaching.

- **Focus on Collecting "Multifunction Tools":** The most valuable items for you to have in your teacher's toolbox are those that can be used effectively in multiple situations, with learners of different ages and language levels, with different content themes and language concepts, etc. For example, you don't need dozens of ideas for vocabulary practice; you just need a handful that can easily be adapted and used for any set of vocabulary you are teaching, with multiple age groups, and with learners of various ability levels.

- **Ask Specific Questions:** Make the most of the time you do spend attending workshops by asking very specific questions of the speaker and even other audience members

if the format is open to it. The presenter is doing their best to cover the issues they believe most teachers need to know, but they cannot always predict exactly what your struggling with individually. Online CoPs are also an excellent place to ask very specific questions to your professional peers.

- **Be Persistent:** If you get a new idea from a workshop or other PD source, try it, and it doesn't seem to work for you, go back to the discussion boards, explain what you tried that didn't work for you and ask if anyone has other ideas. What works for one teacher's style may not work for your teaching style. Learners are all different; teachers are all different.

- **Create Solution Case Files:** You may encounter different challenges and problems with different learners, not because of the content or curricula, but because of how individual learners react and interact with you in the learning process. Therefore, it is very useful to create a case file to write down particular strategies that work and contextualize it. It is suggested that you create case files based on categories such as vocabulary, grammar, pronunciation, listening, speaking, reading, and writing. Every once in a while, you are going to review them and, when ready, you can summarize what strategies are useful for what kind of learners. Building this habit will not only make you a reflective teacher but also help others learn from you. This network of support among teachers will greatly enhance on-line teachers of English for professional development.

Reflection

- What is your current approach to professional development?
- Consider an area of your teaching in which you would like to improve. Set a goal using the suggested strategies above.

02 | LEARNING OBJECTIVES

How can I focus my instruction on helping my learner meet learning objectives?

Keywords
#extend #extension #objective #recycled language

► The Situation

Sometimes, in a 25-minute lesson, I will spend time focusing on important topics but at the expense of the stated learning objectives. I feel like I need to be responsive and cover issues as they come up in class, but I think I need to find better ways to keep the learning objectives front and center. *How can I focus my instruction on helping my learner meet learning objectives?*

Analyzing the Situation

- One of your first priorities as a teacher is to teach the lesson's learning objectives.
- The curriculum you follow is carefully designed to cover a wide range of topics, vocabulary, sentence structures, and grammatical concepts; it can be a disservice to the learner if any of these is not covered in the assigned lessons.
- A learner (or a teacher, for that matter) may get off topic for several reasons, including lack of interest in the topic or existing familiarity with the topic, which can lead to boredom.
- Sometimes a learner does already know all or most of the targets of a lesson, especially if they have learned English in the past with a different program.

Suggested Strategies

Keeping your lessons focused is not always

easy. But you can keep your lessons focused on the learning objectives found in the curriculum. Here's how.

- **Use Your Planning Time:** Typically, you will have a variety of types of targets to cover within a certain lesson. Use your planning time to consider how much of a lesson should be spent on each activity or series of activities. A simple timetable can help you keep yourself on track during class. Make sure to build in flex time to allow for unexpected issues.
- **Bring Them Back:** Should your learner lose focus on the topic at hand, very quickly bring the practice back to the topic and the learning objectives specified. Try using gestures or props to give your learner a visual cue that it is time to return to the task.
- **Level Up:** When you preview the activities provided in the curriculum, think about ways you could increase the challenge level incrementally. For example, perhaps first, the learner may be using a single adjective to describe a noun. If a learner meets that challenge easily, have them use two adjectives in a series to describe nouns. Can they come up with three to describe various nouns? The increasing levels of challenge will keep them interested much like the increasing difficulty levels of a video game do.
- **Gamify:** Even if a learner is already fairly familiar with the objectives, it never hurts for them to be reviewed. Mastery of the targets

of one lesson or unit is likely a prerequisite to mastery of an upcoming set of targets. You can make practice more exciting for learners by adding a timing element, point-keeping, having learners try to outperform their previous record, or adding an element of chance using the roll of a die, etc. to impact the number of points they earn (or even lose) during practice.

- **Extend Strategically:** Try to extend from the learning objectives instead of with an unrelated topic. For example, if the learning objectives involve learning some simple adjectives (*big*, *small*, *tall*), consider recycling nouns from previous lessons or encourage your learner to identify things in their own environment that can be described with those words.
- **Watch Your Lessons:** Depending on what platform you are using, all of your lessons may be recorded by the system and available for you to review. If you feel you are struggling to keep lessons focused on the topic and learning targets of the lesson, go back and watch a few of your past lessons to look for any common missteps.

- **Encourage Pre- and Post-Class:** Check to see that your learner has done any pre-class activity they may have been assigned. Ask them if they did it, if they liked it, and why. Give them verbal praise for finishing these activities. For post-class, make sure to encourage your learner at the end of class and try to be as specific as possible about what they should do.

Reflection

- Consider a lesson you will teach soon. What are the stated learning objectives? How much time will you spend addressing each objective? What are possible **scaffolds** or extensions you might need to support your learner?
- Watch a few of your recent lessons. Can you identify where you taught each of the stated learning objectives? How long did you spend on each? Did you extend beyond the objectives? If so, were these extensions connected to the learning objectives?

PLANNING

How can I make the most of limited planning time to support my learner during class?

Keywords
#curriculum #planning #prepare #time #transition

► The Situation

I do not always have a lot of time to prepare for my classes. I take some time to skim through the slides, but I often think of ideas in class, not before, which makes my ideas harder to implement. I know that the basic lesson planning has been done and materials have been created for me, but there seems like so much more I should be doing. *How can I make the most of limited planning time to support my learner during class?*

Analyzing the Situation

- Although some elements of planning may be included in the curriculum, every teacher is expected to prepare for class. Familiarizing yourself with the curriculum by reviewing slides and learning objectives is a start, but that should only be the beginning.
- Your comfort in class is transferred to your learner. The more prepared you are for the class, the more comfortable a learner will feel. When goals and/or content are ambiguous, learning is more difficult. Support your learner by being as prepared as possible for a range of scenarios.

Suggested Strategies

You do not have to spend an hour preparing every lesson, but you do need to be intentional and strategic about your planning. Here's how.

- **Use Feedback as a Tool:** Use previous teacher feedback or your own experiences with a learner to inform your planning. Consider what seemed challenging in the past or any interests that could be referenced in class. Consider the feedback you leave for other teachers about your own learner and how you hope teachers will use that feedback in future lessons.
- **Keep Wild Cards Up Your Sleeve:** Make sure you have a good set of adaptable language practice activities that don't require special materials and that can be used to teach almost any vocabulary set, sentence pattern, grammatical concept, etc. Possibly even post a list of the names of these activities in your classroom where you can see them, but the camera can't. Then, if you find the need to provide additional practice, you just glance at the list, pick one of your adaptable activities for teaching vocabulary, structures, dialogues, etc. and go into it, no preparation required.
- **Scaffold and Extend:** Be prepared with strategies to **scaffold** or extend activities in the lesson. Consider which activities are likely to challenge your learner the most and which may go quickly. For potential or likely trouble spots, prepare explanations or other examples at the appropriate level. For extension opportunities, select resources or consider recycling as a way of inspiring extended language use. Think of ways your learner can use the newly-learned language with language that is already

familiar to them.

- **Assemble Props and Other Resources:** Be prepared with the visual resources you need to support your learner. Arrange props and **realia** so that they are easy to access. Using class time to search for missing props or find a video clip is inefficient and can give your learner the impression that you are not prepared.

- **Plan Transitions/Phases:** Know where you will need to provide a meaningful transition and get familiar with the transitions that already exist in the curriculum. Planning for these transitions can make a big difference in the learner experience. A lesson should feel cohesive and coherent. Planning transitions can have a big impact. If there are slides that are back-to-back that seemingly have nothing to do with each other (like a grammar practice slide followed by a phonics input slide), consider how you can make these two slides seem like they belong next to each other. Is there a word on one of the grammar slides that

demonstrates an upcoming phonics rule? Can you use some of the just-practiced grammar to ask your learner a question about phonics?

- **Prepare Options:** Especially when working with a new learner, be prepared with options for reward systems or modes of interactions. This not only allows you to pivot if something is not working, but it also can allow for learner choice: "Do you like stars or rainbows (for a reward system)? Do you like puppets or stick figures (for facilitating interaction)?"

Reflection

- How do you currently plan for class? What do you typically add to or omit from lesson slides?
- What situations do you feel most prepared for and least prepared for with your current approach to planning? Which suggested strategies could strengthen your planning?

GIVING INSTRUCTIONS

How can I successfully give instructions so I am confident that my learner knows what to do?

Keywords
#checking #classroom management #grading language
#instructions #instruction checking questions (ICQs) #planning

▶ The Situation

When I teach my learner, she struggles to understand what I want her to do. I end up trying to explain the task to her on the spot, but she obviously doesn't understand me. By the time we get close to doing the task, we have already wasted so much time, or she has lost interest. Teachers are often told that they do not need to know Chinese in order to teach English online, but it seems like knowing some Chinese would help me with this problem. *How can I successfully give instructions so I am confident my learner knows what to do?*

Analyzing the Situation

- While receiving instructions, a learner with limited English may struggle more than a learner who knows more English.
- Providing detailed explanations can be frustrating for both the teacher and learner; the teacher feels misunderstood, and the learner does not know what is expected of them.
- Trying to think of instructions on the spot is stressful and can give the impression that a teacher is unprepared or unable to handle spontaneous situations that inevitably occur in the classroom. Instructions are a critical component of **classroom management**.

Suggested Strategies

You do not need to speak Chinese in order to deliver your instructions in English or model tasks for your learner, regardless of their age or language level. You do need to be patient and prepared. Here's how.

- **Set Clear Expectations:** Your learner wants to know what to do as much as you want them to know what to do! Be sure to include time limits and dos and don'ts as you give instructions.
- **Model Tasks:** Just because you can explain a task doesn't mean that you should. Showing a learner how to do a task is likely to be more successful than trying to explain the task, especially with a language learner who may be afraid of making mistakes.
- **Grade Your Language:** The instructions to your task or activity should not be more challenging than the activity itself. "Grading" your language means making yourself understood in order to set your learner up for success. This does not mean you need to give an explanation, but try to rely on the instructional language they may have already learned or a combination of gestures and physical modeling with very simple words, phrases, or sentences.
- **Script or Preplan:** Every class includes some level of unpredictability that you must deal with on the spot. It makes sense, then, to be prepared with your approach to instructions. This can include writing

or preplanning a "script" of instructions, including how and when to include any necessary gestures and physical modeling, so that you feel prepared.

- **Ask the Right Questions:** If you ask, "Do you understand?" your learner may respond in a variety of ways (e.g. head nod or reply, "Yes, teacher," because they feel embarrassed to not know). If you give clear instructions, you need evidence your learner knows what you want them to do. This is where you should ask **instruction checking questions (ICQs)**. You should ask these questions each time after you give instructions (e.g. "How much time?" "What color?")

- **Break It Down:** If a task includes multiple steps, break the instructions into multiple, incremental steps as well. Consider what the learner needs to know in order to do the task (or part of the task) at hand.

- **Roll with It:** Sometimes, it is not necessary for a learner to do an activity in the exact way the curriculum designers meant for it to be done. If the learner starts doing the activity in a slightly different way, but you feel the way they are doing it will just as adequately provide the needed practice, just let the learner do it their way.

- **Watch Yourself:** If you felt you struggled to communicate instructions to a learner for a given activity, go back and watch the recording of your lesson (if you have access to such a recording). Did you use overly complicated language (vocabulary, tenses, sentence structures)? Did you stick to simple sentences rather than compound or complex sentences? Often watching your lessons (or parts of them) afterwards can help you to improve your delivery in the future.

- **Use Gestures and Mime:** Sometimes learners will understand you better if you speak with appropriate gestures and mime. Children with limited language proficiency will understand and follow instructions if you use gestures that are expressive and can interpret what you are trying to say. For example, if you raise your right thumb to praise a good answer while saying, "Excellent job!" the learner will feel rewarded. Likewise, if the learner is not following directions, and you want the learner to understand, you can give a few choices and use gestures to indicate "No," and "Yes," to confirm the learner's comprehension.

Reflection

- What is your current approach to giving instructions?
- Are there specific activities for which you struggle to give instructions?

MONITORING WORK

How can I monitor my learner's work without class seeming too quiet?

Keywords
#classroom management #instructions #instruction checking questions (ICQs) #monitor(ing) #teacher talk quality (TTQ) #teacher talk time (TTT)

▶ The Situation

It takes a long time for my learner to start working after I give instructions or tell her to start a task. It can lead to some awkward silence while I wait for her to jump in. Usually, I try to talk her through the task some more, but we end up wasting time and not being very productive. I want to make sure she is working, but I am afraid that if I don't help talk her through the task, she won't ever complete it. *How can I monitor my learner's work without class seeming too quiet?*

Analyzing the Situation

- Your learner may struggle to start a task if they are unsure of what to do or how to interact with materials.
- Checking that your learner knows how to do a task does not stop with instructions and **instruction checking questions (ICQs)**. Part of a successful **classroom management** strategy includes monitoring your learner. When you monitor your learner's work during class, you check to make sure they are doing the task as originally intended from start to finish.
- Monitoring is especially important once you move out of the instructions phase of a task into the task itself. This is when it can be especially difficult, as a teacher, to stop yourself from talking. Your learner may need time to process instructions and

expectations before jumping in, and an abundance of **teacher talk time** (**TTT**) or poor **teacher talk quality** (**TTQ**) (where a teacher uses level-inappropriate language) can actually hurt a learner's confidence.

Suggested Strategies

You do not need to be afraid of a little quiet in your classroom. You do need to monitor your learner's work in a way that shows intentional restraint and patience. Here's how.

- **Start Over:** If, after giving instructions and getting appropriate feedback on your instruction checking questions, you monitor and see that your learner still does not start the task or demonstrates that they do not know what to do, start over. Stop any video or pause a reading, give the instructions and instruction checking questions again, and start over.
- **Have Clear Steps:** Break your task into steps if needed. It is easier to monitor tasks if they have a clear beginning, middle, and end. Consider the following task:
  - Your learner will listen to an audio recording of a child describing what they did on their summer vacation. Your learner will write down past tense verbs they hear. Then your learner will choose three of the verbs from the audio and add three new verbs to write or speak about their own summer vacation.

○ There is no need to explain the entire activity to your learner beforehand. Instead, you should lay out the different steps to the activity. This will make it clearer to the learner what they should be doing at any given point, and it will make it easier for you as a teacher to monitor that they are doing each step as intended.

- **Give It Time:** Try drawing out any quiet time at the beginning of a task even longer than you are comfortable. This may actually be the right amount of time for your learner, and it is a good opportunity for you to practice restraint and not fill up space with TTT. Remember that your learner might require more silence than you as a teacher feel comfortable providing.

- **A Little Background Music, Please:** Play some lyrics-free background music at a low volume while your learner is working. Tunes that are short and can be looped to repeat are best so you can provide as much time as the learner needs. (Think, for example, of the instrumental theme music played on the TV quiz show "Jeopardy" while contestants are writing their answers to the final question. "Pomp and Circumstance" is the instrumental loop music played during graduation ceremonies as diplomas are slowly handed out.) Music can also be used as a timing mechanism if you use a tune the child is familiar with (as in they should finish the task by the end of the song).

- **Play Along:** Consider doing the same activity your learner is doing. In this way, while your learner is working, you will also be working. (The task should be relatively simple for you, so you can still keep an eye on how your learner is performing while you are doing the task yourself.)

- **Take Notes:** If your learner sees that you have something planned to do while they are working on a task, it may help them focus on their own work without the quiet seeming awkward for either of you. Taking notes on a learner's pronunciation as they are reading or writing down follow-up questions to ask after a task are good ways to be engaged and monitor your learner's work.

- **Make Quiet Time Active:** Sometimes learners can concentrate in quiet moments. If you give a definite task with timing, then learners will think actively during quiet time, so for them, it is actually active time. Hence, quiet time is purposeful and facilitates thinking and reflection. A busy classroom and over-instruction might not generate a good learning outcome. It is the pacing of class mixed with talking, interaction, and silence that will do the trick.

Reflection

- What do you currently do in a lesson if a learner demonstrates that they do not understand what to do?
- Think of a listening task you conducted that was unsuccessful. Did this task have a clear beginning, middle, and end?

USING RUBRICS

How can I use rubrics to help my learner understand expectations?

Keywords
#expectations #Likert scale #praise #rating scale #rewards #rubrics

► The Situation

I often feel like my learner does not understand some of my basic instructions during an activity or what I expect from them in class. I find it tricky to link these expectations to rewards because I am not sure they understand why they are getting praise; I don't want to confuse them. ***How can I use rubrics to help my learner understand expectations?***

Analyzing the Situation

- A **rubric** is a tool for measuring learner performance involving some kind of rating scale. Rubrics can give your learner, their parents, and teachers a clear picture of strengths, weaknesses, and opportunities for improvement. In language classrooms, they are primarily used for assessing productive skills and behavior.
- Rubrics may be new or unfamiliar to your learner. They may not have ever been assessed in this way, so be intentional with how you introduce built-in rubrics or any that you create on your own.

Suggested Strategies

Rubrics can be a teacher's best friend. You can begin incorporating rubrics into your teaching to help your learner make sense of new expectations and get more out of each lesson. Here's how.

- **Use Existing Rubrics:** In some courses, there are rubrics built into lessons to assist teachers in assessing things like projects or other formative assessment. You could also consider a feedback form at the end of lessons as the start of a simple rubric and bring those expectations to the start of class.
- **Create Your Own:** As long as you keep things simple, feel free to incorporate rubrics of your own design. There are two important pieces to consider: the criteria and the rating. Make sure criteria are specific enough to be useful but not so specific as to be confusing for the learner. For example, a rubric intended to get your learner to interact more during class could include three points per criteria:
  ○ Asking Questions—Ratings: 3: three or more questions, 2: two questions, 1: one question;
  ○ Answering Questions—Ratings: 3: attempted all questions; 2: attempted some questions; 1: attempted at least 1 question.
- **Tie Them to Rewards:** Think about how your reward system or praise could be supported by a rubric. The more meaningful rewards are, the more effective they will be.
- **Go Visual:** Whenever possible, and especially for any lower-level learner, provide a visual representation or nonverbal explanation of every criteria and rating.
- **Checklist:** Write a simple checklist of required assessment tasks on a small

whiteboard. As your learner completes each task, put a checkmark next to that task. (Keep the items on the list limited to one or a few simple words.)

- **Have Your Learner Use Rubrics:** You can create a simple rubric or Likert scale (i.e. usually 1-5 or 1-7 ranging from "Strongly Disagree" to "Strongly Agree") to allow your learner to provide feedback on specific activities they like/don't like or different tasks they think are most/least valuable for them as a learner.

- **Share in Advance:** In advance of an assessment lesson, send the learner and their parents a checklist of tasks the learner will (or may) be expected to perform for the assessment and the order in which they will be expected. Be sure the items on the list are not so specific as to provide the answers to the assessment, or the learner will simply memorize responses before the lesson. You want it to be more like a study guide than an answer sheet!

- **Keep Rubrics Visual and Simple:** Try to use simple and consistent rubrics that can be easily understood and use them repeatedly to reinforce the understanding and reaction of the learner. Rubrics should be demonstrated and communicated to learners before being used. Good teachers know ahead of time what to use, such as "Good," "Bad," and "Excellent!" for learners' imitation of words or phrases, and examples should be given to learners ahead of time before using them.

Reflection

- What are your basic expectations for your learner in class? How could you use a rubric to support your learner's awareness of these expectations?
- Consider the rubric described in the Suggested Strategies. How could you provide visual support to help your learner understand the criteria and ratings?

 | # UNDERSTANDING ASSESSMENT

How can I help my learner overcome a fear of testing and see the value of assessment?

Keywords
#affective filter #assessment #evaluation #formative #gaokao #item
#summative #test

▶ The Situation

My learner gets very stressed out about tests. I try to get her prepared by telling her to breathe, practice, and study hard, but I am concerned that I am just making her anxiety worse. *How can I help my learner overcome a fear of testing and see the value of assessment?*

Analyzing the Situation

- While the idea of assessment is likely to cause some level of anxiety in a learner, your Chinese learner has a different relationship with tests, specifically because of the **gaokao.** The gaokao is a high-stakes assessment that a learner takes a while in high school to determine which university they will attend. Your learner grows up knowing about the importance of this test, so it is easy to see why they might think of assessment as a dirty word.
- Many courses include both ongoing, **formative assessments** to determine how a learner is doing throughout a course, as well as **summative assessments** that determine how much a learner has learned over a specific period of time. The assessment data that your employer gathers from these assessments is important, but ideally, the platform you are using should be fun and engaging for your learner to practice their English; it is not supposed to be as stressful

as their regular school experience. This is why assessments may appear as gamified components in some courseware.

Suggested Strategies

You do not need to treat each lesson before an assessment as a cram session. You do need to try to make your learner feel comfortable with assessment as an integrated and ongoing part of their experience. Here's how.

- **Highlight Learner Strengths:** You can ask your learner where they feel confident and which parts of an assessment they think they will do well on. It is easy for a learner to focus on where they need the most help, and as teachers, we spend quite a bit of time targeting tricky areas in order to help our learner improve. This is critical in class time, but it is not necessarily the best approach right before any kind of evaluation because it can make a learner start an assessment already feeling like they are disadvantaged.
- **Don't Tell Them How to Feel:** Avoid placing labels like "easy" or "difficult" on a task or an assessment. What seems easy or difficult to us as teachers might be the exact opposite for a learner. If they think they are supposed to do well on an "easy" test but find themselves struggling, it can raise their **affective filter** and influence the way they interact with an assessment as well as how

they perform on an assessment.

- **Give Testing Strategies:** Especially for your older learner who might be more mature about/familiar with testing, consider giving them some ongoing testing tips. Depending on the item (question) type, share with your learner different techniques they can use to better respond to an item. For example, if a multiple-choice item is based on a reading passage, encourage your learner to try to answer the question without looking at the options first. Then they can look at the options to see which one is closest to their original idea.

- **Think About Either Outcome:** Another strategy for an older learner involves asking them to consider different outcomes from an exam. If they do well on the exam, how will they celebrate? If they do not do as well as they would like, what do they plan to do? Encouraging your learner to have a plan on the other side of an assessment can make them focus and have realistic expectations.

- **Explain the Purpose:** If your learner knows enough English to understand the concept, let them know that these minor tests, unlike the *gaokao*, are used to help the learner and the teachers. It doesn't matter if they get some things wrong. This just lets them and their teachers know what they need to work on together. This sort of testing is just

as much about seeing how well we have taught as it is about how well they have learned.

- **Stick to Your Routine:** If you usually start class in a good mood with a song, do not change that on "test day." It is important that your learner sees test day as an integral part of the learning journey, and that is not necessarily more or less important than some of the other ways they spend time in their lessons. You can help with this by instilling in your learner a sense of familiarity and expectations.

- **Maintain Positivity:** Maintain a positive and cheerful persona throughout the assessment. If a learner makes a mistake, show no negative reaction during the assessment. If a learner sees you react negatively to one item during the assessment, it may severely shake their confidence through the remainder of the assessment.

Reflection

- How do you prepare your learner for tests? How does your learner respond?
- Which strategies from above do you want to try? How could you tweak your approach to fit the needs of your learner?

08 GATHERING FEEDBACK

How can I gather real-time feedback about how my learner feels about activities?

Keywords
#evaluation #feedback #satisfaction #take cues

▶ The Situation

I always want to make my classes fun and engaging for my learner. I reflect on how I think each class goes or how I think my learner performs in class, but I notice that even though my learner always does a good job, sometimes she doesn't seem to like doing OR working through the activities. *How can I gather real-time feedback about how my learner feels about activities?*

Analyzing the Situation

- It is important to gather feedback and evaluate how your learner feels about activities. If a learner enjoys an activity, they are more likely to engage with the content of the activity.
- Your learner is likely to feel more connected to your class if they think that their voice and opinions are being heard. Feedback allows your learner to have a voice in class and helps the lesson feel more like a partnership.
- Learners like routines (including routine activities) because they enjoy the satisfaction of predicting or anticipating what comes next; not knowing what comes next can make an already difficult language learning environment that much more difficult and intimidating. If you gather feedback on the activities your learner enjoys and dislikes, you can more easily personalize each lesson and make it more satisfying to your learner.

Suggested Strategies

Your learner will vary in the activities they like and dislike. Gathering real-time feedback from them after each activity will help inform how you navigate future lessons. Here's how.

- **Face the Camera:** Look at your learner's face. Do they seem happy or upset? Sometimes their feedback about a task is written all over their face, even if they cannot explain why they feel the way they do.
- **The "Eyes" Have It:** Learn to understand the reasons learners (or anyone) moves their eyes in various ways. Nonverbal communication using the eyes tends to be universal across cultures. Rapid eye movements can mean impatience. Slow eye movements indicate fatigue. Eye movement up and to the left—visual recall; up and right—visual construction; left—auditory recall; right—audio construction; down and left—Internal dialogue; down and right—kinesthetic. If you know enough about eye movements, they can tell you when learners are happy, excited, sad, disappointed, etc. (For more, search for "saccades" or "saccadic eye movement.")
- **Use Your Thumbs:** Getting into a habit of soliciting thumbs up, thumbs down, or thumbs sideways from your learner after each activity is a good way of getting real-time feedback without wasting precious class time.
- **Color Code It:** Once your learner knows colors, consider having them use colors

to give feedback and rate each activity. For example, model for them that green means, "Yes, I like it!"; yellow means, "It's okay,"; and red means, "No, I don't like it," and ask them to assign a color to each activity once it is complete.

- **Rank It:** Using a ranking system to solicit feedback can help you get a better understanding of how your learner feels about activities. This can include ranking lesson activities favorite to least favorite. You can take screenshots of different activities from the lesson and ask your learner to give a number from one to five or assign faces that represent least to most favorite.

- **Take Cues:** Sometimes your learner does not interact with material or activity in a way you anticipate or intended. This does not mean that all is lost. Pay attention to how your learner seems to think they are supposed to interact with a task. Does your learner sort flashcards onscreen instead of matching them? Do they try to drag vocabulary words or letters rather than circling them? Think of these missteps as cues or feedback about how a learner expects to interact with materials. These cues can help you get a better sense of how your learner wants to interact or communicate and can help you prepare for the next lesson.

- **Experience:** If you have not been teaching for long, recognizing how your learner feels about various activities and so on is challenging. Rest assured that with experience, you will be able to tell very quickly how a learner is feeling about an activity (or anything else) just through their nonverbal communication.

Reflection

- What is your current approach to soliciting learner feedback on activities?
- Which strategy(ies) from above do you think would work in your lessons?

USING THE LEXICAL APPROACH

How can I incorporate the principles of the lexical approach in my lessons?

Keywords
#chunking #collocations #lexical approach #fixed expressions #vocabulary

▶ The Situation

My learner seems to pick up on words quickly, but I am concerned because she can only really recall or remember these words in isolation. I can show a flashcard of an apple, and she can identify it in English, but the moment I try to ask her what it is or if she likes it, she cannot respond. She simply says "apple." I want her to be able to relate the word to an appropriate context. *How can I incorporate principles of the lexical approach in my lessons?*

Analyzing the Situation

- Your learner is used to translating word for word (e.g. *apple* is *pingguo* in Chinese) or associating a single word with a concrete representation of that image (e.g. an apple is represented by an image of an apple). This identification of vocabulary is a fantastic start, but it does not really demonstrate much about a learner's ability to communicate.
- The **Lexical Approach** began in the early 1990s and is a method that focuses on breaking language down into chunks rather than by grammatical structures. These chunks are lexical units and are critical because they promote communication more than **accuracy**. Consider the sentence, "She plays basketball on Fridays." We could break this sentence down into

meaningful **chunks**, for example "plays + basketball" and "on + Fridays."
- Collocations are words that are commonly found together, like the word *get* and other words that may be associated with it (*get a job, get online, get lost*, etc.

Suggested Strategies

You do not need to completely rewrite your lessons; chances are you will see many nods to the lexical approach in the curriculum already. You do need to have some strategies in your back pocket in case you see a moment where targeted work might lead to learner success. Here's how.

- **Use Substitution Drilling:** Consider the sentence above: "She plays basketball on Fridays." If you chunk this into "plays + basketball" and "on + Fridays," you can invite your learner to swap or substitute a word in each chunk to still make meaning. For example, *football* could be substituted for *basketball* or *Mondays* could be substituted for *Fridays* to make "She plays football on Mondays." A learner can make a lot of progress by using and building those collocated word relationships.
- **Finish the Sentence:** Build upon chunks and word relationships that are likely fixed expressions your learner knows by writing a single word on the screen, like the word *what's*. Then invite your learner to fill in

the next word they can think of. If they still struggle, provide the next word until they get the gist of the activity. You can do this with quite a few *wh-* questions or other chunks and collocations (and once your learner gets the hang of it, you can even do a word at a time).

What's _____ ?
What's your _____ ?
What's your name?

- **Promote Collocations:** Encourage your learner to think about words that are regularly partnered together, whether phrasal verbs like *put on* and *put up* or collocations like *fast food* and *hard work*. You can do this by putting a single word on the screen and brainstorming partner or companion words, then looking at those words in context (or vice versa).

- **Use Substitution Tables:** You can create simple graphic organizers on your screen that are either filled in already (as below) or that have certain elements missing or needing additions. Then have your learner practice building sentences. If you solicit the words from your learner and fill in the table, your learner will be able to more clearly demonstrate how much they know about language chunks. You can also show how fun (and funny) language can be.

| Dogs
Cats
Pigs
Rabbits
Horses | can | fly.
swim.
run. |
| | can't | jump.
eat pizza.
speak English.
play mahjong. |

- **Gamify It:** Add a point-keeping system to the exercise in which the learner earns a point for each word she uses in her response. A response of "apple" earns one point. "Yes, I do,"— three points. "Yes, I do like apples,"—five points. "No, I don't like apples, but I really do like peaches,"—eleven points. (Of course that last one is not going to really happen at this level, but you get the idea.)

- **Go Bananas:** Draw your learners' attention to the structure rather than the substitution vocabulary. Often you can do this by having them use the same (perhaps silly) vocabulary item while the rest of the sentence changes, but still uses the grammatical concept being taught. For example, have the learner insert the word banana or bananas into the slots in grammatically similar questions:

My dog eats bananas,
My dad makes bananas.
My mom drives a banana.
My teacher reads bananas.
My grandma lives in a banana.

The learner will pay more attention to the structure than the silly word inserted because it is the structure that makes it funny.

Reflection

- How do you currently present new vocabulary words? How does your learner respond?
- Which strategies from above do you want to try?

10 | TEACHING VOCABULARY

How can I teach vocabulary that is especially difficult or is challenging to explain?

Keywords
#chunking #high frequency words #immersion #lexical chunks #vocabulary

▶ The Situation

Sometimes I want to provide a definition or present new vocabulary that is hard to explain or define (e.g. the word *use*). When I think of how to explain it to my learner in the lesson, I find myself overcomplicating the definition and using an explanation that is more difficult than the word I'm actually trying to teach! I don't speak Chinese so I cannot translate, and I struggle to let my learner know the meaning clearly and quickly. These words are simple but very important for learning. ***How can I teach vocabulary that is especially difficult or is challenging to explain?***

concrete illustrations of *is*, *the*, or *a/an*, for example. These words don't have recognizable associations with gestures or illustrations. However, the learner needs to know them in order to understand phrases and sentences.

- It is important to remember that there is not a one-to-one correlation between every word English and Chinese. This is why it is important to think about presenting language in **chunks** instead of as single vocabulary words that might not make sense or have an easy explanation in isolation.

Analyzing the Situation

- Teaching these seemingly simple (yet abstract) vocabulary words is challenging but important, especially in language learning. About 220 of the highest frequency words used in print make up 75% of all words used in books. Being able to quickly recognize **high frequency words** (**HFWs**) without decoding will help your learner better understand the meaning of print and can help them become more fluent readers.
- Sometimes vocabulary and high frequency words cannot be defined by using a prop, gesture, or picture, making it difficult for a language learner to understand the meaning. Think about how to provide

Suggested Strategies

You do not need to be afraid of teaching abstract words. You do need to help your learner by putting new vocabulary in a meaningful context for them. Here's how.

- **Plan It!:** Plan ahead and think about which vocabulary words have clear explanations and the best way to explain them. Consider which vocabulary words will require a simple synonym; which vocabulary words will need gestures, **realia**, or pictures; and which vocabulary words will be more complicated explanations.
- **Be Age Appropriate:** Whatever method you use must be appropriate for the age and ability of your learner. For lower levels, examples in context are better than

definitions. Examples also help a learner learn to predict meaning based on context, prior knowledge, and experience.

- **Build on Prior Knowledge:** Think about when and how your learner has interacted with vocabulary in prior units or learning cycles. If you are presenting colors for the first time and know that your learner has already had success with classroom items (e.g. *book, crayon, pencil*), consider presenting colors using different colored books, crayons, and pencils. This way, even in your learner struggles to retain the new vocabulary, they will not feel totally defeated because they are familiar with school supplies vocabulary.

- **Chunk It:** Instead of presenting the vocabulary word *dog* in isolation, consider presenting and practicing the phrase "a dog" or the complete sentence, "It's a dog," so the entire phrase or sentence becomes committed to memory rather than individual words that comprise the phrase or sentence. Use your fingers to present as well (three fingers for, "It's a dog," where each finger represents a word and can act as a **recasting** tool during error correction).

- **Hit the Boards:** We cannot possibly explain ways to teach every abstract English word in this publication without it being as bulky as an unabridged dictionary. Rather, we recommend that if you have a concern about a certain abstract word you need to teach, go to the online discussion boards for professional English as a second/foreign language teachers and ask how others teach that word. Often different abstract words can be taught using totally different techniques.

- **Bricks vs. Mortar:** Understand that a learner need not understand every word in a sentence in order to comprehend its meaning. Firstly, know that some words are **content words** while others are **function words**. Content words are those that carry a lot of meaning (typically concrete nouns, action verbs, adjectives, and adverbs).

These are the bricks. Function words are either abstract or carry little meaning. These are the mortar. It takes time and multiple usages in different contexts for learners to fully understand function words, but they can usually understand the meaning of a sentence as long as they know the meanings of the content words. This is similar to the way we describe a wall as a brick wall rather than a brick and mortar wall.

- **Ask for Help:** Perhaps the child's parents speak English well enough to explain the meaning of certain abstract words to their child (using Chinese). Perhaps you have access to Chinese speaking colleagues who can help to explain it. Ask for help from such people if you feel it is imperative that the child understand the usage of the word immediately rather than over time through regular exposure to it.

- **Understand the Culture:** Chinese parents tend to put a lot of emphasis on learning vocabulary, and they focus on the learning of content words rather than including function words. First, understand and accept this. Second, explain to parents that some abstract words (and almost all function words) will take a while and regular exposure before the learner fully understands how to use them. Also explain that as long as the learner understands the general meaning of the sentences, they will come to understand how certain abstract words are used.

Reflection

- How do you usually teach simple words that have more abstract or hard to explain meanings? How do you plan for these words while preparing for your lesson?
- Which strategies from above do you think would be most successful in your lessons?

11 | VOCABULARY STRUGGLES

How can I help a learner who struggles with new vocabulary?

Keywords
#chunking #context #lexical approach #realia #subskill #vocabulary

▶ The Situation

It seems like each time I present new vocabulary to my learner she struggles to recall it or pick it up quickly enough to move into practice. When she struggles, I try to explain what the word means or provide more examples of it in dialogues, but nothing seems to work. ***How can I help a learner who struggles with new vocabulary?***

Analyzing the Situation

- Vocabulary is a sub-skill of all other linguistic skills (reading, writing, speaking, and listening), so it is an incredibly important component of any language learning environment.
- Before you can tackle the learner's struggles with new vocabulary, you need to pinpoint how they are struggling. Is there an issue with pronunciation when your learner repeats? Are some vocabulary words more prone to difficulty because of **L1** (first language) **interference**? Is the issue with remembering the word or with using it incorrectly? Does the problem arise consistently with tenses or **collocations**?

Suggested Strategies

Your learner is more likely to retain new vocabulary if it is in a context that is meaningful to them. The curriculum usually tries to account for this, but sometimes you need to take an extra step based on what you know about your learner. Here's how.

- **Make Every Word Intentional:** Every word you use in your lesson, from your first hello to your final goodbye, should be intentional, even (to some degree) your "free" talk. This is because if your learner does not know the words you are using, they do not know how to distinguish which words are the most important or the target language. This can make new vocabulary easier to forget.
- **Show First, Explain Later:** For vocabulary that has a pretty clear or concrete image associated with it, just show the image and say the word, versus trying to explain what it is. Also, keep in mind that if you show the image of a new vocabulary word alongside the text of that word (especially with an early or young learner with a low level of English), you have already doubled the amount of information a learner is supposed to take in. Adding an example sentence or even two adds significantly more to their cognitive load. Do this intentionally and only as your learner is ready.
- **Use Realia:** Using a real object when you present can be preferable to using a flashcard or image of an object. While you don't have the ability to physically share **realia** with your learner, your use of it communicates that an apple in a teacher's home office is the same as an apple in a Chinese grocery store.
- **Chunk It:** Instead of presenting the

vocabulary word *cat* in isolation, consider presenting and practicing the phrase "a cat" or the complete sentence "It's a cat", so the entire phrase or sentence becomes committed to memory rather than individual words that comprise the phrase or sentence. Use your fingers to present as well (three fingers for, "It's a cat," where each finger represents a word and can act as a **recasting** tool during error correction).

• **Focus on Lexical Sets:** Separate the vocabulary you need to teach into any existing **lexical sets**. For example, if you are teaching the word *cat*, there's a good chance you will be teaching *dog* and the words for other pet animals. Do an activity in which you practice that lexical set of vocabulary together. The existence of the set will give your child additional information about all of the words in a set. They will realize, "Oh, these are all words for pet animals."

• **Substitution Practice:** Words are almost always taught within certain sentence structures. Provide your learner with a sentence frame into which a lexical set of words can fill a blank slot, then practice the words by using picture cues and having the learner use the pictured word in the empty slot of the frame. You can turn this into a simple game by first going through the list of words in a particular order a couple of times, then have the learner try to guess which word you are going to show next (as they can recall the order). Then make the

activity more challenging by going through the words in the list backwards and see if your learner can still guess which word is next.

• **Be Silly:** If you are teaching a list of pets (for example) using the sentence frame, "I want a pet _____," slip a picture of an elephant or dinosaur into the stack of pictured words. Your learner will find it very fun to say something like, "I want a pet dinosaur." A child who is having fun and is mentally engaged tends to learn more readily than a bored child.

• **Use Graduated Interval Recall:** After you have introduced a new vocabulary word, sentence structure, grammar concept, etc. and practiced it a few times, bring it up again after a couple of minutes. Then bring it up again after ten minutes, then after twenty minutes, in the next lesson, and several lessons later. Even make notes of which words your learner is struggling the most with and bring up these words more frequently than those they seem to have already committed to their **long-term memory**.

Reflection

• Do you have a way that you prefer to present new vocabulary? How does your learner usually respond?
• Which strategies from above have you tried? How could you tweak your approach?

UNDERSTANDING PHONICS

How can I use a phonics approach to help my learner become a better reader?

Keywords
#analytic phonics #blending #decode #encode #grapheme #high frequency words #phoneme #phonics #reading #receptive skills #synthetic phonics

▶ The Situation

It is usually very difficult for my learner, who is younger and lower level, to pick up basic reading skills like sounding out words and noticing patterns. It seems like one minute they remember the word perfectly, then the next time I show it to them, they do not remember. *How can I use a phonics approach to help my learner become a better reader?*

Analyzing the Situation

• Phonics approaches are more difficult for a Chinese learner in part because they are based on a language, English, that has letters instead of characters. Chinese learners practice memorization of whole characters, and these characters are strung together as concepts versus English letters that follow phonics rules to form words and build up from there. This means that your learner may attempt to memorize the entire word *basketball* or even *basket* and *ball*, but breaking down the word into separate **phonemes** will be difficult and unfamiliar.

• There are two main schools of phonics instruction. **Synthetic phonics** involves building words up from their most basic parts, phoneme by phoneme and discovering the word that way. **Analytic phonics** involves **noticing** patterns or rules within whole words once the word has been identified. There are plenty of pros and cons of both approaches, and both of them should be reflected in the phonics

offerings of a good curriculum.

• Generally speaking, it is easier for a learner to practice **decoding** (or **blending**) the letters together to "read" words or parts of words, than it is to encode. **Encoding** refers to using letter/sound knowledge to write. If you build confidence in decoding, your learner will be more willing to take risks and apply that knowledge to encoding.

Suggested Strategies

You do not need to be a literacy specialist or phonics master in order to help your struggling or beginning reader. You do need to have a basic familiarity with phonics and think about how you can implement elements of a phonics approach in your lessons. Here's how.

• **Sound Subtraction:** In the very early stages of letter phonics learning, consider using a technique called sound subtraction (if the learner already knows the names of the letters of the alphabet). Most letter names contain the most common letter phonics sound they represent. All you have to do is to drop the vowel sound from the letter name and you have the letter sound only. This can be taught in groups according to what vowel sound you need to drop:

B		/b/
P	drop the long e sound	/p/
D	from the letter name	/d/
T	to get the letter sounds	/t/
V	(the phonemes)	/v/
Z		/z/

Other sets of letters you can drop a vowel sound from to get the phoneme include *F, L, M, N, S, X* (drop the short e sound from the beginning of the letter name to get the phonemes) and *J, K* (drop the long a sound from the end of the letter name to get the phonemes). For long vowels, the name of the vowel itself is the most common long sound it makes. Short vowels and *C, F, G, H, Q, R,* and *W* cannot easily have their most common phonics sound derived from the letter name in this way.

- **Step-by-Step:** Once you have taught the most common single-letter sounds, including both long and short vowels, your next step might be to practice two letter consonant blends such as *st, bl,* and *rp.* Then you need to teach multi-vowel sounds such as the usual sounds of *oo, ow, ai,* etc. Then you have digraphs like *sh, th,* and *ch.*

- **Sound it Out:** Start by sounding out sounds and associating the most typical sounds (phonemes) with the most typical written representation (graphemes) of the sounds. If you use this approach, you need to be consistent and include some element of practice in each lesson to help your learner build up a memory of these rules.

- **Work in Threes:** Before tackling multi-syllable words or words that include phonics rules that are a little more difficult for your learner (e.g. digraphs like *ch, th, sh*), practice with consonant-vowel-consonant (CVC) words. These are common three letters words or nonsense words. (Nonsense words may end up being components of larger words later on.) If that is still a struggle for your learner, try starting with just VC combinations.

- **Practice "Easy" Words First:** Start practicing with words like *dog, pig, pen,* and other words that follow pretty straightforward phonics rules. You can even focus on parts of words or nonsense words. Reading can be especially tricky for a language learner because many of the common vocabulary words for a lower-level learner do not follow an easy phonics rule. Consider the

words *pencil* and *scissors,* which are pretty common, low-level words that do not necessarily have an easy (early) phonics rule for a learner to pick up.

- **Look for "Good" Errors:** Look for opportunities to praise your learner's phonics knowledge, even if the word is spelled incorrectly while writing (encoding). If a learner spells "pensul" or "sizzers", these are good errors for them to make, because they acknowledge some level of phonics knowledge in the spelling. If your learner is able to blend letters together as they decode, it is easier to appreciate spelling errors.

- **Explain Exceptions:** Let your learners know that just like certain elements of English grammar, verb conjugation, etc., there are exceptions in phonics. For example, usually the combination of letters *eigh* makes the long a vowel sound (the sound in *tape*). Take for example the words *eight, weight,* and *neighbor.* However, there are exceptions to this rule. For example, the word *height* has the long *i* sound (the sound in *type*).

- **Site Words:** Although this question is about phonics, realize the importance of leveraging both phonics decoding and sight word recognition. Many very frequently used words in English use fairly advanced phonics. Consider *the.* It must be learned early in any program, but it consists of a diphthong followed by a schwa vowel. The most common word in English is *of.* Why isn't that one spelled "uv"? Such words are better taught as sight words, and do not even get us started on words like *queue* and *colonel!*

Reflection

- How do you currently implement elements of phonics instruction in your lessons? How does your learner respond?
- Which strategies from above do you want to try? How could you tweak your approach to fit the needs of a learner?

13 | READING COMPREHENSION

How can I help my learner move beyond reading the words on the page to comprehending the text they just read?

Keywords
#blend #comprehension #decode #extensive reading #intensive reading #reading task #receptive skills #skim #scan #segment #text-dependent questions (TDQs) #text to self questions

▶ The Situation

I have a learner who can decode words and sentences on the page, but when I ask about the content of the reading, he seems lost. I want to help him become a more proficient reader, but I just don't know the best approach. *How can I help my learner move beyond reading the words on the page to comprehending the text they just read?*

Analyzing the Situation

- **Decoding** and reading are very different things, but it is a good start that your learner is able to decode. **Chunking** together letters (**blending**) and breaking down words (**segmenting**) is a difficult task in its own right.
- Moving your learner from understanding how the language works on the page to comprehending and responding to the content can be challenging but rewarding.
- Once you help your learner unlock their ability to **read intensively** (structured, focused reading that usually takes place in the classroom), you might be able to spark the desire to **read extensively** (reading away from the classroom).

Suggested Strategies

You do not need to start over with your learner or find all-new texts for them to explore. You do need to have specific tasks in mind as your learner develops different reading skills. Here's how.

- **Scan or Skim:** It may be easier for your learner to start by scanning or looking for particular bits of information, within a text. Scanning a text can make the purpose of a task seem more clear or immediate. After doing some scanning activities, it may make it easier to approach skimming, or quickly reading to get a general idea.
- **Have Clear Pre- and Post-Tasks:** A pre-reading task might include showing some pictures to establish context for you learner and to help them warm up to reading. A post-reading task could be as specific as highlighting words in a text and asking what they suggest about the passage overall. (E.g. Highlight all the adjectives the author uses to describe her vacation. Did she have a good or a bad trip?) or encouraging your learner to rewrite the ending to a story.
- **Break It Up:** If a passage is long or complicated, a learner may feel fatigued and less likely to interact with it. Consider breaking a reading task down or offering time to dissect and discuss certain portions of the text. This may mean breaking a

sentence down into chunks of words, breaking a paragraph down into sentences, or breaking down a longer text into paragraphs. Have the learner read a single sentence or two, then ask them direct questions to make sure they comprehend just that small portion of a larger text.

- **Ask Text-Dependent Questions:** Have your learner answer **text-dependent questions (TDQs)**, questions that can only be answered if your learner refers back to the text. Get your learner into the habit of relying on the text to support analysis, even at lower levels. Consider the following sentence: "Julie goes to the park on Sundays." You could ask the following TDQs:

    Who goes to the park on Sundays?
    Where does Julie go on Sundays?
    When does Julie go to the park?

- **Ask Text-to-Self Questions:** Sometimes it is appropriate to encourage a personal connection to the text. If you read a passage about a summer camp, for example, ask your learner questions like, "Have you ever gone to a summer camp?"; "Do you want to go to a summer camp?";

or "What kinds of things do you do at a summer camp?" These kinds of text-to-self questions help a learner personalize the information they've just read. They are a good companion to TDQs.

- **Question the Teacher:** After reading a portion of the text (or even the entire text) encourage the learner to ask you questions related to the content of the text. This technique works better if you tell the learner before reading that you will have them ask you questions about the text. Then, as they read, they will concentrate very much on the content so they are prepared to question the teacher.

Reflection

- Are there certain reading activities and texts that seem more challenging to your learner than others?
- Think of a successful reading activity you may have done recently. Why was it successful? How did your learner engage with the text and the reading task(s)?

14 | READING STRATEGIES

How can I incorporate top-down and bottom-up reading strategies into my classes?

Keywords
#**bottom-up** #**decode** #**high frequency words (HFWs)** #**prediction** #**reading** #**sight words** #**top-down**

▶ The Situation

I have a young learner who is starting to read fairly long passages. She can usually read the text, but I am not sure if she really understands everything or if she is just sounding out the words. I know that reading can be approached top-down or bottom-up like this, but I'm not sure how to encourage the right strategies at the right time. *How can I incorporate top-down and bottom-up reading strategies into my classes?*

Analyzing the Situation

- **Bottom-up** reading involves the learner knowing phonics rules and sight words, then assembling sounds to form words and words to form sentences. Basically, all of the information comes from decoding the text. Top-down reading requires the learner to apply background knowledge and higher-level thinking skills when encountering a text. Trying to predict the content of the text and skimming text are examples of **top-down** reading strategies. Some of the information and understanding actually comes from the learner's background knowledge rather than from the text.

- Beginning readers rely on bottom-up reading strategies like decoding when learning to read, but more advanced readers should also regularly practice top-down reading strategies. Most researchers agree that a model allowing for both processes to interact is ideal.

Suggested Strategies

By understanding how these bottom-up and top-down processes can work together, you can help your learner read more confidently. Here's how.

- **Start with Bottom-Up:** For beginners, start with letter phonics, followed by combining sounds to form words and building up phonics "rules" (what the letters sound like by themselves or when partnered with other letters, like blends and digraphs).

- **Remember L1:** Keep in mind that Chinese does not use an alphabetic writing system but rather one made up of symbols (called characters) that represent entire words. For this reason, it is important to reinforce the relationship between individual letters and their sounds (and why it might be even more difficult for beginning readers to pick up on the principles of decoding).

- **Introduce Sight Words:** It is also helpful for beginners to learn to recognize some **high frequency words** (**HFWs**) on sight (e.g., *this, the, and*). This is called **sight word recognition**. It is important for your learner to distinguish between sight words that they need to recognize immediately and words that they need to decode. A good way to introduce and practice sight words is to have them flash on-screen quickly as a whole word to promote quick recognition, versus blending and segmenting words piece by piece while decoding.

- **Introduce Skimming:** Give the learner a fixed time limit in which to just skim the text trying to notice key words such as nouns, verbs, adjectives, and adverbs. Then ask them generally what the selection is about.
- **Encourage Predicting:** If a learner can speak enough English to explain things simply, each time you do a reading activity, have them look at the pictures or illustrations, then guess what they think the text selection will be about. You can also

do this with titles and headings.
- **Make Connections:** Before reading, ask the learner what they know about the topic or what their opinions about it are.

Reflection

- Are there certain types of reading activities and texts that seem more challenging to your learner than others? If so, what do these activities and texts have in common?
- Think of a successful reading activity you may have done recently. Why was it successful? How did your learner engage with the text and the reading task(s)?

15 | READING STRUGGLES

How can I help a learner who struggles with reading?

Keywords
#blending #high frequency words #phonemes #phonics #reading #reading strategies #reading struggles #SQ3R #text

▶ The Situation

My learner has a difficult time with reading activities. I am concerned that if I cannot help her, she is going to end up hating reading, which is such a valuable skill for a successful language learner. I have tried having her repeat after me while she follows along, but I am afraid that I am just helping her develop bad habits. ***How can I help a learner who struggles with reading?***

Analyzing the Situation

- Reading struggles can look very different for different learners. Some learners may not even be able to string letters together to make simple words (blending), and others may be able to read the words on the page but not necessarily comprehend what they are reading.
- Having your learner read after you and follow along may seem valuable, but if your learner is just repeating after you, then they are focusing more on listening and speaking than on reading rules or pre-literacy skill building.

Suggested Strategies

You do not want your learner to be nervous every time they see a printed word. You do want them to feel like they are capable of being successful readers. Here's how.

- **Highlight What Your Learner Knows:** It is common for a learner to look at a page or a screen and highlight or draw attention to all of the words they don't know. This can be incredibly de-motivating to a learner. Instead of highlighting the words your learner doesn't know, try highlighting all the words they do know. Then you can work together to figure out the meaning of the other words, with the goal of highlighting the entire page, screen, or section of text.
- **Get Back to Basics:** If your learner struggles to even string letters together, consider doing some blending work and reviewing letter sounds (**phonemes**).
- **Highlight Content Words:** Have your learner go through the reading selection and, with your help, highlight or underline the **content words** (concrete nouns, action verbs, adjectives, and adverbs). When it comes to comprehension tasks such as reading, just focusing on the content words will give your little reader a very good idea of the full content of the reading selection.
- **Have a Purpose:** Establish which kind of reading task you want to do. Perhaps ask your learner to skim the text to get a general idea of it or to scan the text for specific details. Whichever task you choose to accompany a reading text, make sure your learner knows beforehand.
- **Engage with the Text:** When your learner is reading, encourage them to focus on

sentences that they think are important or the most meaningful. This will be an important skill for them to develop as they start to write and focus on supporting ideas with text evidence. This could be as simple as starting with questions like, "Which sentence from the text is your favorite?" and "Why?"

- **Start Small:** Your learner may often struggle to come up with big ideas after reading. After/while reading, encourage them to put a sentence at a time into their own words. Then ask them to approach paragraphs the same way, putting a series of paragraphs into their own words.
- **Use the SQ3R Method:** SQ3R stands for Survey, Question, Read, Retrieve/Recite, Review, and it may be an effective method for a higher-level learner, as it is a good way to combine some of the strategies included above. Survey: scan the text for purpose and main ideas. Question: create your own questions. Read: be an active reader based on the previous two SQ steps. Retrieve or Recite (often used interchangeably): put the information into your own words, from memory, as if retelling the text to someone else. Review: share the purpose of the passage in your own words and ensure you are able to answer all the questions you formed early on.

Reflection

- What are some examples of reading activities and texts that seem more challenging to your learner than others?
- Think of a reading task you did that got a positive response from a learner. Why was it well-received? How did your learner engage with the text?

NEW GRAMMAR

How can I help a learner who struggles with new grammar?

Keywords
#concept checking questions (CCQs) #grammar #inductive #rules

▶ The Situation

Teaching grammar can often be frustrating. My learner doesn't seem to pick it up easily, and I cannot seem to figure out how to help her. I try and correct errors related to the new grammar we are learning, but it doesn't seem to be enough. *How can I help a learner who struggles with new grammar?*

Analyzing the Situation

- English grammar "rules" almost always have exceptions, which can confuse someone learning English as a foreign language.
- Early and young language learners learn grammatical concepts differently from adolescent and adult learners.
- Children have an innate ability to learn languages, but in the process, they must be exposed to many examples of correct usage of English grammar, which takes time but may also allow for greater fluency.

Suggested Strategies

Teaching new grammar does not have to be intimidating, and you do not have to be a grammar wiz to be effective in your instruction. Here's how.

- **Use Examples:** Young learners tend to learn language **inductively** from repeated exposure. Be sure to expose your learner to multiple examples of sentences using a certain grammatical concept correctly, then put them into a situation in which they need to speak using the same grammatical concept.
- **Same Grammar, Different Context:** Think of ways the target grammar structure at hand can be used with different themes or contexts the learner has experienced earlier in the curriculum and show the learner how the same grammatical concept can be used in multiple contexts:

  I really like baseball. (sports, the context of the current unit)
  I really like mangos. (food, previous topic)
  I really like robots. (toys, previous topic)

- **Be Patient:** Inductive learning does require using many examples and plenty of practice, but a learner who learns through such inductive learning usually has much better fluency than those who learn from direct instruction.
- **Use Visual Cues:** For differences like relative pronouns, consider other visuals to prompt your learner. For example, simple, brightly colored props with pronoun labels could be used to remind a learner during class. Later, you can even remove the pronoun label for a less **scaffolded** prop. You could apply this same strategy to articles. Color coding different parts of speech or the negative forms can be an effective way to draw attention to particularly tricky grammar components.
- **Use Timelines:** Think about specific strategies relevant to the common errors

above. For teaching and reinforcing verb tenses, timelines can help your learner visualize the language in a clearer way.

- **Use Concept Checking Questions (CCQs):** Ask your learner **concept checking questions** to ensure that they understand new grammatical concepts.

17 | CONCEPT CHECKING QUESTIONS

How can I integrate concept checking questions into my lessons?

Keywords
#CCQs #concept checking question #grammar #input #practice #questioning #timeline #vocabulary

▶ The Situation

It seems like every time I teach my learner new language, we struggle to get going. I'll present new language or provide input and ask her if she understands. She always says yes, so I feel like it is time to move on. Then, when we start to practice using the language, she freezes or makes mistakes, and I have to go back. I want to ensure she feels comfortable with the new material before moving on. ***How can I integrate concept checking questions into my lessons?***

Analyzing the Situation

- We need to ask **concept checking questions (CCQs)** to let our learner demonstrate that they understand concepts the way they are supposed to before they try to practice using them. While CCQs are often thought about with regard to grammatical concepts, they can be used for vocabulary as well.
- If you ask "Do you understand?", "Got that?", or "Okay?", a learner may exhibit behavior that suggests you can move on, but that is no guarantee that they actually do understand. There are three things that could be going on: 1.) the learner thinks they understand, but they do not; 2.) the learner knows they do not understand, but they are afraid to admit it; 3.) the learner may partially understand and not realize that they do not fully understand.

Suggested Strategies

You do not need to feel helpless as you try to get an honest response from your learner about whether they understand new language. You do need to be proactive and think about CCQs while preparing for your lessons. Here's how.

- **Write Them Out:** It is best to think about and account for CCQs before your lesson rather than on-the-spot (as that is when we tend to overcomplicate our language). Consider the following conditional sentence: "If I had a million dollars, I would buy a yacht." A series of CCQs might look like this:
    Do I have a million dollars? (No.)
    Can I buy a yacht now? (No.)
    Is a yacht expensive? (Yes.)
    When will I buy a yacht? (When I have a million dollars.)
- **Check Often:** You cannot move on to new material without checking that the new input has been understood. Teach a little, then check for understanding and determine if you can move on or if you need more input.
- **Play "Silly Teacher":** With a younger or low-level learner, concept checking questions can be as simple as showing a flashcard of a cat and declaring, "It's a dog," or asking, "Is it a dog?" Your learner will likely correct you very quickly, demonstrating that they recall two vocabulary words. If they do not respond, then you know you need more

input in the **target language**.

- **Start Small and Work Up:** You want to concept check by using language that is simpler than the language being presented. When asking concept checking questions, it is best to start with a *yes/no* question (or short series of *yes/no* questions) before working to with a short-answer question or, in some cases, an "I don't know," answer. This is because CCQs should be easy to answer.

- **Throw a Curve Ball:** It may be helpful to ask one question you know will be challenging for the learner—but only one. If the learner can respond correctly to a challenging prompt, they likely do fully comprehend the target concept. If they cannot, then they may not. Never throw more than one "curve ball" so that your learner does not become discouraged and, if you do throw one, praise them for doing their best and tell them it was a very hard one to get right.

- **Use Timelines:** Especially once you start working with mixed verb tenses, timelines are an effective way for your learner to visualize events that happened in the past,

events that happen regularly, events that are currently happening, etc. For example, consider the sentence, "She will be seven on Tuesday." On a timeline this sentence may look like this, followed by appropriate CCQs:

Is it Tuesday now? (No.)
What day is it? (Whatever day it actually is.)
Is she seven now? (No.)

Reflection

- How do you currently check to make sure your learner has understood a newly presented concept? Do you struggle more with checking new grammar or new vocabulary?
- Which strategies from above do you want to try? How could you tweak your approach to fit the needs, age, and level of your learner?

FORM VERSUS MEANING

How can a teacher balance their focus on grammatical forms and meaning?

Keywords
#error correction #grammar #grammatical form #meaning #function
#inductive #deductive #noticing #recasting #overt correction
#communication

▶ The Situation

My learner often struggles trying to get the grammatical form of what they want to say correct. I wish they would pay less attention (at least at first) to the form of what they are trying to say and put more emphasis on getting their meaning across. I can help them improve their grammar once they have at least communicated what they mean (even if it wasn't entirely grammatically correct), but it is sometimes difficult to do this in class. *How can a teacher balance their focus on grammatical forms and meaning?*

Analyzing the Situation

- The goal of learning a language is communication, and this is reflected in the language standards followed by most curricula. Often, a learner can communicate meaningfully without using perfect grammar.
- It is common and expected for a language learner to produce sentences that are both grammatically incorrect yet still clear in their meaning. Learners tend to benefit significantly from making errors and mistakes as long as they **notice** them (or are helped to notice them).
- Especially with a young learner, teachers should focus more heavily on **function** (meaning) than on grammatical **form**.

Suggested Strategies

You do not need to completely kick grammar out the door. You do need to find a balance between grammar and meaning and leverage techniques to help your learner communicate clearly within this balance. Here's how.

- **Leverage Inductive Teaching:** Inductive learning allows your learner to notice patterns in language and work out language rules on their own. Provide multiple examples of a grammatical form being used correctly and encourage your learner to produce similar language based on their own points of view. **Deductive** learning involves providing a rule that your learner practices with specific, provided examples.

- **Recast:** When your learner makes mistakes, but their meaning is clear, it is best to use recasting. This means you acknowledge the learner's conveyance of meaning, but you repeat what the learner said using the correct grammatical structure. You do this with minimal interruption of the flow of the lesson so that the learner notices their mistake so they can try to correct it in future utterances.

- **Start with Content Words:** First, have your learner just say the subject noun, the verb, and the object noun or whatever **content words** (concrete nouns, action verbs, adjectives, and adverbs). Their meaning will probably be clear just from those words. Put these in a list, then work with the learner to add any content words they may have missed then **function words** like articles, determiners, prepositions, and conjunctions to complete a grammatically correct sentence.

- **Get the Gist:** Once your learner has provided the content words, show them you can already understand the gist of their meaning by adding function words and using a questioning intonation at the end of your sentence so they can correct you if you have it wrong.

> S: Like eggs breakfast.
> T: You like to eat eggs for breakfast?
> S: Yes...I...like to eat eggs for breakfast.
> T: Oh. I like to eat bread for breakfast.

- **Take Out the Grammar:** Consider providing your learner with key words that have any grammatical forms missing and asking them to connect these words using any grammar they see fit. If you can share one learner's

work across lessons with other learners, it can be a powerful way to show how we balance meaning and grammar.

- **Sentence Jumbles:** Take sentences and mix the words up. Have your learner put the words back in the correct order. If they stumble, consider providing the first word or the last word (then additional words as needed) until they are able to do the task successfully on their own. Your learner may not realize they are combining meaning and form as they navigate the words that belong in the sentence.

Reflection

- How do you currently balance your focus on form and meaning?
- Think of a particular learner who struggles in this situation. Which strategies from above could you try in your lessons to help this learner?

19 | BALANCING FLUENCY AND ACCURACY

How can I balance my focus on fluency and accuracy?

Keywords
#accuracy #error correction #fluency #rules

▶ The Situation

I always want to teach lessons that help my learner communicate in English, but I feel like when I focus on accuracy through a lot of error correction, I see a drop in fluency. When I focus on fluency, I see a drop in accuracy. I've heard some people say that we should prioritize accuracy and others who say fluency should be the target. ***How can I balance my focus on fluency and accuracy?***

Analyzing the Situation

- **Accuracy** involves the learner following a system of "rules." **Fluency** involves how easily or fluidly a learner can communicate. Both are important aspects of language use, and you will indeed notice trade-offs as your learner focuses on one or the other with new language. This is normal; with time and a balanced approach, both accuracy and fluency can be achieved.
- Typically, accuracy-focused activities come before fluency-focused ones in a lesson. This is to focus a learner's attention on the **target language** before encouraging freer production.
- A good teaching platform should focus on helping each learner develop the ability to communicate comfortably and confidently in English. While errors can get in the way of communication and can be especially important in certain contexts, an overemphasis on accuracy can also get in the way.

Suggested Strategies

Accuracy and fluency are critical in language teaching and learning. You can confidently integrate accuracy and fluency into your lessons. Here's how.

- **Know the Culture:** Understand that in Chinese culture, perfect accuracy is paramount. You can try to reduce your learner's focus on accuracy, but that focus is already ingrained in them. Praise learners for grammatically incorrect answers as long as they were said fluently. (Keep notes and go back at the end of the activity to correct accuracy.)
- **Know Your Goal:** Understand ahead of time whether an activity should have a fluency or accuracy focus. Add this to other considerations, like what props you will use, as you prepare for your class. You can also encourage a higher-level learner to guess whether an activity will have a fluency or accuracy focus (or both) and which cues help them make this assumption.
- **Share Expectations:** Let your learner know whether they should focus on ignoring accuracy while getting their message across or if they should try to produce grammatically accurate responses.
- **Go Familiar for Fluency:** If your target is fluency, use content that is already familiar to your learner and ideally high-interest. Introducing new language can derail a learner's fluency as it adds additional cognitive load, and low-interest topics can make it difficult for your learner to stay

engaged.

- **Communicate!:** One of the features of fluency activities is a focus on communication in real time. These activities focus on whether the learner's message can be understood and whether the appropriate meaning is being shared.

- **Provide Support:** To support fluency, provide resources like a word bank to enable the learner to push beyond their current proficiency and hold back on most error correction until the end of an activity. To support accuracy, limit the focus of the activity and provide targeted feedback on the spot.

- **Establish Routines:** Choose some common activities to practice either fluency or accuracy with your learner. This way your learner will associate a kind of activity with a fluency or accuracy focus. For example, if you regularly start each class with your

learner speaking freely for 30 seconds, you want them to associate this activity with fluency; do not change course and start picking apart your learner's grammar. Similarly, if you use sentence jumbles to encourage your learner to think about word order, you want to consistently do this to practice accuracy.

Reflection

- Consider your current approach. Do you think you tend to favor a focus on accuracy or fluency? If so, which of the suggested strategies could you use? If not, how do we achieve a balance with your learner?

- Consider one of your current learners. Which of them could benefit from additional attention to fluency or accuracy? How could you apply the suggested strategies above to support this learner?

PRACTICING SPELLING

How can I help my learner practice spelling?

Keywords
#decode #encode #grapheme #high frequency word (HFW) #phoneme #pinyin #spell

▶ The Situation

I know that I should not conduct an entire lesson practicing spelling with my learner, but I want to help give her the skills to succeed when she writes and spells. I do not want to make her hate spelling or doubt her ability. *How can I help my learner practice spelling?*

Analyzing the Situation

- Spelling is a difficult skill for many language learners, especially for Chinese learners of English because the two systems of writing are completely different. Chinese learners do learn to write using *pinyin*, which is the romanization of Chinese characters and literally means "spell sound," but there are still sounds in each language that do not exist in the other.
- Consider a word like *judge* /dʒʌdʒ/, where the /dʒ/ **phoneme** (sound) is represented by both **graphemes** (letters) *j* and *g* versus the word *go* (/goʊ/). The letter *g* looks the same in both words, but it sounds different each time. English is full of many of these kinds of complications, and they can make it tricky to be a successful speller.

Suggested Strategies

You do not need to prepare your learner for a spelling bee every time you meet. You do need to have some ideas about how to practice spelling quickly and reinforce its importance in the language classroom. Here's how.

- **Teach Your Learner to Ask:** Once your learner is able to identify letters of the alphabet and write them accurately, get them in the habit of asking, "How do you spell...?" so that they can take ownership of this question and acknowledge when they need your help. If they are able to actually write while you spell something out for them, try to give them the opportunity to show you what they have written down or typed out.
- **Know the Difference:** Once you have worked with phonics, make sure your learner knows early on if they are being asked to recall and write a **high frequency word (HFW)** or **sight word** from memory or a **decodable** word that can be sounded out before being **encoded** (written). Being able to distinguish between these two kinds of words will help a learner develop their own strategies for spelling.
- **Use Vowels:** Once a learner is familiar with vowels, make sure you regularly draw attention to their placement in words. If a learner feels comfortable with vowels, it can help them be more confident spellers.
- **Keep the Words Up:** If you do a spelling game or activity with your learner, make sure they have enough time to see the fully spelled out word on screen or a mini whiteboard before clicking to the next slide or erasing. It is common for teachers to do a spelling game (like Hangman or any other guess-the-letters game), where the bulk of the activity involves seeing only part

of a word, then erasing or clicking away as soon as the full word, phrase, or sentence is complete.

- **Go Incremental:** Show the learner a word you want them to spell. Then show them a jumble of the letters of that word above a series of blanks and challenge them to re-arrange the letters into the blanks to spell the word. If they are struggling, put one of the letters into the blanks for them (preferably a vowel) then if they still can't progress, put in another letter or move one they may have already placed in the wrong position:

  e l e p h a n t

  _ _ _ _ _ _ _ _

  _ _ e _ _ a _ _

  _ _ e p _ _ a _ _

- **Use Crosswords and Word Searches:** These types of word puzzles can be especially motivating for learners of different ages and levels, and there are many free puzzle generators available online. Consider providing these for your learner to work on independently outside class and give them the opportunity to share their work briefly at the beginning of your next lesson.

- **Show Your Vulnerability:** Tell your learner that even you can't always spell some English words correctly without looking them up. What is the word's spelling for someone or something from the island chain south of Eastern China? Is it P-H-I-L-O-P-I-N-E, P-H-I-L-L-I-P-I-N-E, F-I-L-I-P-I-N-E, F-I-L-L-I-P-I-N-E, P-H-I-L-O-P-P-I-N-E, P-H-I-L-I-P-I-N-O, F-I-L-I-P-P-I-N-A? (We'll let you look it up.) Also, as a native speaker of English, can you spell the word pneumonoultramicscopicsilicovolcanoconiosis? And how many native Chinese speakers can correctly write the character biáng used in the phrase biáng biáng noodles?. (That one Chinese character requires 57 pen or brush strokes to write.)

Reflection

- How do you currently practice spelling in your lessons?
- Think of a particular learner who struggles with spelling. Which of the strategies from above do you think would be successful?

EXPRESSIVE WRITING

How can I encourage my learner to express themselves while writing across the curriculum?

Keywords
#colorful language #expressive writing #stative verbs #varied sentence structures #variety

---

▶ The Situation

When I challenge my learner to write anything—from sentences to paragraphs to essays—their writing is made up of short, choppy sentences that are not very detailed or colorful. Even if their work is grammatically accurate, it is just not as expressive as I would like, and it does not have a varied sentence structure that you would hope to see in good writing. ***How can I encourage my learner to express themselves while writing across the curriculum?***

Analyzing the Situation

- Out of the four primary language skills of listening, speaking, reading, and writing, writing is usually the most challenging for learners.
- Many English language learners tend to write using only simple sentences rather than ever using varied sentence structures (e.g., compound, complex, or even compound-complex sentences). Often language learners write very generally rather than about their personal opinions and feelings.
- It is not uncommon to see your language learner do the bare minimum when forming sentences. Thus, they may write with little or no use of adjectives and adverbs, which would make their writing more detailed and colorful.

Suggested Strategies

Writing may feel very difficult, even daunting, to your learner, but there are some simple ways to help your learner become more expressive in their writing. Here's how.

- **Include Stative Verbs:** Try giving your learner a short list of stative verbs such as *like, want, hate, love, feel,* and *think* to include in their sentences along with the pronoun I. This way, your learner will have to come up with a sentence that expresses their personal feelings about a topic. This slight personalization might make your learner feel more motivated to participate in a writing task.
- **Use Adjectives and Adverbs:** Have your learner write a sentence (or even a paragraph), then go back and focus on finding a way to insert an adjective or adverb into each sentence. It may be useful to brainstorm a list of adjectives or adverbs your learner has studied to get them thinking how to best incorporate them into their writing. Then you can build after that. (Your learner can go through and add two adjectives or adverbs, etc.)
- **Start with Their Interests:** Learners are more likely to express themselves when talking about things they like. For a younger learner, start class with pictures of a superhero or animal. Hold up a picture and ask the learner to tell you about it and why they dislike/like it. For older learners, use a

picture of a celebrity and ask the learner to tell you about them and why they like/dislike them.

- **Give Them Sentence/Paragraph Frames:** Build toward more expressive writing by providing partially complete sentences/paragraphs, or "sentence/paragraph frames." These are anything that Includes a part of an idea, then usually a blank or ellipsis (...) to represent what the learner should complete. Give learners very complete frames (requiring only words or short phrases from the learner) early on, but transition to less complete frames (requiring phrases and sentences).

- **Put It in Context:** Learners are much more likely to be expressive if there is something to be expressive about. Even with simple sentences, provide context where none is provided. For younger learners, when the activity includes the sentence, "I like red apples," mime picking an apple off of a tree and eating it. For older learners,

when the activity includes the sentence, "I like books that have surprise endings" say, "Imagine you are at the library. Say this to the librarian."

- **Provide Linking Words:** Give learners a list of linking words they can use in their writing to encourage them to write using diverse sentence structures for specific reasons. These words may help them feel more inspired or confident to actively put pen to paper. Categories may include emphasis (e.g., *particularly, especially*), addition (e.g., *in addition, furthermore*), contrast (e.g., *unlike, despite*), or order (e.g., *above all, finally*).

Reflection

- How do you currently encourage your learner to vary their writing?
- Which writing strategy from above are you eager to try with your learner?

22 | WRITING FEEDBACK

How can I provide appropriate feedback on learner writing?

Keywords
#direct feedback #errors #feedback #indirect feedback #rubric #writing #written corrective feedback

▶ The Situation

Whenever I work on writing with a learner, they always want me to correct every error. When I try to explain or ask them to think about their writing, I get little to no response. I want my learner to become a more independent writer, but it feels like my feedback is not helping. ***How can I provide appropriate feedback on learner writing?***

Analyzing the Situation

- There are two main categories of **Written corrective feedback (WCF)**: **direct**, in which a learner is given a correct form, and **indirect**, in which errors are only indicated to the learner. Both can be effective strategies for providing feedback to learner writing.
- A learner's previous experiences with writing and writing feedback can impact how a learner engages with feedback. You will sometimes encounter older learners who may have experienced different types of feedback and prefer one type over another.
- Beliefs and preferences can also play a role. A learner who believes that **accuracy** is the target will often appreciate more direct feedback.

Suggested Strategies

Giving feedback on learner writing does not have to be stressful. In fact, helping your learner develop writing skills can be a valuable and productive exercise for both you as the teacher and your learner. Here's how.

- **Explain Feedback:** When explaining feedback, which should happen anytime a learner will receive feedback, always include 1.) what type of feedback learners will receive (i.e., what it will look like, e.g., comments, underlines, circling, codes, etc.) and 2.) what the feedback means (i.e., what learners should do with it).

- **Give Attention to Process:** By introducing writing as a process, there are multiple built-in opportunities for feedback. Focus on certain elements of writing with first drafts (usually structure and organization) and wait until later drafts to address other issues (like fine-tuning and accuracy-related issues, such as spelling and grammar). For shorter writing tasks, such as sentences, you can also build a process that focuses on particular elements of the sentence (such as the subject) in one step and others (the verb and object) in the next.

- **Be Consistent:** Once you introduce a system of feedback with a learner, use it consistently. It requires some time for learners to adjust to new forms of WCF. Take a moment at the beginning of every class to remind your learners how they will receive feedback. For new learners, spend a little more time modeling a feedback interaction (i.e., the teacher asks a question, S writes a response, T provides feedback, S revises based on feedback).

- **Get Them Involved:** Before an activity, tell your learner that they will help you decide how they will be scored. Discuss the characteristics of a good response or successful participation in the activity and write them down. This could also mean including specific areas a learner struggles in or would like feedback on. For younger learners, provide options for them to pick from, either on a whiteboard or with cards. Then, during the activity, use the rubric to provide feedback.

- **Mistake Scavenger Hunt:** Tell your learner that there are a certain number of a certain type of mistake in their writing (e.g., "You have four spelling mistakes."). Then ask them to find the errors and underline or circle them. This often demonstrates how much a learner is capable of on their own, despite still needing some support.

Reflection

- What is your current approach to giving feedback on learner writing?
- Consider a recent writing lesson that was successful. What strategies did you use to engage your learner in feedback?

23 | READING-WRITING CONNECTION

How can I help my learner make the reading-writing connection?

Keywords
#**construct knowledge** #**encoding** #**subskill** #**transfer**

▶ **The Situation**

I have a learner who does well with specific tasks that focus on a single skill, but he has trouble transferring from one skill to another or seeing the connection between them. I want him to realize that all linguistic skills are connected, and I am confident that once it "clicks" it will make him a more successful language learner. I want to start with two skills first, since my learner is especially strong in reading and writing. *How can I help my learner make the reading-writing connection?*

Analyzing the Situation

- It can be difficult for a young learner to understand the importance of integrating linguistic skills for communication.
- Writing is a skill that typically develops after listening, speaking, and reading. A focus on writing skills can help other linguistic skills develop at the same time.
- When people communicate, they typically listen then speak, or read, then write. Language skills are interconnected.

Suggested Strategies

Each component of language builds upon and helps another component of language. You should think of teaching the four linguistic skills (listening, speaking, reading, and writing) as interconnected. Here's how to focus on a connection between reading and writing.

- **Prediction:** Before your learner reads, have them preview a text by looking at the title or perhaps reading the first sentence or first paragraph, depending on the length of the text. Your learner can then write about what they think the text will be about. Then, after reading the text, have your learner go back and see if their predictions were correct or not.

- **Write After Reading:** Think about it: if you were asking a learner to write a haiku poem, you would likely give them a haiku as a model; you wouldn't just try to explain what a haiku is. The same can be said with reading a sentence or text that models grammatical forms or reading an informational essay that shows what a learner would need to include as they draft their own essay.

- **Think About Transfer:** Similar to above, if you work on identifying vocabulary words in a reading task, make sure your learner gets to transfer that language through practice using the vocabulary in a writing task. For example, if your learner reads about a dream vacation, have them circle the reading's adjectives. Then have them identify the opposite adjectives and write a new text about the worst vacation.

Dream Vacation	Nightmare Vacation
On my dream vacation, I would wake up late in my soft, comfortable bed and eat delicious, fresh food every day.	On my nightmare vacation, I would wake up early in my hard, uncomfortable bed and eat disgusting, stale food every day.

• **Provide Exposure to Interesting Texts:** Make sure your learner has the opportunity to see examples of texts that they might not otherwise see in classes. For a more advanced learner, consider giving examples of music reviews and having them write their own reviews about songs or albums they enjoy. For a lower-level learner, consider having them look at the text that appears in popular children's comics then try to write their own.

• **Get Graphics:** Make sure your learner knows that written texts do not always look like expository writing or involved stories. Sometimes writing looks like infographics that accompany informational texts. Demonstrate for your learner how to create infographics based on information in a text. Also, give your learner the chance to fill out graphic organizers based on an existing reading text then use graphic organizers to arrange their own ideas before writing.

Reflection

• What is your current approach to teaching reading and writing?
• Consider one of your current learners. Which strategy from above could you use to help develop the reading-writing connection for your learner?

24 | PRONUNCIATION STRUGGLES

How can I help a learner who struggles with pronunciation?

Keywords
#intonation #minimal pairs #productive skills #pronunciation #receptive skills #speaking #stress #subskill #syllable

▶ The Situation

My learner often struggles with pronunciation, especially because she is a younger learner who is still relatively new to learning English. I know that there are differences between Mandarin and English, but sometimes it is difficult to know how serious the issue is. There are times I think I should spend more time on an issue and dig deeper and, other times, I think it might just go away with normal practice and exposure. ***How can I help a learner who struggles with pronunciation?***

Analyzing the Situation

- Pronunciation is a subskill of both speaking and listening, which means it connects **productive** and **receptive** skills.
- In English, we often change our intonation to indicate sarcasm or emphasis. Because Chinese is a tonal language, even the slightest intonation change can completely change the intended meaning. Depending on the tone you use, you could be saying the word *mother (mā), hemp (má), horse (mǎ),* or *scold (mà).*

Suggested Strategies

You do not need to spend each lesson as an accent coach. You do need to think of how you want to implement more targeted pronunciation work in your lessons. You can do this in a few different ways.

- **Know Your Learner:** Different regions of China have different regional dialects that may interfere with your learner's pronunciation in English. For example, in certain parts of China, there is a difficulty distinguishing between /l/ and /n/. This means that in Chinese (e.g., in Nanjing), something like *south (nán)* might sound like *blue (lán)*. In your classroom, this might mean that a word like *no* sounds like *lo* or *banana* sounds like *balala*. You should check with your Chinese colleague to find out where your learner is from and find out which regional dialects might exist.
- **Practice Minimal Pairs:** *Minimal Pairs* primarily refers to spoken words that share similar and commonly confused **phonemes** like *sheep* and *ship* or *bad* and *bat*. Give each learner plenty of opportunities to distinguish these similar sounds, drawing attention to the specific phoneme that is different each time. See more examples below.

ship	sheep
bad	bat
bad	bed
hat	rat
wet	wait

- **Sound It Out:** It can be difficult for a language learner to hear and acknowledge the different syllables in words, especially in a **lexical set** where the majority of the words are the same number of syllables except for one outlier (e.g., *cat*, *dog*, *fish*, *rabbit*). Practice snapping or lightly clapping while sounding out syllables in words. Remember not to snap or clap so loudly that you cannot actually hear the word being spoken.

- **Use Bubbles:** For a learner who struggles with placing stress on the correct syllable of a word, use bubbles to illustrate how to stress each syllable. Similar to the use of bubbles you might see on a karaoke screen, draw different-sized bubbles over each syllable with the stressed syllables having a larger bubble. For an alternative, try using a rubber band that stretches or a fist that opens when the stress happens in the word.

apple

- **Provide More Examples:** If you are working on distinguishing the number of syllables in

a word, consider categorizing other words your learner already knows according to syllables and encouraging **noticing** of syllabication that way. If your learner still cannot seem to pronounce a single specific word correctly, consider repeating the word or playing someone else's pronunciation of the word. Consider putting the word in a full sentence to provide context for your learner. Also, keep in mind how sounds in words change based on the words they are next to (linking, etc.) You want to make sure your learner is practicing pronunciation in a realistic way.

Reflection

- What are some ways you currently teach pronunciation (including stress, intonation, syllabication, etc.)?
- Which strategies from above are you most confident to try? Which will you need to practice more?

MOVING PAST REPEATING

How do I encourage my learner to respond to questions instead of just repeating the question back?

Keywords
#comprehensible input #productive skills #receptive skills #repeating

▶ The Situation

I have a new learner who always repeats the questions back to me rather than answering them. The learning objectives suggest that I should get my learner to respond to or answer questions rather than just repeating them, but this always proves to be a struggle. *How do I encourage my learner to respond to questions instead of just repeating the question back?*

Analyzing the Situation

- Repetition is a natural part of children's language acquisition. In the beginning stages of language learning, imitation is automatic and effortless. Children (our learners) are attempting to communicate, learn, and practice language.
- When teaching a learner, we have to remember to develop **receptive skills**, those involved in reading and listening, in addition to **productive skills**, those involved in writing and speaking. We do this by providing **comprehensible input** and modeling interactions.

Suggested Strategies

There are many simple activities that you can do with beginners to interact with and practice the language. With a few tweaks, you can be on your way to encouraging effective interaction in your classroom. Here's how.

- **Scaffold the Interaction:** Many Chinese learners are not used to the type of interaction that is common in North American classrooms. Be patient and recognize that your learner may be slow to pick up these new patterns. Take a moment before the activity to model and practice the interaction using **Total Physical Response (TPR)** and pointing to yourself when asking the question and pointing to the learner for the response. Emphasize the learner's turn by saying, "Now, it's your turn to answer."
- **Assign Roles:** Using images on the slide, assign roles to yourself and your learner. Then, write a question mark above your role and a checkmark above your learner's role. Practice with an example question.
- **Use Props:** Write the words *question* and *answer* on two different flat-prop gift boxes. Then, mime giving the "question" to the learner and receiving the "answer." Encourage learners to mime along. Display these question models behind you on a bulletin board or whiteboard. flat-prop microphones and questions marks could also be used.
- **Have Learners Correct You:** If your learner only wants to repeat after you instead of answering questions, consider using what they know to help them answer questions. For example, if there is a particular word or **lexical set** that you feel confident your learner knows (e.g., numbers 1-5, colors, domestic animals, etc.), ask the question,

"What's this?" and answer incorrectly. (show an image of *blue* and instead say, "It's red.") Children are typically pretty passionate about correcting their teacher, so your learner may be more eager to let you know you are wrong by saying, "It's blue." This gives you an opportunity to praise them for correcting you, which may motivate your learner to respond or interact rather than just repeat.

- How do you currently model interaction? What's working and what's not?
- Consider a current learner who struggles to follow patterns of interaction in class. Which of the following strategies will you try to support this learner?

26 ASKING QUESTIONS

How can I help my learner ask questions more independently?

Keywords
#anxiety #fear #questions

▶ The Situation

I worry that my learner does not ask questions when she is unsure of something or needs help. I want to help her, but it is hard to know what the problem is. Sometimes she will nod and smile along even when she does not understand, and other times she will try to ask questions but struggles to find the words. *How can I help my learner ask questions more independently?*

Analyzing the Situation

- Chinese classrooms tend to have very different norms around asking questions than those in North American classrooms. Active participation in class by asking questions, contributing ideas, and sharing opinions is not a basic expectation, and in some cases, it is actively discouraged. Keep these different cultural expectations in mind when encouraging questions in class. Asking questions directly to a teacher may be very new for your learner, and it can take time for them to get comfortable with it.
- Fear and anxiety can also get in the way of independent question asking by raising the **affective filter** and reducing your learner's appetite for risk-taking.
- Encouraging learner questions can help a learner feel more interested in the content and make more meaningful connections.

Suggested Strategies

You do not need to stress out about how to get your learner asking questions in class. You do need to consider ways to get your learner more involved. Here's how.

- **Model It:** Provide clear models that give your learner appropriate **scaffolding** to more independent questioning. For a younger learner, this can mean providing the full question form (e.g., "How do you spell...?") For an older learner, this can be providing the five *whs* and *h* questions (*who, what, when, where, why, how*).
- **Give Them Time:** Formulating questions in English can be challenging for your learner. Give them time to process content or feedback before you move on. Also, do not be afraid of silence. Reducing **teacher talk time** (TTT), in general, can open up space for your learner to contribute more in class, even if it seems awkward to you that there is dead air.
- **Use Your Classroom:** Props like a flat-prop question mark could remind and encourage your learner to ask questions. Question models can also be displayed on a bulletin board or whiteboard.
- **Tie to Rewards:** Use rewards to encourage questions. After setting simple, clear expectations at the beginning of class, reward your learner each time they ask a question using one of the models you introduce.

Reflection

- Consider your current approach. How do you encourage your learner to ask questions in class? What's working, and what's not?

- Consider a current learner. How can you use the suggested strategies to encourage more independent questioning?

SUMMARIZING

How can I help my learner who struggles to summarize thoughts or text?

Keywords
#graphic organizer #paraphrase #productive skills #receptive skills #summarize

▶ The Situation

When I ask my learner a specific question that uses essentially the same wording from a text or audio, she can handle it and provide mostly accurate answers. However, when we work on trying to summarize thoughts or text, she tends to shut down. It seems like she cannot focus on building up to or down from a big idea. It is hard to determine how much of a big picture she gets if she only shares or recalls details. *How can I help my learner who struggles to summarize thoughts or text?*

Analyzing the Situation

- Summarizing is a key academic skill that not all learners will have been introduced to.
- While there are certainly other reading skills and subskills that are important, learning how to summarize is particularly tricky for the learner who struggles to put things in their own words or who struggles to determine which information is more/less important than other information.
- We need to help each learner understand that a summary is much shorter than the original text. It may also be important to introduce the concept of main ideas and details. Being ready and able to explain the differences between a main idea and details (as necessary and appropriate) will help your learner improve their English skills.

Suggested Strategies

You do not need your learner to rephrase every bit of text or audio you encounter in your lessons. You do need to consider some simple strategies to help your learner think big-picture. Here's how.

- **Explain It:** Perhaps your learner has never had a clear definition of what a summary is. Be sure they clearly understand what a summary is (shorter than the original and explained in their own words).
- **Model It:** Your learner may be struggling because they do not understand the summary's goal. Give them a concrete model using a story about yourself or one that your learner has shared. This increases their interest and teaches them the skill in a communicative manner. (They like hearing about personal information.)
- **Break It Down and Build It Up:** Encourage your learner to read a single sentence and paraphrase it or put it in their own words. Then have them read a few sentences and put them into their own words using one single sentence. Then, do the same thing at a paragraph or multi-paragraph level until your learner feels more comfortable.
- **Think of the Five *Whs* (& *How*):** The questions to consider begin with *who, what, when, where, why,* and *how.* Your learner needs to know which questions to ask to begin to identify main ideas and locate key information. This helps your learner

recognize the most important information and only include it in a summary.

- **SWBS:** When working with literary texts, provide your learner with a framework that helps them identify main ideas. An easy one to use is SWBS, introduced by Keylene Beers. **SWBS** stands for *Someone, Wanted to, But,* and *So. Someone* refers to the main character in a story. *Want to* and *but* capture the central problem the main character is facing. Finally, *so* represents the solution. Consider Goldilocks and the Three Bears as an example. Someone: Goldilocks; wanted to: eat and sleep, but: she was away from home, so: she entered the bears' house and tested their food and beds.

- **Use a Graphic Organizer:** You may have a learner who responds well to visuals. A graphic organizer to assist your learner can be a successful tool. There are many kinds of organizers and some are introduced in

curricula. Be sure to understand the format and how detailed a graphic organizer needs to be depending on your learner's needs.

- **Play "Odd Man Out":** After reading or listening to a text, provide your learner with a short list of possible paraphrases or summaries. Encourage your learner to identify which options are not summaries. This can help them think about which parts of a text are most important to include.

Reflection

- What is your current approach to helping your learner summarize the text?
- Consider one of the courses you currently teach. Which strategies above could you apply to improve your learner's summary skills?

LISTENING

How can I better help my learner remain on task during listening activities?

Keywords
#active listening #extensive listening #instructions #intensive listening #listening task #listening text #receptive skills

▶ The Situation

My learner always seems to struggle with listening activities. She often seems bored or like she is unsure of what she is supposed to do. She also gets distracted and starts doing something else like doodling or looking at her phone. When we have a follow-up task, it is as if she did not hear the listening task or does not know how to respond. I know how important it is for her to have strong listening skills, and I want her to be a well-rounded learner. ***How can I better help my learner remain on task during listening activities?***

Analyzing the Situation

- Your learner may shut down and be unwilling to participate if unsure why or how they are supposed to interact with a listening text before listening.
- A **listening task** here and throughout refers to the activity a learner does in relation to the listening text. A listening text is the actual resource (e.g., recording, video, song) being used.
- While there is always an argument to be made that we listen for enjoyment or for listening's sake (**extensive listening**), our lessons usually have a specific reason we are asking a learner to listen (**intensive listening**).
- Consider your instructions. If a task does not go as planned, it is often because instructions and expectations are not clear. Learners typically like to know what they are supposed to be doing before they start a task, regardless of the linguistic skill being practiced.

Suggested Strategies

You do not need to avoid listening tasks in your lessons or throw your hands up in frustration. You do need to think of ways to keep your learner engaged once you press play. Here's how.

- **Promote Active Listening:** If you want your learner to be engaged during a listening task, give them something to do. This can be as simple as having them count how many times a character says a target word or phrase or as creative as having your learner watch playback from their class and acknowledging which new words they picked up on the fastest.
- **Break It Up:** If a listening text is long or complicated, a learner may feel fatigued and less likely to interact with it, especially without established expectations. Consider breaking a listening task into parts or offering time to dissect and discuss certain listening text elements before moving on.
- **Consider Turn-Taking:** Have your learner practice listening to respond. If a learner does a listening task and is expected to respond or ask follow-up questions, they are

going to be more likely to fully interact using **receptive skills** to transfer to productive skills. You can provide support and parameters as necessary (e.g., telling your learner they will need to ask *wh-* questions as a follow-up to a listening task).

- **Get Them Ready:** Unless you are starting your lesson with a listening routine, your learner needs to get ready to listen. This may include looking at pictures to provide context (e.g., pictures of a train station before listening for a scheduled train to be announced) or doing an activity connecting to background knowledge or material from previous lessons.
- **Use the Listening Text:** A good listening text can be used in many different ways. Considering fatigue, think about different

ways for a learner to interact with a listening text to make it worth a learner's time to engage with the text in the first place. Consider having your learner listen to a text while putting the sentences back in order or do a gap fill with missing words provided in a word bank.

Reflection

- Are there certain listening activities and texts that are more problematic than others in your lessons?
- Think of a successful listening activity you may have taught recently. Why was it successful? How did your learner engage with the listening text and the listening task(s)?

LISTENING STRATEGIES

How can I incorporate top-down and bottom-up listening strategies in my classroom?

Keywords
#**bottom-up** #**listening** #**listening strategies** #**top-down** #**receptive skills**

▶ The Situation

I realize that listening skills are incredibly important in a language learning environment, so I want my learner to have the tools she needs to listen confidently. I don't feel that I am truly giving my learner the best opportunities to practice listening because I usually just play the songs or audio twice then move on. I want her to listen closely and pay attention, but so far, it hasn't clicked. ***How can I incorporate top-down and bottom-up listening strategies in my classroom?***

Analyzing the Situation

- When we use **bottom-up** listening, we start small. This kind of listening can refer to a learner working their way up from individual sounds into words into phrases, sentences, etc., eventually relying on the meaning and context of surrounding words to help make out the overall meaning. It can also describe listening with more of a focus on details. **Top-down** listening, on the other hand, starts with the big picture first and works down to details. This is similar to top-down and bottom-up approaches to reading as reading is a **receptive skill** as well.
- Each learner will need to have a combination of both bottom-up and top-down listening skills in order to be stronger listeners. That being said, there may be an emphasis on one more than the other

depending on why the learner is listening. Imagine the amount of fatigue a learner might feel if they try a bottom-up approach for every task.

Suggested Strategies

You do not need to pack every lesson full of new listening activities. You do need to have a better understanding of how to structure different listening activities. Here's how.

- **Have Specific Expectations:** Each time you listen, whether using a bottom-up or top-down approach, your learner needs to know why they are expected to listen before they listen. Just because you can listen to an entire pop song or podcast with your learner does not mean you should. Perhaps your learner needs to listen for a grammatical point that is repeated throughout a song. You would want to find ways for them to notice this grammar.
- **Think Real-World Context:** When considering a listening task or text, think about why a person would need to listen to it in the real world. You wouldn't expect a learner to listen to a train announcement then respond to questions about how the announcer is feeling. You could use a train announcement with elements of top-down (listen for background and determine where you might hear this announcement) and bottom-up (listen for specific details related to departure time and gate).

- **Be a Human CD Player:** A fun way to practice listening is by pre-teaching the different buttons on a CD player: pause, play, go back, go forward. Encourage your learner to either complete a gap fill or take dictation (depending on skill level) as you read a text aloud. At first, you can start very quickly until your learner tells you to "pause," "go back," and "play." Then you can move back in your reading or the text and encourage your learner to pick up where you start. This is a good way for a learner to give their teacher clues about the pace at which they are able to work; it also allows the learner to give commands, which may be motivating for certain learners.
- **Practice Notetaking:** For a higher-level learner or for a learner who is good at dictation and ready to move on, notetaking is a very useful skill. Your learner will need to learn this skill for classes in their native language, but taking notes in a foreign or second language can be especially intimidating. Consider starting small (with a listening text of a few sentences or a brief paragraph). Encourage your learner to listen first and write down what they remember. Mix it up by including longer listening texts or shorter listening texts that may seem more complicated. Then move on to trying to take notes in real time while listening.

Reflection

- What are some examples of listening activities and texts that seem more challenging to your learner than others?
- Think of a successful listening activity you may have done recently. Why was it successful? How did your learner engage with the listening text?

 **LISTENING STRUGGLES**

How can I help a learner who struggles with listening?

Keywords
#**authentic text** #**inauthentic text** #**listening** #**listening strategies**
#**listening struggles** #**listening text** #**receptive skills** #**scaffold**

► **The Situation**

My learner has a difficult time with listening activities. Unfortunately, she shuts down or gives me a blank look whenever I try to play audio in class. It doesn't even matter which kind of audio it is. I've tried playing her pop songs and clips from the internet in addition to the materials included in our lessons. She gets a sad look on her face and just tries to wait it out. I ask her afterward to talk about what she listened to, but she doesn't seem to understand. *How can I help a learner who struggles with listening?*

Analyzing the Situation

- It is critical that a learner is given reasons to listen, regardless of what listening text is being used. If you only wait to ask questions until after the learner has listened, a learner can get fatigued or overwhelmed quickly.
- Every learner needs to have a balance of **authentic materials** and **inauthentic materials**. *Authentic materials* refers to listening texts that were not necessarily created for language learning (e.g., a pop song on the radio or a weather report on TV), and *inauthentic materials* refers to instructional materials created for specific, pedagogical purposes (e.g., songs with specific **target language** created specifically for language learning). Authentic materials can seem daunting

because they often include language beyond a learner's language level, but if you set up the right task (e.g., listen for each time the singer uses an "I am verbing" phrase), you can still use authentic texts as a valuable resource.

Suggested Strategies

You do not have to make your learner sad every time you press play. You do have to be clear in your intentions and use the right resources most beneficially. Here's how.

- **Give Them Time:** If your learner is struggling with listening tasks, there is a chance that they feel overwhelmed by the sheer amount of **listening text**. Play chunks of the text at a time. Then set a timer to allow time for processing and questions before moving on.
- **Exploit Your Resource:** If your listening text includes multiple opportunities for listening tasks, make it worth your learner's time to listen to it. Consider different ways to have a leaner interact with a dialogue they listen to. Perhaps on the first listen, they identify different speakers. Then on the second listen, your learner finds specific vocabulary words or words that have the same number of syllables. On the third listen, your learner identifies locations being referenced in the conversation.
- **Listen for Different Reasons:** If you plan

to have your learner listen to the same listening text multiple times, change up the reasons your learner needs to listen each time. Consider starting with the least challenging task first and building up to the most challenging task after subsequent listen so that your learner has time to get accustomed to the listening text.

- **Use Transcripts:** Provide a transcript of a listening text on the screen so that your learner can follow along. Slowly build up to include transcripts with single-word gap fills and, ultimately, remove the transcript completely and include follow-up questions.
- **Reorder Text:** Include sentences from your audio on screen and encourage your learner to put the sentences in the correct

order as they listen. Once your learner becomes more comfortable with this kind of task, consider adding "decoy" sentences that are not included in the audio so that they have another level of rigor; your learner will still have text on the screen as a **scaffold**, or support, as they listen.

Reflection

- What are some examples of listening activities and texts that seem more challenging to your learner than others?
- Think of a listening resource you used that your learner seemed to love. Why was it well-received? How did your learner engage with the listening text?

31 | LISTENING-SPEAKING CONNECTION

How can I help my learner make the listening-speaking connection?

Keywords
#comprehension #early learner (EL) #input #listening #noticing #output #reinforce #scaffold #silent period #speaking #transfer

► The Situation

I have a learner who does well with specific tasks that focus on a single skill, but she has trouble transferring from one skill to another or seeing the connection between them. I want her to realize that all linguistic skills are connected, and I am confident that once it "clicks" it will make her a more successful language learner. I want to start with two skills first since my learner is especially strong in listening and speaking. ***How can I help my learner make the listening-speaking connection?***

Analyzing the Situation

- It can be difficult for beginners and young learners to understand the importance of integrating linguistic skills, for communication. Frequently, lessons do not dedicate equal time to all of the skills, or they focus on one or two more than the others; this means making the connections between them adds an additional layer of learning.
- A focus on listening (a receptive skill) generally precedes a focus on speaking (a production skill). Learners need **comprehensible input** prior to being able to produce output.

Suggested Strategies

Each component of language is interconnected in that it builds upon and helps another language skill. You can help put these skills in conversation with each other so that your learner has a more well-rounded language experience. Here's how.

- **Be Patient:** It is not uncommon for a beginner language learner, especially an **early learner (EL)**, to go through a **silent period** in which they are listening and mentally processing input but are not yet confident enough to try to produce (speak) the language. Although we must understand this, we can still use **positive reinforcement** and gentle **scaffolding** to help learners emerge from their silent period into **production**.
- **Use Audio Intentionally:** When listening to an audio recording included as part of the lesson or listening to audio that you provide, encourage noticing. This noticing can be supported by providing an incomplete transcript (even of only a sentence) or by encouraging note-taking. Then, after listening, encourage the learner to use the language they **noticed**. This can mean using vocabulary that was used in a song or information from a recording.
- **Use Hints:** Provide hints, but do not provide a full response. A teacher may ask, "What does he have?" then after a long pause and gesturing for the learner to respond,

hint at the beginning of the response as in, "He…" or "he has…." This scaffolding is non-intrusive support for the learner so that they can produce more of the response on their own.

- **Encourage Pre- and Post-Class Work:** Check that the learner has done the assigned pre-lesson activity. Ask if they did it, if they liked it, and why. Be sure to give verbal praise for finishing these activities. Make sure that at the end of class, you encourage your learner to complete post-class activities. There are often listening components to pre-class activities and production components to post-class activities to help build this connection.

- **Finish the Audio:** Think about playing audio and strategically pausing so that your learner can finish the sentence. For example, if you play the audio of, "I like to play basketball," consider pausing after, "I like to _____," or even after, "I like to play _____." This will help your learner predict and feel more comfortable speaking on the spot.

Reflection

- What is your current approach when teaching listening and speaking skills?
- Consider one of your current learners. Which strategy from above could you use to help develop the listening-speaking connection?

MISMATCHED SKILLS

How do I facilitate a worthwhile experience for a learner with mismatched skills?

Keywords
#automaticity #four skills #mismatch #productive skills #scaffolding

▶ The Situation

I have a learner who is very good at writing but still struggles when she tries to speak. This makes lessons challenging for me to teach because it limits how much we can interact. I know she understands the content, but her speaking skills are so low that it is hard for her to demonstrate that knowledge. *How do I facilitate a worthwhile experience for a learner with mismatched skills?*

Analyzing the Situation

- Sometimes a learner who struggles more with speaking than other skills is particularly shy about speaking for fear of making mistakes. After all, with writing, the learner has time to think carefully about constructing sentences, but, with speaking, they have very little time to think before uttering a verbal response.
- If a learner has experienced an environment in which reading and writing are the focus, they may not have enough practice speaking to develop oral fluency and **automaticity**, so they may need to apply conscious mental thought before constructing a sentence.

Suggested Strategies

Helping your learner improve a particular skill to catch up with their other language skills can be a challenge. However, you are capable of handling these situations with confidence. Here's how.

- **Take the Time:** It is probably necessary to allot more lesson time to practicing the weak skill (speaking, for example), while still making sure to cover all required content. This kind of practice can be brief and is often best before an activity that requires the weak skill or at the end of a lesson.
- **Be Patient:** Be sure to pause and give your learner time to respond to a speaking prompt or question. Remember that your learner is probably still depending on conscious mental thought, and reaching the goal of automaticity takes a good deal of time and practice.
- **Praise Them:** By using rewards tied to performance on the target skill (e.g., giving a reward for using complete sentences), you can encourage your learner's focus and attention. Just be careful to provide enough accessible opportunities for the learner to accomplish what is needed in order to earn the reward.
- **Transfer Skills:** If your learner is strong with one productive skill but not the other, or one receptive skill but not the other, considering using their strength in one domain to help the other. For example, if your learner struggles during listening tasks but is great at reading, show them that most listening tasks can be transformed into reading tasks by using transcripts. If your learner struggles to express themselves through a speaking

activity, encourage them to respond to a prompt by writing first. Then give them the opportunity to transfer back to the weaker skill. After you have turned a listening task into a reading task to build confidence, remove the transcript and try again with the originally intended listening task. If you have your learner write a response, encourage them to block out the text and try to articulate what they wrote in their own words.

Reflection

- Consider one of your learners with mismatched skills. Which of the suggested strategies could you try next time you teach that learner?
- Have you studied another language, and if so, do you feel that you are stronger in one or more of the four skills? If so, why do you think that is?

33 | WRONG-LEVEL LEARNERS

How do I facilitate a worthwhile experience for a learner who is in the wrong level?

Keywords
#engagement #instructions #planning #prepare #simplify

▶ The Situation

When I teach my learner, she struggles to understand the lesson. She cannot read simple CVC words and only repeats after me instead of answering my questions. I also see that sometimes her parents give her answers. I feel like she should be placed at a lower level. When I have to spend a lot of time on one or two tasks in order for her to feel comfortable moving on, I lose a lot of class time. I often end up unable to complete all the slides in the lesson. *How do I facilitate a worthwhile experience for a learner who is in the wrong level?*

Analyzing the Situation

- During a lesson, a low-level English learner may struggle more than a learner who knows more English; it also might take a low-level learner more time to feel comfortable participating.
- Teaching a lesson that is too difficult can be frustrating for both the teacher and learner; the teacher feels misunderstood, and the learner does not know what is expected of them.
- Try to think of ways to engage the learner at the appropriate level while still covering the lesson content.

Suggested Strategies

Even if there is some sort of remediation plan in place for your learner, you still want them to have a memorable and engaging lesson while they are online with you. You do not always need to skip tasks in your lessons or completely fabricate activities on the spot. You do need to think of ways to adapt and keep your learner engaged once class starts. Here's how.

- **Break It Down:** If your learner struggles with **consonant-vowel-consonant** (**CVC**) words, focus on isolated, individual **phonemes** and build up from there. Once your learner seems to get the hang of isolated phonemes, combine them in CV or VC combinations and repeat the process.

- **Use a Bottom-Up Approach:** When a learner struggles to understand longer readings or specific reading subskills like paraphrasing or summarizing, highlight what your learner does know in the simplest ways possible first in order to build confidence before moving on. Show a picture of an apple to try to elicit the word before showing the word or highlight the isolated word *apple* in a sentence before trying to read other words in the sentence.

- **Adapt Activities:** Find opportunities for a learner to be successful by adapting activities. For example, if a learner is struggling or unable to respond orally during an activity, provide the option of responding nonverbally. Use these responses as opportunities to give praise and rewards. Also, adapt activities by breaking them down into smaller chunks.

- **Simplify the Language:** Simplify the language expectations you have for your learner. If your learner does not understand how to respond to specific content-related questions (e.g., "Which animal do you like?") reframe the question to be simple identification (e.g., "What's this?" while pointing to the image on screen). This way, learners get to interact at their own, appropriate level.
- **Prepare Them for Success:** If you are having the same issues with a regular learner, leave feedback that you will ask certain questions at the beginning of the next lesson (and precisely include which questions and

sample answers). If your learner can practice towards very explicit expectations, it may make them feel more comfortable in the next lesson when you engage.

Reflection

- What do you currently do in a lesson if a learner demonstrates that they do not understand what to do?
- Think of a learner you have who may be placed at the wrong level. How can you apply a strategy from above to reengage that learner?

34 | MORE ADVANCED LEARNERS

How should I differentiate lessons for a more advanced learner?

Keywords
#engagement #extend language #personalize #reinforce #zone of proximal development (ZPD)

▶ The Situation

Sometimes when I teach a specific learner, I get through the slides in about 15 minutes. I usually try to go back to the vocabulary and have my learner repeat after me or recall the words again. This particular learner's pronunciation is better than most of my other learners, and she can speak in complete sentences. I want her to get the most out of each lesson and not waste her time. ***How should I differentiate lessons for a more advanced learner?***

Analyzing the Situation

- Every learner should be learning within their **zone of proximal development (ZPD)**, which is the difference between what a learner can do without any help and what a learner can achieve with some guidance and encouragement.
- By teaching one-to-one lessons, a teacher can really personalize and take the time to ensure the learner is getting the most from each lesson. This allows the teacher to adjust how they teach and which classroom activities are best for each learner.
- With a good curriculum, teachers have what they need to teach, but differentiating instruction is how teachers can reach each individual learner.
- Adjusting the pace of teaching can also enable you to teach based on an individual learner's situation. You may need to move

quickly when the learner demonstrates an understanding of activities, and you may need to slow down if the learner needs more time to digest or comprehend.

Suggested Strategies

Language learners are not always at the same level in their knowledge and skills development. It is normal to have more advanced learners in certain dimensions such as oral or written skills. As a teacher, you can always find a way to make those learners active. Here's how.

- **Let Your Learner Take the Lead:** If your learner is able, ask them to give you ideas about how they might like to extend the language in class. They will likely appreciate having their voice heard, and it will help them build confidence to assert themselves in English. For starters, you could ask your learner to choose three free-talk topics loosely related to the lesson theme or grammar point then pick one topic at random at the end of the lesson.
- **Reinforce Vocabulary and Grammar:** After completing the core activities in a lesson, go back and reinforce vocabulary and grammar for more intensive work. This can include adding a writing activity for a previously-completed speaking activity or having your learner practice listening if they completed a reading activity. Use the same activities in the lesson but try them in

a different domain extending to other skills. It will help your learner look at the activities differently and also see how language is connected.

- **Extension Activities:** Work with a learner on extending activities from the lesson. If the activity was only reading, ask some follow-up questions. Try to extend past main ideas and key detail questions and ask more in-depth questions, such as prediction or inference questions. Have the learner ask you questions about the reading. If there is a nice image in one of the lesson slides, have the learner write a description of the image then read it to you.

Reflection

- What is your current approach to working with a more advanced learner? How do you change up your lessons accordingly?
- Consider one of your upcoming lessons. Using the strategies above, how could you differentiate the activities of your lesson?

35 | LESS ADVANCED LEARNERS

How should I differentiate lessons for a less advanced learner?

Keywords
#**break down** #**personalize** #**routine** #**scaffold** #**simplify** #**zone of proximal development (ZPD)**

► The Situation

I have a learner who struggles to get through each lesson. He loses interest quickly, especially when working on something that he finds difficult or has trouble understanding. Sometimes he makes it clear that he is interested in the material and wants to engage with it, but that is usually all in Chinese. Then when we try to practice with it, he shuts down. I think the material is just too advanced for him. *How should I differentiate lessons for a less advanced learner?*

Analyzing the Situation

- Your learner should be learning within their **zone of proximal development (ZPD)**. The ZPD refers to what a learner can do without any help versus what a learner can do with the appropriate guidance and encouragement.
- Techers need to remember that every learner can learn, but they learn in different ways. By teaching one-to-one lessons, a teacher can really personalize content and take the time to ensure the learner is getting the most from each lesson. This allows the teacher to adjust how they teach and determine which classroom activities are best for each learner.

Suggested Strategies

Your learner will vary in the activities they like and in the activities in which they excel. Observe your learner during each lesson and tweak your lessons for the future. Here's how.

- **Scaffold:** Support your learner by **scaffolding** the material in the lesson. Break down activities into smaller steps. In addition to simplifying, you can provide your learner with other ways of doing the same activity. Scaffolding can help your learner complete an activity that they otherwise would not be able to complete on their own. Over time, the learner should need less and less support, and the teacher can adjust their level of help. Scaffolding should provide the learner with the necessary skills so that the learner will be able to complete activities in the future with less help. Consider the following skeleton dialogue and how it provides scaffolds that can be removed or added back as needed.

With More Scaffolding	With Less Scaffolding
A: Hi, _____. How are you?	A: Hi, _____. How are you?
B: I'm fine. How are you?	B: I'm _____. How are you?
A. I'm okay. What are you doing?	A. I'm _____. What are you doing?
B. I'm listening to music. What are you doing?	B. I'm _____. What are you doing?
A. I'm reading a book.	A. I'm _____.

- **Follow Routines:** Providing a routine in your lessons can help your learner feel more comfortable and less anxious about what comes next in the lesson. Routines provide a sense of familiarity; this familiarity with routine can make incorporating new information go smoother.
- **Explain the Importance:** Your learner should know the importance of why an activity is taking place. For a lower-level learner, the activity's goal might be something like receiving rewards (and this might be a

way you frame it for lower levels). It can be difficult for a young learner to step back and understand the whole reason for doing an activity.

Reflection

- What is your current approach to working with a less advanced learner?
- Consider one of your upcoming lessons. Using the strategies above, how could you differentiate the activities of your lesson?

36 | ADAPTING MATERIALS

How do I adapt material for an older learner who is in a lower level?

Keywords
#adapt #language function #personalize #purpose #relevance

► The Situation

I have a learner who is older but a true beginner with the English language. The beginner level course material is geared more towards younger learners. I am afraid she will lose interest, or her parents will ask to put her in a higher level because the topics might seem more appropriate for her age, even though she needs the lower level to learn English language basics. *How do I adapt material for an older learner who is in a lower level?*

Analyzing the Situation

- It can be frustrating for an older learner who has beginner English language proficiency, but it is very important that the learner masters the basics before moving on, even though the class may seem childish.
- It is important to consider how to make tasks relevant for a learner while keeping the **language function** the same. This way the learner can benefit from the language they need to practice, but at the same time, they can feel like the lessons are more tailored to their interests.

Suggested Strategies

Every learner is different and will vary in the activities they like. Be patient and prepared to teach each learner as an individual. Here's how.

- **Preplan:** Every class and every learner

presents some level of unpredictability that you must deal with on the spot. You can prepare for your lessons with an older learner who is learning lower-level material. Look through the lesson ahead of time and look for places to personalize or adapt the material to the learner's interests. Look at the teacher tips and extension opportunities and anticipate which suggestions might actually be successful for your learner.

- **Explain the Purpose:** It is often important for your older learner to be treated as the mature individual they are trying to be. By explaining the purpose of a game or fun activity with an older learner, you can make it clear to the learner what they will be practicing, and therefore, the learner may respond more positively. Have your learner repeat the purpose back to you if they are able.

- **Know Your Learner:** Find out more about activities your learner likes or does not like as well as any interests or other relevant information that might help you personalize and adapt your lesson to fit their needs. If your learner feels like you are making an effort to relate to them, they may be more willing to do tasks they might not enjoy otherwise.

- **Personalize:** Think about how you can personalize a task in the lesson and make it more relevant for your learner. Help your learner develop real and personal reasons for learning the language. If a task contains a situation to which your learner would not be able to relate, keep the learning objective and language skills the same but adjust the situation to be more applicable to your learner's age. If you have a lesson related to shopping, but your learner is not interested in shopping, consider changing the theme to be about something your learner enjoys or ask them to choose a scenario to use the same kind of language.

• **Think Outside the Slides:** A low-level older learner might not appreciate the cutesy nature of the course's characters in lesson settings. If possible, prepare some additional images to share with your learner that might help the material seem more mature. For example, instead of relying on a school supply store's cutesy image, consider showing an image of a stationary or office supply store.

Reflection

• Consider an older learner who is currently in a low-level English class. What current struggles do you have as you teach the material?
• Which of the suggested strategies could you try in your next class?

PLAYING CATCH-UP

How can I help a learner who is behind when there are only 25 minutes in class that do not account for "catch-up"?

Keywords
#assumed knowledge #catch-up #homework #post-class #recycled language #review

▶ **The Situation**

Sometimes, reviewing content at the beginning of class involves more than just review. I feel like I have to spend time teaching content that my learner was supposed to have already learned. I know we have to finish teaching all of the slides, but sometimes there isn't enough time in one lesson to catch up with the old material and teach the new material. *How can I help a learner who is behind when there are only 25 minutes in class that do not account for "catch-up"?*

Analyzing the Situation

- Your primary role is to teach the current lesson. Of course, taking time to address previous learning can be helpful. Still, future teachers depend on you to cover the assigned content.
- **Recycled language** is often included throughout good courses. Before using class time to address a "catch-up" issue, consider opportunities that may exist later in the lesson to address the issue.
- Your learner may struggle to warm up at the beginning of the lesson. This means that it is important not to make assumptions based on the first few slides. Make a quick note to keep this in mind, but give the learner time to demonstrate what they might know.

Suggested Strategies

You do not have to feel overwhelmed by trying to cram review, input, and practice all into one lesson. You should be responsive and help your learner engage with the lesson in front of them. Here's how.

- **Set Expectations:** It is very important to make sure a learner knows what is expected of them for each task. Sometimes they do not need a significant review overhaul. Still, they seem like they do because they are unsure what is expected of them at any given moment.
- **Keep Moving:** In 25-minute classes, there is just no time to dwell on a particular issue. As a reminder, just five minutes of review equals 20% of total class time.
- **Provide Support:** Using effective feedback and scaffolding strategies, you can often provide the support a learner needs to engage with an activity. If your learner struggles to remember vocabulary words, consider including a word bank on screen that travels with them from task to task. If your learner struggles with a particular grammar point, consider providing a "useful language" table somewhere on screen for them to reference. For subject-verb agreement, this may look like a table including sentence starters (e.g., "I like…," "You like…," "He/She/It likes…," "We like…," "They like…")

- **Keep Resources Handy:** As you review the lesson slides before class, think about areas that might need extra support. Select appropriate props and other materials (as necessary) and think through how you might help a learner get through the current lesson content with the help of the prop or other resources, even without mastering previous content.
- **Suggest Review:** Take time at the end of class to suggest activities to help the learner review the content they are still struggling with. Remind them that resources like homework and a digital library can be used to help them catch up outside of class.
- **Hold Off:** If there are particular lesson slides that you do not feel will benefit your learner or that may take up precious time (e.g.,

song, transition, **Total Physical Response**), consider cutting them or saving them until the end of the lesson so that you can spend more class time targeting a specific language point.

Reflection

- What is your current approach to helping a learner catch up during a lesson when they do not remember the content or have the required skills?
- Consider one of the courses you currently teach. Which areas always seem to need a review? Which resources could you use to help your learner with those trouble spots?

RUSHING

How can I help a learner who tries to rush through tasks?

Keywords
#classroom management #instructions #modeling #routine #pacing #planning #rushing

▶ The Situation

I have a learner who always rushes ahead and tries to do the slides without listening to the instructions. Because he rushes, he has many incorrect answers. When I restore the slide and let him try again, he gets very frustrated. He does not want to participate, probably because he feels like he is doing the same thing over and over. Then I get frustrated because I feel like we are wasting our class time. **How can I help a learner who tries to rush through tasks?**

Analyzing the Situation

- Every learner wants to know what they are supposed to do during a task or how they are supposed to interact with materials. This is why instructions are such an important part of classroom management. Effective teachers can prevent many problems like rushing by providing proper instructions.
- A learner may rush through activities due to excitement or to gain power or control. Exciting activities can make your learner overeager to rush through them. Suppose a learner is unsure of what you want them to do (e.g., because they do not understand instructions). In that case, they might think that taking control of the class by rushing is a way for them to be proactive about tasks.
- Your young learner might rush more than an older learner because they are still in the process of learning how to follow instructions and are not familiar with the pacing of lessons. This means that, especially for a young learner, it is important to start establishing routines and familiar instructions from the get-go.

Suggested Strategies

You do not need to be afraid of a learner who rushes through tasks. You do need to be patient and prepared to help your learner follow routines. Here's how.

- **Use Your Tools:** If your learner insists on rushing and not listening to instructions, first praise their eagerness to engage. Then bring them back into focus. You can do this by revisiting important words or phrases on the screen. For example, if your learner confidently responds, "I'm happy!" even though the question on screen reads, "How old are you?" you could say, "Yay! I'm happy, too!" or "I'm glad you're happy!" Then, revisit the original question, and underline, highlight, or otherwise emphasize the word *old*. When your learner successfully and appropriately answers, be sure to respond with praise and rewards.
- **Bring Them Back:** Do not be afraid to start activities over if it means the learner will better understand what to do. It can be difficult to regroup, but if you do not, you are in danger of having the same issue persist beyond a single lesson. This may mean doing things like turning off a

learner's mouse. If you are worried about your learner feeling like they are repeating the same task, be sure to praise the way they initially interacted, then reframe the transition back to the original task. For example, you can say, "Very good, Lucy. Now let's do it a different way!"

- **Anticipate:** Look at each slide of a lesson as though you are a learner with limited English. What does it look like the slide wants you to do? How does it seem like you are supposed to interact with it? Thinking this way will help you anticipate parts of the lesson where rushing may occur.

- **Take Cues:** Sometimes, when a learner rushes through an activity, they are demonstrating how they would like to interact with a slide or an activity, either because the way they have envisioned it makes more sense than the task at hand or because they are used to doing something similar in a different lesson. For example, if a learner consistently wants to drag flash cards instead of match them, they are telling us they either prefer dragging or they are more familiar with dragging than with matching.

- **Place Accuracy over Fluency:** If a learner tends to be fluent at the cost of accuracy, then the teacher should help the learner to focus on accuracy by asking the learner to repeat what is said and use **corrective feedback** to question, confirm, or engage in meaningful conversation by focusing on accuracy.

- **Set Up a Time:** For mini-tasks, the teacher can set up a time, say one minute or 90 seconds, for a mini-task and let the learner maximize that time without rushing. For example, a teacher can say that if the learner finishes the task earlier, they can use the remaining time to double-check what they have done. This can help the learner build the habit of consciousness of being accurate.

Reflection

- How do you currently handle lessons where your learner tries to rush through activities?
- Which of the above strategies do you think is most effective or could be implemented in your lessons?

39 | USING ROLE PLAY

How can I facilitate role-play activities in a one-to-one classroom environment?

Keywords
#affective filter #interaction #listening skills #role play #speaking skills

▶ **The Situation**

I love role playing with my learner, but I feel like role playing with me, their teacher, can be harder than with their peers. I want to make sure they have plenty of opportunities to practice interaction and speaking skills, but I want it to be easy and fun—just like it would be with their friends in a brick-and-mortar classroom. ***How can I facilitate role-play activities in a one-to-one classroom environment?***

Analyzing the Situation

- Role plays can be fun and entertaining and help lower the **affective filter** and practice speaking and listening skills. These activities are also wonderful opportunities to inject humor and practice real language in a low-stakes context.
- In one-to-one role plays, your role as the teacher shifts to one of model or performer. Since one of the goals of role plays is to simulate real-life social interactions, learners need to see this modeled as authentically as is practical.
- This does not mean that all feedback or error correction should be avoided, but it should be done intentionally to make sure your learner has a clear understanding of the purpose of these activities: to interact meaningfully in English.

Suggested Strategies

Role plays are common on many platforms and in language classrooms around the world. You can make sure your learner reaps the benefits of this communicative activity. Here's how.

- **Make Expectations Clear:** Moving into role plays, make sure that expectations are clear. This means making sure your learner understands their role. This includes understanding what they should say and when. For example, if you are doing a dialogue with two people, use a scaffold onscreen (like a typed-up dialogue) to make it clear who is supposed to speak and when. This can be as simple as assigning each line of a dialogue A or B. You can assume the role of A, and your learner can assume the role of B. (It makes it easier to change roles afterwards and extend language that much more.)
- **Model It:** You might choose to start with a dialogue on the screen where each person is assigned a color (or letter, as suggested above) so that it is very clear who should speak. Then start just reading assigned lines. You can then always swap roles or remove some of the words and allow a learner to fill in the missing information.
- **Sufficient Time:** These social interactions can be intimidating at first, especially for a young language learner. Give your learner the time they need to process instructions and prepare silently. Providing this time can

be the difference between a successful role play and one that is rushed, confused, and unsuccessful.

- **Use Props and TPR:** You can make role plays special by using specific props and routines to model the activity. Consider microphones, **Total Physical Response** (**TPR**) sequences, and other resources to make expectations and role assignment crystal clear. Puppets are an excellent option for younger learners, as they can help simulate the entire interaction.
- **Take Notes:** Role plays can be a great opportunity to see your learner apply language they are learning in less

contextualized activities. Keep track of where your learner struggles to provide appropriate follow-up. You can also note areas where your learner is strong and extend or personalize these role plays.

Reflection

- What is your current approach to facilitating role-plays in your classroom? What's working and what's not?
- Consider a lesson you teach with a built-in role play. How could you use the strategies above to help your learner get the most out of the activity?

USING GAMES

How can I use games to help my learner in the classroom?

Keywords
#**cognitive load** #**games** #**interaction** #**play** #**practice**

▶ The Situation

One of my regular learners loves the games we play at the end of class, but I question whether they really help him learn. Last week he had to apply some of the languages we had been practicing in games in a new activity. I thought it would be simple for him to make the connection, but it turned out to be a real challenge. I know games can be effective, but for some reason, mine do not seem to be helping. ***How can I use games to help my learner in the classroom?***

Analyzing the Situation

- Games used for learning should include interaction, feedback, goals, and other motivating elements that connect them to course content.
- There should always be attention to when and why you introduce a game. Keep in mind how a game might fit with the other input the learner is receiving (pre-class, lesson content, enrichment, props) and avoid adding unnecessary cognitive load.
- Learners at different ages and skill levels will react differently to games. Select games carefully based on learner interests, the language needed to play, and the lesson objectives.
- If designed well, games can be an extension of learning after the class, as much of the time in class should be spent on interaction.

Suggested Strategies

Do not stress about incorporating games into your lessons. You can make games fun and worthwhile for both you and your learner. Here's how.

- **Know Your Purpose:** Use games to meet a clear learning objective. For example, play games to review. If a game's goal is to review, include only the **target language** to review; review games should not require too much class time to pre-teach vocabulary or specific instructions.
- **Use Game-Like Elements:** Set up a game with basic cues like, "Ready, set, go!" This makes even a simple flashcard activity seem more like a game and that much more enjoyable for a learner.
- **Make Games Appropriate:** With a younger learner, try hiding and revealing props on different sides of your screen for a quick hide and seek game. In the game, use props that are within the scope of the lesson and support the learning objectives. For an older learner, try Twenty Questions. In the game, use questions that encourage the use of target vocabulary and target question formation. To find out if your game or prop is appropriate, ask yourself two questions:
  ○ Does its content relate directly to the learning objectives?
  ○ How could its images or features distract from learning?
    If you answer "yes" to the first question,

you then should flag potentially distracting images or features in answering the second. Quickly note when you may need to redirect attention.

- **Make Practice Fun:** Get your learner engaged in content and offer them opportunities to practice the target language in fun and authentic ways. Introduce a simple game and its rules using adverbs of sequence (*first, next, then, finally, etc.*) and conditionals ("if you draw this card, then this happens…"). Then have your learner repeat back the rules. The context of the game makes practicing adverbs and conditionals more fun!

- **Consider Class Time:** Find the best moments to use games. Consider these potential issues before including a game in your lesson:
  - How long will it take to set up, play, and transition?
  - What will you do if we run out of time?
  - Is the game the best choice to support the learning objectives?
  - What else could you do with class time?
  - A game may be the best choice in your situation, but it is always good to consider these questions given a 25-minute lesson.

- **Don't Play a Game Just for the Sake of Playing a Game:** Make sure the games you introduce will require intensive language practice preferably even more intensive than other classroom activities. Do not play a game that takes an inordinate amount of time and results in very little language production by the learner.

- **The Point Is…:** Often, you don't need to think too hard to come up with a complicated game that will take a long time to explain. Many times, you can add point-keeping or a timer to your usual classroom activities, and it becomes a game to the learner (and motivates them to practice more intensively).

- **Chance:** Add an element of chance to your games. Perhaps the roll of a die will determine how many points they receive. Perhaps a flip of a coin will determine if they will receive two points or their opponent (the teacher in a one-to-one class) will receive one point as a result of their correct answer. This will lower the learners' **affective filters**, as winning the game is no longer completely dependent on their language performance.

Reflection

- What kind of games do you currently use in your classes? What seems to work, and what doesn't?
- Reflect on one of your current learners. How could you use a strategy above to engage and support your learner with gameplay?

41 | USING MUSIC

How can I effectively use music in class?

Keywords
#chants #music #productive skills #receptive skills #songs

► **The Situation**

I've heard many teachers talk about using music in lessons and how much their learner loves interacting with the songs. I have not felt comfortable trying to use music, though. I am a little reserved when it comes to singing, and I am unsure about what music can add to my lessons. I do not want my learner to miss out on a fun opportunity that another teacher is more eager and able to offer. ***How can I effectively use music in class?***

Analyzing the Situation

- Using music in language classes can be intimidating if you don't think of yourself as a singer. The good news is that you do not need to be a karaoke star to use music or musical elements successfully in your lessons.
- Music is not just entertaining; it is also proven to help language learners retain the language and develop **productive** and **receptive skills** and subskills.
- Musical elements can also make teachers and learners feel more comfortable repeating sentences or phrases that might seem silly or awkward if just spoken over and over again. Think about the opportunity to use **chants** as well as (or in place of) songs.

Suggested Strategies

You do not need to sing well in order to effectively engage your learner using music or musical elements. However, you do need to have an open mind and be prepared. Here's how.

- **Know Your Skills:** Music and musical elements can be used to improve various linguistic skills and subskills. A chant-like "Patty Cake" is memorable because of its rhythm; use this kind of chant to target intonation and demonstrate a more fluent cadence, which helps learners improve their listening and speaking. Also, use simple rhythmic repetition to help your learners with stress. Take the word watermelon, for example. Chinese young learners often place the stress on the third syllable instead of the first (wa-ter-MEL-on). A short "watermelon, watermelon, yum, yum, yum" chant will help target this pronunciation issue and can be used as reinforcement.

- **Have a Plan:** It is important to have a plan, not only for the skills you want to address but for what your learner should do on the first or second listen. Even if you do not want to sing, your learner can still engage with songs in class. Encourage your learner to provide a missing word upon second listen or pause the song to have the learner fill in the rest of a phrase. Perhaps ask your learner to stand up and wiggle when they hear the word *she* and crouch down and wiggle when they hear the word *he*. There are many creative ways to engage your learner with music and musical elements. Neither teacher nor learner must know how to sing.

- **Beat Box:** Even if you feel you cannot sing

well, you can still participate with your learner by keeping the rhythm. You can do this vocally, keeping the rhythm with a simple beatbox (rhythmic sounds made vocally) such as "boop, chee, boop, chee". You could also use an inexpensive children's tambourine or even simple clapping to keep the beat while your learner sings.

- **Use Background Music:** Once in a while, consider playing music in the background during class to help your learner concentrate during longer or more involved tasks. Using songs as background music too can offer built-in amounts of time (i.e., you have a song's worth of time to complete a particular task.) When choosing background music, be intentional. Songs that are loud or unnecessarily busy wordy might backfire and create anxiety for your learner. The same can be said for music that includes dramatic builds. Always listen to music you plan to use beforehand to make sure it is appropriate for the learner and your online classroom.

- **Use the Right Type of Background Music:** Using music well can help enhance learning and improve concentration. Sometimes, selecting the right type of music is crucial, depending on the type of activity. If music is used in the background, usually baroque music helps learners relax and reduce anxiety. If students are doing vocabulary exercises or doing question and answer tasks, rock or light rock might help create an atmosphere for concentration and time urgency. Background music with lyrics is not encouraged, as students could be carried away by the words in the song and become distracted.

Reflection

- What is your current approach to using songs and music in your classes?
- Consider one of your upcoming lessons. Using the strategies above, how could you incorporate music into your lesson?

42 | TAKING RISKS

How can I encourage my learner to be a risk-taker?

Keywords
#affective filter #environment #risk #scaffold

▶ The Situation

My learner seems afraid to try speaking using new sentence structures. Sometimes he is even shy about saying new target vocabulary words. I think he is afraid of making mistakes. I want him to be more comfortable with at least trying to use new language. ***How can I encourage my learner to be a risk-taker?***

Analyzing the Situation

- It is very common for learners to be shy, nervous, or afraid of making mistakes, especially when they are just beginning to learn English. These sorts of feelings raise what researcher, Stephen Krashen, would call the learner's **affective filter**, or the learner's attitude about their performance with the new language. If a learner has a high affective filter, it is very difficult for them to learn or take risks necessary to help them improve quickly.
- Lowering your learner's affective filter will help them be confident to take more risks.

Suggested Strategies

It may take some time for your learner to become more outgoing and take more risks, but teachers can help them be comfortable producing new language. Here's how.

- **Provide Good Examples:** Before expecting your learner to produce new language, make sure that you first provide multiple examples of the structure or other target being used correctly. This will help your

learner feel more confident that they can at least approximate a similar utterance with some degree of accuracy.
- **Break It Down and Build It Up:** Break down examples and build up toward more complex language. By starting with a more accessible version of the **target language**, your learner has to take less of a risk. Thus, they may have more confidence to attempt. For example, if you are working with the auxiliary verb *do* in questions, instead of focusing on the entire questions like, "What do you like to eat?" or "Where do you want to go?" etc. instead focus on the phrases "do you like" and "do you want". This will help the learner focus on the form before extending out to the full questions.
- **Create Space:** Your learner needs to feel like they are part of a comfortable, non-threatening environment. Be sure to make eye contact with your learner and use a soft, reassuring voice, yet be upbeat and friendly. Comedy, illustrations, music, and educational games are all things that can help lower a learner's affective filter.
- **Be Careful with Correction:** If you use too much correction, a learner may shut down. If you use too little correction, the learner may not have enough guidance. To encourage risk-taking, consider providing feedback only after completing an activity.
- **Put Yourself Out There:** It is one thing to encourage your learner to take risks, but it is another thing to show them it is okay to take risks and fail. This means that as a

teacher, you can make language mistakes or errors in class (and you can plan these out intentionally beforehand); then you can either encourage your learner to correct you or you can correct yourself. If you have a lesson where you need to refer to a journal entry that includes grammatical errors or that could be improved by adding descriptive adjectives, tell your learner it is from your own journal and that you would like a second set of eyes on it. This simple gesture may communicate that it is okay to take risks with language, get feedback, and use this feedback to improve.

Reflection

- Have you studied another language? If so, were you a confident risk-taker, or were you also afraid of making mistakes? If you haven't studied a second language, have you ever been faced with other learning tasks where you were afraid to take risks?
- Consider one of your learners who has struggled with taking risks. Which of the suggested strategies could you use with this learner in their next lesson?

References

Aliakbari, M., & Jamalvandi, B. (2010). The impact of "role play" on fostering EFL learners' speaking ability: A task-based approach. *Journal of Pan-Pacific Association of Applied Linguistics, 14*(1), 15-29.

Anderson, N. (2003). Scrolling, clicking, and reading English: Online reading strategies in a second/foreign language. *The Reading Matrix, 3*(3).

Barekat, B., & Nobakhti, H. (2014). The effect of authentic and inauthentic materials in cultural awareness training on EFL learners' listening comprehension ability. *Theory and Practice in Language Studies, 4*(5), 1058-1065. doi: 10.4304/tpls.4.5.1058-1065

Beers, G. K. (2003). *When kids can't read, what teachers can do: a guide for teachers.* Portsmouth, NH: Heinemann.

Brophy, J. (1998). *Motivating students to learn.* Retrieved from http://www.erasmusgrobina.lv/images/motivation/JereE.Brophy.Motivating-Students.pdf

Budden, J. (2008). *Adapting materials for different age groups.* Retrieved from https://www.teachingenglish.org.uk/article/adapting-materials-different-age-groups

Bui, G., & Skehan, P. (2018). Complexity, accuracy, and fluency. *The TESOL Encyclopedia of English Language Teaching,* 1-7.

Cameron, L. (2001). *Teaching languages to young learners.* Cambridge: Cambridge University Press.

Cervantes, I. M. (2013). The Role of risk-taking behavior in the development of speaking skills in ESL classrooms. *Revista de Lenguas Modernas,* (19), 421-435.

Elsheikh, A. (2018). Rubrics. *The TESOL Encyclopedia of English Language Teaching,* John Wiley & Sons, 1-8. doi: 10.1002/9781118784235.eelt0368

England, L. (2018). Communities of practice. In J. I. Liontas, T. International Association, & M. DelliCarpini (Eds.),

The TESOL encyclopedia of English language teaching. doi:10.1002/9781118784235.eelt0396

Goswami, U. (2005). Synthetic phonics and learning to read: A cross-language perspective. *Educational Psychology in Practice, 21*(4), 273-282. doi: 10.1080/02667360500344823

Grabe, W., & Stoller, F. L. (2011). *Teaching and researching reading* (2nd ed.). New York, NY: Routledge.

Graham, C. (1979). *Jazz chants for children: rhythms of American English through chants, songs and poems.* New York: Oxford University Press.

Harley, B. (2000). Listening strategies in ESL: Do age and L1 make a difference? *TESOL Quarterly 34*(4), 769-777.

Harmer, J. (2001). *The practice of English language teaching* (3rd ed.). London: Pearson Education ESL.

Hedgcock, J., & Ferris, D. (2009). *Teaching readers of English.* New York, NY: Routledge.

Hinkel, E. (2017). Teaching speaking in integrated-skills classes. In J. I. Liontas, T. International Association, & M. DelliCarpini (Eds.), *The TESOL encyclopedia of English language teaching.* doi:10.1002/9781118784235.eelt0256

Lewis, M. (1993). *The lexical approach: The state of ELT and a way forward.* Heinle ELT.

Levine, L.N., Ur, P., & Nunan, D. (2009). A TESOL symposium on differentiated instruction: Meeting the needs of large groups of diverse learners. *TESOL International Association.* Retrieved from https://www.tesol.org/attend-and-learn/tesol-academies-conferences-symposiums/upcoming-tesol-symposiums/symposiums/a-tesol-symposium-on-differentiated-instruction

Lin, C. C. (2017). Inviting diverse participation: The role of student-generated questions in classroom

collaborative inquiry. *NYS TESOL Journal, 4*(2), 66-77.

Lyster, R. (1997). *The classroom and immersion pedagogy.* Retrieved from https://pdfs.semanticscholar.org/cfea/da24fbe084bd44f9be0a2c80bd014b0427c0.pdf

Ma, J. J. (2020). L2 students' engagement with written corrective feedback. In J. I. Liontas, T. International Association, & M. DelliCarpini (Eds.), *The TESOL encyclopedia of English language teaching.* doi:10.1002/9781118784235.eelt0966

McFadden, T. U. (1998). Sounds and stories: Teaching phonemic awareness in interactions around text. *American Journal of Speech-Language Pathology, 7,* 5-13. doi: 10.1044/1058-0360.0702.05

McLeod, S. (2019). *What is the zone of proximal development?* Retrieved from https://www.simplypsychology.org/Zone-of-Proximal-Development.html

Mertler, C.A. (2000). Designing scoring rubrics for your classroom. *Practical Assessment, Research, and Evaluation, 7*(25).

Moon, J. (1999). *Children learning English.* Oxford: Macmillan Heinemann.

Nadolny, L., Alaswad, Z., Culver, D., & Wang, W. (2017). Designing with game-based learning: Game mechanics from middle school to higher education. *Simulation & Gaming, 48*(6), 814–831. doi: 10.1177/1046878117736893

Nation, P. (2003). Materials for teaching vocabulary. In B. Tomlinson (Ed.), *Developing materials for language teaching* (pp. 394–405). London, England: Continuum.

Oxford, R. (2001) Integrated skills in the ESL/EFL classroom. *The Journal of TESOL France,* (8), 5-12.

Reilly, V., & Ward, S. (1997). *Very young learners.* Oxford: Oxford University Press.

Savage, J. (2014). Lesson planning: key concepts and skills for teachers.

London: Routledge.

Scrivener, J. (2005). *Learning teaching.* Oxford: Macmillan Heinemann.

Taguchi, N. (2018). *Presenting new language items.* In J. I. Liontas, T. International Association, & M. DelliCarpini (Eds.), *The TESOL Encyclopedia of English Language Teaching, 1–6.* doi:10.1002/9781118784235.eelt0193

Tennant, A. (2007). Listening matters: Top-down and bottom-up listening. Retrieved from http://www.onestopenglish.com/skills/listening/teaching-tips/listening-matters/listening-matters-top-down-and-bottom-up-listening/154567.article

TESOL International Association (TESOL). (2019). Standards for initial TESOL pre-K-12 teacher preparation programs. Retrieved from: https://www.tesol.org/docs/default-source/books/2018-tesol-teacher-prep-standards-final.

pdf?sfvrsn=23f3ffdc_6

Underhill, A. (Ed.). (2000). *Teacher development series.* Oxford: Macmillan Heinemann.

Ur, P. (1996). A course in language teaching: Practice and theory. Cambridge: Cambridge University Press.

Workman, G. (2005) *Concept questions and time lines.* Chadburn Publishing.

Part 3
Case Analyses in Techniques & Strategies in Online English Teaching

▶ Introduction

Technology has broken down barriers to education and created new online learning opportunities for hundreds of thousands of children. This has revolutionized tutoring and extracurricular learning as we know it by removing location restraints, saving time, and creating a new level of access to teachers. This has also allowed for more opportunities and equity in education. In the next decade, AI technologies will be part of learning at all levels and blur the line between formal classroom education and self-paced, individual learning. In language teaching, likewise, we shall integrate technologies in order to stay competitive in the years to come.

Because teaching English online is relatively new to many language teachers, there are a lot of issues, challenges, and teaching problems that we encounter on a daily basis. What are considered to be useful activities in traditional language classrooms, such as pair work or group work, cannot be applied to one-to-one teaching. Due to each lesson's limited class time, some activities (e.g., writing or silent reading) might not be appropriate or effective. Pre-class or post-class review or preview, which greatly ensure the learning outcome, should be integrated into the curriculum, but how to ensure that all the learners do what is required is uncontrollable. When teachers

teach different learners all the time, how do we establish rapport and sustain continuity? Also, when a lesson is only 25 minutes long, how can we warm up the learner without taking too much time, and how can we meaningfully use the last few minutes to check how well the learner has learned according to the lesson objectives? These are the questions our teachers often encounter, and we have provided cases and recommendations in this Part.

Skills transfer is always a critical point as many teachers teaching online are experienced language teachers offline. How can we use what we are good at and apply it to online teaching? For instance, when we use **TPR (Total Physical Response)** very successfully in regular classrooms, we find it hard for learners to move the body as they sit, and sometimes the camera of the computer will not be positioned to show the whole body for the teacher to know whether they are moving according to the right directions. For another example, the use of Artificial Intelligence (AI) is always a great idea as we know that AI can provide personalization at scale, but quality education will always require active engagement by human teachers. Teachers should be prepared to use AI tutors to assist them. We encourage our teachers to personalize their teaching and make adaptive learning possible. However, how are we going to use software to modify content and pace of delivery based on each learner's language proficiency? Many teachers are aware that we can utilize **augmented reality** (a view of a real-world environment enhanced with computer-generated information); **blended learning** (a hybrid of online and face-to-face learning); a **flipped classroom** (a teaching model in which an instructor asks students to first engage with materials on their own, often online, then uses the class to deepen their learning); **gamification** (an educational model that incorporates elements of video-game design to more deeply engage students, who may choose from options that lead to different exercises and outcomes), and a **learning management system** (software that delivers and tracks academic courses and student data), among other elements in our language teaching. How can we play a role in contributing ideas rooted in our teaching to enable computer scientists and engineers to develop these to suit our needs?

A digital library is a great resource for our learners as learning requires extended continuity Only learning English online for a limited period of time will not get our learners too far. By utilizing our digital resources, our learners will be exposed to more authentic input and have more opportunities to familiarize themselves with what they have learned and what they are going to learn. How to utilize our digital library is certainly a strategy a language teacher should know about. We have provided cases on this subject in this part as well.

Apart from technology requirements, facilities, and digital resources, professionalism in online language teaching is also an important aspect in providing quality online teaching and a virtual online classroom. For instance, punctuality is greatly appreciated by both parents and learners. Also, because parents are paying for a certain period of lesson

time, it is advisable that teachers completely fill the allotted lesson time using review activities or extensions if needed. It is also highly recommended that teachers appear professional. In order to make the virtual classroom professional and appealing, some things a teacher might want to consider include attire, grooming, positioning in front of a camera, background, and eye contact with the camera lens.

Teaching online from home can make one feel rather isolated, but there are many opportunities for online teachers to interact with others using social media. Teachers are encouraged to ask other online teachers questions regarding improving their professional delivery, share ideas, and share resources. Teachers are strongly encouraged to do outside reading, look for online webinars, join online ESL and EFL teacher discussion groups, or even join professional TEFL and TESOL organizations and attend conferences. This allows you to better understand the research and advances being made in this field.

As a language teacher, you are wise to become involved in online teaching. Although the field is still somewhat new and is adjusting to better work with new challenges, online language learning is here to stay and will likely become a mainstay of the children's language education field for years to come.

Question	Sub-Topic
1. How can I build rapport with my online learner?	**Online Rapport**
2. How do I promote meaningful interaction in my online classes?	**Meaningful Interaction**
3. How can I appropriately share more of my own background and experience to support learning?	**Background & Experience**
4. How can I make simple, yet effective activities seem more engaging to my learner?	**Engaging Activities**
5. How can I make the most of the first five minutes of class?	**First Five Minutes**
6. How can I make the most of the last five minutes of class?	**Last Five Minutes**
7. How can I help learners who move quickly through lesson activities and content?	**Quick Finisher**
8. How can I create a professional and comfortable learning environment online?	**Learning Environment**
9. How can my online classroom and bulletin boards enhance my online teaching?	**Online Classroom**
10. How can I better use props to enhance my online teaching?	**Using Props**
11. How can I use TPR effectively in my online classroom?	**Using TPR**
12. How can I help my learner transfer skills from our online classroom back to their regular classroom?	**Skills Transfer**
13. How can I help my learner benefit from the flipped classroom model?	**Flipped Classroom**
14. How can I help my learner understand the value and importance of pre- and post-class activities (e.g., pre-class videos, homework, self-study)?	**Pre- & Post-Class**
15. How can I help my learner and their parents benefit from AI components in courses?	**Benefits of AI**

Question	Sub-Topic
16. How can I help my learner benefit from digital library resources?	**Digital Library**
17. How can I help learners better understand the language needed to interact with our courseware?	**Courseware Interactions**
18. How can the teacher and learner respond to and overcome unexpected technical issues?	**Overcoming Technical Issues**
19. How can I adjust my teaching methods when teaching a one-to-many class online?	**One-to-Many Methods**
20. How can I make sure that all learners participate equally in a one-to-many class?	**Equal Participation**

ONLINE RAPPORT

How can I build rapport with my online learner?

Keywords
#**meaningful interaction** #**new learner** #**rapport** #**relationships**

▶ The Situation

As a teacher, I teach both new and regular learners. Some learners are really shy and don't want to even speak a single word no matter how much I encourage them. It is a bit awkward, especially in the first lesson. I want to make sure that my learners and I get to know each other, but it seems so much harder to do through a webcam than in real life. It is also difficult when my learners do not always have the language to express themselves or understand what I am sharing. ***How can I build rapport with my online learner?***

Analyzing the Situation

- It is possible to build deep and meaningful relationships with your learners online, even with new learners. In fact, many teachers cite the relationships with their learners as part of what they love most about their job.
- Children may experience anxiety when meeting strangers for the first time. When they are anxious, they may choose to remain quiet, act passively, or even avoid eye contact. Depending on each child, anxiety can go away in a few minutes or last a long time.
- Building rapport with learners can make a difference when in language classes. With rapport, learners are more likely to use the **target language**, have a solid learner-teacher relationship, and engage in activities.
- Having a good rapport with your learners involves intention and attention. You are

with your learners for a short period of time each week, so you must think through a routine for building rapport. Then, keep an eye out for new opportunities to further develop your relationships with learners down the road.

Suggested Strategies

You don't have to be your learner's best friend to have a good rapport. You do need to be intentional and have patience. Here's how.

- **Say Their Name:** Names are the quickest way to build rapport in the first moments of class. For younger learners, you can refer to characters on a welcome slide and ask, "Is this [learner's name]?" Then, you can say, "No, you are [learner's name]?" For older learners, you can ask them to tell you more about their name, whether it is their Chinese name or their chosen English name. Sometimes the stories behind these names are wonderful!
- **Be Playful, Humorous, and Happy:** Children are playful. You, too, can be playful in the classroom while still maintaining your role and responsibilities as a teacher. You can crack jokes, ask random questions, and tell funny stories on the topics you are teaching. Always remember to smile! Show your learners you are excited to see them and get to know them.
- **Share:** Do not rely solely on the learner for rapport-building opportunities. Often, when teachers make the first move with a personal detail like, "My favorite animal is…"

or, "I have a big family, but..." you will be surprised how quickly learners will be more inclined to offer up their own stories.

- **Remember the Details:** From the T-shirt they are wearing to the stuffed animal on their desk, always take opportunities to connect with what is in the learner's environment. Then, make a note of these details for the next time you see them. Learners love talking about their things, and they love it even more when their teacher remembers them and seems interested.

- **Use the Whole Class:** The best opportunity to connect with a learner could be at any time during a lesson. Don't think about rapport as something that can happen

only in the first and last minutes of class. If your learner feels comfortable with you throughout the class, they will be more likely to take risks and handle mistakes with the confidence to move forward, trusting that you will be there to help them navigate it all.

Reflection

- What is your current approach to building rapport with your learners?
- Consider one of your regulars with whom you have a great rapport. How did you develop it? How long did it take?

02 | MEANINGFUL INTERACTION

How do I promote meaningful interaction in my online classes?

Keywords
#interaction #online #rapport #relationship #transactional distance

▶ The Situation

I am so thankful for the opportunity to teach Chinese learners on the other side of the world with just a computer and a webcam. Still, I can't help feeling like my learner and I are missing out on a connection that might be easier for us to have if we were in a traditional, face-to-face classroom. ***How do I promote meaningful interaction in my online classes?***

Analyzing the Situation

- It can be tough to form a quick bond with a learner you only see at the other end of a webcam. The theory of transactional distance refers to the development of a unique relationship or interaction between teacher and learner as a result of being geographically separate. This necessitates a different pedagogical approach to teaching. The challenges of online teaching and learning mean teachers may have to try harder to create and shape a bond with learners.

- Remember that you only see your learners for a short time each week; they likely have very busy lives outside of their time with you. Understanding your learner as a developing human can help you approach your time with them as a learner.

Suggested Strategies

You don't need to be your learner's best friend or cater to every detail of a lesson to topics that interest them. You also don't need to pretend that your classroom isn't online. You do need to find creative and thoughtful ways to allow your learner to open up while learning English. Here's how.

- **Know Your Learner:** Interaction in class is a two-way street. If you demonstrate a willingness to know more about your learners, they are often more willing to reciprocate. Take time to find out what kinds of clubs your learner is involved in or what hobbies they enjoy. Is there anything going on in your learner's life that might affect how well they perform in classes or how motivated they are about learning English? Understanding just a bit more about your learner can help you tailor your lessons, where possible, to fit their needs. To ease into this effort of getting to know each other, try using an "I share"/"You share" approach. This can be as simple as saying, "My favorite color is blue. What's your favorite color?" and soliciting the appropriate response.

- **Personalize Your Interaction:** Once you find out more about your learner, think of ways you can inject a bit of their personality (or your own) into your lessons. This could mean learning the name of your learners' friend or pet and including that name in dialogues or sharing pictures or stories about your own family.

- **Prepare for All Learners:** Teachers do not always get to teach the same learners regularly. Therefore, it can be challenging for you to learn who your learners are. Be prepared with a repertoire of strategies that will enable you to pivot in class and try different strategies until you find one that fits the needs of your learner. The best way to do this is to try them out and experiment regularly until you find techniques that work. One strategy includes writing down a series of "getting to know you" questions on cards and having your learner choose which card they want to respond to.

- **Put Yourself in Their Shoes:** The stresses of a child's daily life might be difficult to understand when you only see them for a couple of hours a week. Try to imagine all of the activities and routines that learners go through on a daily basis (as well as any other stressors that might be relevant at the time) and consider this as you navigate and deliver lessons. A quick check-in at the beginning or end of class can often give you important information that can help you shape the most effective lesson for that learner.

Reflection

- How much information do you get about your learner before teaching them the first time?
- Which strategies from above have you tried? How could you tweak your approach?

03 | BACKGROUND & EXPERIENCE

How can I appropriately share more of my own background and experience to support learning?

Keywords
#background #diversity #experience #identity #meaningful interaction

▶ The Situation

My learners seem curious and interested in my life and my identity, but I'm always unsure of how much or how little I should share with them or how to incorporate this into our lessons in a meaningful way. With younger learners, I struggle to explain with the limited language they have. With older learners, the conversations can get long and sometimes even very personal. *How can I appropriately share more of my own background and experience to support learning?*

Analyzing the Situation

- Your company's platform may be home to a diverse community of teachers and learners who all bring something valuable to the table. It is important to recognize and appreciate diversity in your peers and in your learners.
- Whether intentional or unintentional, the language you use, the expectations you set, and the connections you make can help or hinder learning. Because language learning is a collaborative endeavor, carefully consider what you share as it can meaningfully shape the learning environment and your learners' experiences.

Suggested Strategies

Use your identity to your advantage while also acknowledging where your learners come from. Cultural exchanges do not have to be scary, especially if you use one of these strategies.

- **Language First:** Any personal stories you tell should have an instructional purpose. For example, when learning the names of family members, a story about your parents or siblings might be very relevant and allow for great **comprehensible input**. This also provides a model for your learners and can encourage them to share more appropriately and meaningfully.
- **Plan Your Sharing:** For topics, you teach regularly (e.g., weather, family), prepare relevant and engaging stories ahead of time. Consider the language you will use and make sure it is appropriate for your learner's age and level. You can even assemble pictures or other **realia** to enhance storytelling.
- **Communicate Interculturally:** Teaching English to Chinese children online involves intercultural communication. Communication norms are not universally shared around the world, and acknowledging those differences in preference (how learners like to communicate) and expectation (how learners expect to communicate) is important.

• **Highlight What You Share:** It can be easy to focus on personal and cultural "differences", but identifying what you share with your learners can be just as powerful. Bonding over a shared love of ice cream or a TV show might be what engages a more reserved learner and gets them talking.

Reflection
• How do you currently share your background and experiences in class? What is working, and what is not? • Consider a recent lesson you taught. How could you have shared something from your background or experiences to engage the learner in the lesson content?

ENGAGING ACTIVITIES

How can I make simple, yet effective activities seem more engaging to my learner?

Keywords
#activities #engaging #technique #TPR #interact #gamification
#competition #reward #token economy #role play #role reversal

▶ The Situation

My learners learn a great deal from very simple activities that encourage them to respond and interact frequently. That being said, sometimes these very simple games and activities seem to bore my learners. I imagine it is very difficult for them because they have to rely on interaction with me instead of their peers. ***How can I make simple, yet effective activities seem more engaging to my learner?***

Analyzing the Situation

- Activities that require frequent learner responses are one of the best ways to reinforce and consolidate learning, but it is also important that learners develop the skills to initiate conversations.
- Many teaching platforms include a variety of tools such as the magnifying glass tool, **augmented reality (AR)** stickers, and rewards that teachers can use to help simple activities seem more engaging to learners.

Suggested Strategies

Not every activity needs to seem like a high-interest game a child might play on a digital pad outside school. That being said, you can use a variety of tools and techniques to make activities fun and engaging for all learners. Here's how.

- **Augmented Reality Stickers:** Use AR stickers, which may be available on the teaching platform you are using or from external tools to add an element of silliness to activities. You can place certain items on the screen, use special screen frames, make it appear that you are wearing unusual hats or glasses, etc.
- **Make Rewards Fun:** In addition to digital rewards such as stars that can be given out when a learner performs well in class, consider other personalized and creative rewards. Many teachers have found success with simple step-by-step drawings where each reward involves the teacher completing one more step of the drawing. With a quick internet search, you can find simple instructions for bringing your learners' favorite animal or superhero to life as they complete activities and earn rewards.
- **Use Total Physical Response (TPR):** Especially if you are working with an active learner, have them first act out their response to a teacher prompt before giving a verbal answer. By acting out a response, they show that they understand the prompt, and it makes the process of providing a response more fun for them.
- **Use Role Reversal:** One way to keep the learner engaged is to have them play the role of the teacher and give you prompts that you must respond to. Of course, your responses could also be accompanied by

physical actions or use of some of the tools discussed above. Encouraging a learner to do this might take extra time and extra rewards, so be prepared.

- **Don't Overdo It:** Engagement strategies should be used deliberately. Pay attention to how your learners react and balance consistency with freshness. The overuse of a particular strategy can lead to learner disinterest and burnout, and the use of too

many different strategies can overwhelm or confuse.

Reflection

- What are some strategies you already use to effectively engage your learners?
- Which strategies from above have you tried? How could you tweak your approach to be more effective?

FIRST FIVE MINUTES

How can I make the most of the first five minutes of class?

Keywords
#engagement #first five minutes #making connections #rapport
#teacher talk time #TTT

▶ **The Situation**

When I first started teaching online, I was always unsure about the first minutes of class with a learner across the globe. I was nervous about meeting new learners and struggled to draw out the quiet ones at the beginning of lessons and first activities. I feel more comfortable now, but I still have those classes where the first minutes drag. Other times, it feels like we're rushing it. ***How can I make the most of the first five minutes of class?***

Analyzing the Situation

- Even without sharing the same physical space, The tone of the class can be set in the first five minutes. In fact, even just the first five seconds can have an impact on how a learner engages with class.
- These moments of greeting are excellent opportunities for engagement and rapport-building. They help you make connections and learn about your learners and their day-to-day lives.
- If a learner is new to you, it is also the perfect time to gather some information like their age and interests while also getting a feel for their language skills.
- Many parents will be pleased to see you encouraging their child to produce as much language as possible in the early part of the class.

Suggested Strategies

Give you and your learners the best chance at a successful lesson; maximize the first five minutes of class. Here's how.

- **Learn and Use Their Name:** Be prepared with your learner's name and incorporate it several times in the first minutes of class. Learners and parents will appreciate this simple personalization. For regulars, you can go beyond the name and find out even more about your learner (interests, etc.) and use that information to personalize the first five minutes.

- **Grab Their Attention:** It is important to display energy and creativity, so plan these moments before you teach. When a learner arrives to class, immediately engage them by being an animated and enthusiastic teacher.

- **Gauge Their Skills:** Since it is very common to teach new learners with most online companies, take the time to gauge a learner's skill level at the beginning of class. With younger learners, ask them about the color of your clothes or objects in your classroom. With older learners, ask them to tell you about what they did over the weekend. These responses can give you tips about where to focus your attention during class, but be careful to avoid too much **teacher talk time (TTT)** that can overwhelm a learner.

- **Accomplish Something:** Make the learner

feel successful early on in the class. If review is the focus, use props or rewards to build your learner's confidence in what they already know. If it is new content, celebrate new words they learn in the first activities early and often. HIghlight new learning early and often in each lesson.

- **Use a Checklist:** Learners and parents both expect the teacher to be prepared and ready for class. Have a checklist for your first five minutes as; it gives everyone confidence that you have set your lesson up for success. Use a simple checklist like this: (1) Welcome learners; (2) Make Introductions;

(3) Make a personal connection; (4) Teach an activity; (5) Highlight new learning; (6) Give a reward; and (7) Provide feedback.

Reflection

- What is your routine for the beginning of class? What is working and what is not working?
- How are the first five minutes different with your regulars compared with your new learners?

LAST FIVE MINUTES

How can I make the most of the last five minutes of class?

Keywords
#**energy** #**interest** #**last five minutes** #**motivation**

▶ The Situation

I often start a class strong, but I feel like the last few minutes of class are the hardest. My learner's energy and interest levels can be lower, and since I do not always know whether we will finish early, I do not always feel prepared to make the most of that time. *How can I make the most of the last five minutes of class?*

Analyzing the Situation

- There are a number of issues that can affect a learner's motivation toward the end of class. In addition to energy and interest, a learner's performance during class—as well as the teacher's energy and interest—can all impact how much momentum is felt in the last five minutes.
- Many learners are juggling other after-school classes and responsibilities. These other activities can also have an impact on a learner's attitude and motivation.
- It is normal for learners to move through a lesson at different paces and occasionally have time after the last slide. Being prepared for this allows you to be responsive and avoid any hesitation on your part that could demotivate your learner.

Suggested Strategies

Don't let the last five minutes of class bring you down. Help make the most of the end of class with the following strategies.

- **Think "Last Five" First:** Plan for your lesson and get set up for class, considering what the last five minutes will look like. What new skills or knowledge will learners have? How will they demonstrate them at the end of class? Use the lesson objectives as a guide to build toward those final minutes.
- **Connect "First Five" and "Last Five":** Remember, psychology tells us that learners remember more of what they were exposed to first and last than what they learn in between. Bookend your lessons with meaningful experiences like greetings and goodbyes to promote authentic language use.
- **Use Existing Resources:** Before considering additional options for the last five, make sure you are familiar with the existing resources in the lesson. Check to see if the lesson has a review or reflection slide you can build on. If there is, you can play related games or songs to extend and engage in the last five minutes.
- **Revisit Trouble Spots:** The last five minutes can be a great time to revisit and work with a tricky topic from class. Choose a narrow topic for review in order for your learner to end the lesson on a high note. Remember, the end of class should give the learner a sense of completion and accomplishment.
- **Extend:** If your learner has demonstrated mastery of the learning objectives, give them an opportunity to go further. For younger learners, recycle language from previous lessons to generate new phrases

that include new vocabulary. (E.g., Bring back colors when teaching vegetables.) For older learners, try and connect language to a different, but related, topic with free talk. (E.g., when learning the names of animals, you also discuss the places they live.)

- **Reward Activity:** If you have been using a **token economy** system to reward learners during the lesson towards a goal of doing a language-learning activity or game at the end of class if time permits, obviously do so

and end it with a bang (a fun ending such as the teacher doing a silly dance, digital confetti, digital fireworks, etc.)

Reflection

- What do the last five minutes of your classes usually look like? What is working, and what is not?
- Consider the different courses and levels you teach. How would you apply the suggested strategies differently?

QUICK FINISHER

How can I help learners who move quickly through lesson activities and content?

Keywords
#planning #prepare #engage #extend #practice

▶ The Situation

For the past few weeks, I have been teaching a learner who wants to go very fast through the slides. I find that we are done with the lesson and still have quite a bit of class time left! I try to go through all of the slides as slowly as I can (or as slowly as I think we need), but we still finish lessons very early. *How can I help learners who move quickly through lesson activities and content?*

Analyzing the Situation

- Sometimes learners want to move forward quickly through a lesson, but lessons are usually very structured and have tight timelines. These structures and timelines are critical to successfully moving through levels and, more accurately, understanding your learner's English level.
- If lesson content is not engaging for your learner, this can be a barrier for them to follow the lesson structure.
- There may be a variety of reasons you are finishing early. Some learners move quickly because they have mastered the content. Others may move quickly out of disinterest. It is important to adjust your approach based on whether the cause appears related to ability or behavior.
- It is also critical to consider how your own behavior impacts the pace of a lesson. Staying alert, patient, and engaged can go a long way to managing the pace.

Suggested Strategies

The time it takes for a learner to move through the slides will always vary. Make sure your learners get the most out of their class time with you. Here's how.

- **Provide Extra Practice:** Find opportunities to engage your learner with related practice. Games like Tic-Tac-Toe and Bingo are great, engaging ways to practice vocabulary and grammar without seeming too repetitive.
- **Extend with Free Talk:** Ask your learner extended questions about the content from the lesson. Ask about their likes and dislikes. Engage in conversational practice that allows for meaningful language skill development.
- **Pre-Plan:** Always prepare extra activities ahead of time in case learners finish early. This can include more work with new vocabulary, recalling previously learned vocabulary, practicing sentence extensions, practicing writing, or practicing more targeted conversation.
- **Manage the Pace:** Ultimately, you are responsible for managing the pace of the class. Use engagement strategies and strategically-placed extensions to make sure that learners feel movement through the lesson. Where learners are strong, a quicker pace may be appropriate for certain activities. But even so, find ways to slow it down and dig deeper.

Reflection	
• What do you currently do in a lesson if a learner moves very quickly through the slides?	• Consider an upcoming lesson. Using the strategies above, what can you add to help the learner actively make the most of class time?

08 | LEARNING ENVIRONMENT

How can I create a professional and comfortable learning environment online?

Keywords
#disrupt #distraction #environment #home #online classroom
#parent portal #professional

▶ **The Situation**

I know that a learner's environment can affect their experience learning English online, but I'm not always sure what that environment should look like. And it's even more complicated because the learning environment includes both my online classroom and the learner's home. *How can I create a professional and comfortable learning environment online?*

Analyzing the Situation

- It is important for teachers to create a welcoming, professional, and practical online classroom that contributes to the learner's environment when they log in to a lesson.
- It is equally important for learners to have a non-disruptive home environment in which to access lessons.
- If either of these environments is less than ideal, it can be very difficult to facilitate a successful language learning experience.
- Although teachers have little control over the home environment, it is often possible to influence it by communicating with parents through an online **parent portal** (used by many online learning companies).

Suggested Strategies

A safe and distraction-free learning environment is critical to a successful language learning experience. Here are some tips for creating this kind of environment.

- **Shh:** Make sure your teaching environment is free of noisy distractions such as traffic, pets, children, noise from other rooms, and so on. Encourage learners and parents to make sure that the home environment is as quiet as possible during lessons.
- **Set Up Your Classroom for Learning:** Use your background and desk setup to enhance learning. You can include a whiteboard to use during a lesson and a bulletin board area you can decorate seasonally (or even decorate to match the theme of your lesson). If you plan to use any **realia** or props in your lesson, be sure they are neatly organized and easily accessible.
- **Be Equipped:** Be sure that you have a good quality camera, multi-angle lighting to avoid shadows, and a good noise-canceling headset with a microphone arm. Detachable cameras are ideal because they are easier to position or even move around. Noise-cancelling headphones are also recommended for learners. If the child is not using good quality headphones, feel free to use the comments section on the parent portal to suggest to the parents that they get a set.
- **Bring the Home Environment into Class:** Learners usually access their lessons from their bedroom or at least their home. This means that you may even be able to

leverage the environment in your teaching. You can instruct a learner to, for example, "Find something yellow," or to "Show me a fruit."

Reflection

- Do you believe your digital classroom environment is professional and practical for teaching online? If not, what could you do to improve it?
- Have you asked parents to help contribute to their child's learning success in other ways? How? How did the parents respond?

ONLINE CLASSROOM

How can my online classroom and bulletin boards enhance my online teaching?

Keywords
#bulletin boards #cognitive load #online classroom #props

▶ **The Situation**

I see other teachers with these amazing online classrooms with bulletin boards, decorations, and props. I was pretty happy with how I have my classroom set up (a simple colored background and my name), but I am starting to wonder if I am missing something. *How can my online classroom and bulletin boards enhance my online teaching?*

Analyzing the Situation

- There is no one "correct" way to set up the space behind you, but most online classrooms fall into one of three categories: (1) those that are decorative and primarily for display, (2) those that are functional and interactive, and (3) those that combine elements of both 1 and 2. Find the setup that works best for you and your learners.
- Always keep the age, gender, and level of your learners in mind when deciding what to post on bulletin boards or what kinds of images and props you want to be displayed. Avoid adding anything unnecessary or potentially distracting. If something is visible in your classroom, make sure it is intentional and that you have a plan to use it.

Suggested Strategies

You do not have to be an expert crafter or interior designer to set up your online classroom. With these strategies, you will be on your way to making choices that will support learning.

- **Put Language First:** Consider how each element of your classroom setup supports language learning and interaction. There are countless opportunities to work on question formation, descriptive language, and much more, and having the right classroom materials can help facilitate these opportunities for your learners.
- **Show Off Rewards:** Try displaying your rewards system. You may not want it to be displayed throughout the entirety of the class, but think about where you can display it when you need it. A small shelf or **pocket chart** might be all you need.
- **Think ABC, 123:** Simple supports like an alphabet or number strip can allow you to turn a mistake into a reinforcement opportunity. By simply turning around and referencing something in your classroom, you can quickly support and redirect your learner.
- **Make It "Interactive":** In addition to rewards and static displays like the alphabet, you can use white boards, felt boards, push pins, magnets, and more to facilitate interaction in your classroom even when you don't physically share the same space.

Reflection

- What does your online classroom look like now? What do you like, and what do you think could be improved?
- Consider your current learners. What is one feature of your classroom and bulletin boards that can help you connect with ALL of your learners? If you cannot think of one, refer to the suggested strategies and get creative.

USING PROPS

How can I better use props to enhance my online teaching?

Keywords
#**cognitive load** #**engagement** #**props** #**realia** #**rewards**

▶ **The Situation**

After six months of teaching online, I have collected or created a few props, but I often feel like they are not as effective as I want them to be. At the same time, I see other teachers show off their props and talk about how well they work, so maybe I just need to be pointed in the right direction. ***How can I better use props to enhance my online teaching?***

Analyzing the Situation

- Props can help facilitate interaction, be part of engagement and rewards systems, and support learners in noticing and recalling new language.
- When using props, it is important to remember that you are introducing something additional to what the learner sees on the screen, which already includes plenty of input (e.g., slides, your webcam, their webcam, the chatbox). This input, combined with the addition of props, affect the number of working memory resources a learner must bring to an activity. This **cognitive load** can greatly impact a learner's ability to interact with new language.
- Since props are another form of content in your classroom, you must also consider their quality and appropriateness for age and level. Some types of props, like puppets, will

be more appropriate for younger learners. Others, like a whiteboard, are more universal.

Suggested Strategies

Props are a great way to freshen up a routine or add variety to your classes. Here's how.

- **Develop MVPs (Most Valuable Props):** Based on the courses and levels you teach, prepare a core set of props that can be used across all (or almost all) of them. This will also help you focus on props that can assist with instructional language and interaction (e.g., microphones and white boards).
- **Get Them Talking:** Props like puppets can help encourage interaction and lower the affective filter for learners who may not feel comfortable participating in class. Use puppets to mimic the question and answer interaction during lessons.
- **Think of Rewards:** Whether you choose flat props like laminated stars or use a whiteboard to draw a reward, props can enhance a variety of reward systems.
- **Get "Real":** Use what you have and do not be afraid to use **realia**. Family photos and real food can be a great way to connect with learners. You can even encourage learners to find their own related props for class.

Reflection

- What are your current MVPs (Most Valuable Props)? Why are these props helpful to you?
- Consider the reward systems you use. Does it involve props? How do learners respond? If you do not use props, how could you use them to enhance your rewards system?

USING TPR

How can I use TPR effectively in my online classroom?

Keywords
#demonstration #props #total physical response #TPR

▶ **The Situation**

One of my fellow teachers recommended I use TPR when I teach. I feel like I cannot teach well when trying to explain all the new content physically. Also, with my limited space and because of the nature of an online classroom, I find that it's hard to use body language effectively sometimes. **How can I use TPR effectively in my online classroom?**

Analyzing the Situation

• **Total Physical Response (TPR)** is an understanding-based approach to language teaching. The goal of TPR is that the learner shows their understanding of a verbal prompt from the teacher by acting out what they hear. For example, when given the prompt, the learner should physically "sit down" or "pick up the paper." TPR encourages learners to respond with their bodies instead of their voices since spoken responses can be difficult for a new language learner. Once the learner is ready, spoken responses become more common.

• Not all new lesson content requires TPR. TPR should build upon prior learning to construct meaning. This means that new meaning can also be understood without physical examples. Knowing when to use TPR effectively and when it is inappropriate or distracting is critical in language teaching and learning.

• Certain physical responses are difficult to convey when interacting through a webcam (e.g., those that require you to stand up or move around). Recognize the limitations and be ready to adapt to online modalities!

Suggested Strategies

You do not need to do gymnastics in your classes to try to get your point across. You do need to consider how TPR can and should help your learner better understand the content. Here's how.

• **Know It:** TPR is not the teacher simply modeling something physically. The R stands for the response. If the learner is not required to respond with a physical motion, what you are doing is not TPR.

• **"Show" and "Tell":** First, demonstrate the action, then invite the learner to do the same. After your learner consistently uses their body to demonstrate their understanding, you can stop using yours. At this point you can start using only verbal instructions. Once your learner responds correctly to spoken instruction, reinforce with written instructions on the screen.

• **I Do; We Do; You Do:** Keep in mind that first the teacher says a word and does an action. Then the teacher and the learner do the action together when the teacher says the word. Then the learner does the action each time the teacher says the word. (Once learners are responding only physically to prompts, you can encourage them to say the word with you, and you both do the action."

- **Use Props:** Use puppets to demonstrate TPR. Introduce the word or phrase, then use the puppet to demonstrate. For example, say "runs quickly," then demonstrate the puppet running quickly. Encourage your learner to physically respond. (That's the point.) They can do this by making sure that they have enough room on their side of the camera to move around. Remember, your learner does not have to speak if they are not ready.

- **Think Outside the Verb:** Keep in mind that TPR does not need to be limited to the learning of verbs. You can also create actions to represent nouns, adjectives, adverbs, prepositions, etc.

- **Develop a TPR Toolkit:** Take three steps to build your TPR toolkit: Make a list of your own most frequently used classroom language and regularly update as you preview your new lessons. In the mirror, test different TPR for your **target language** items. Add finalized gestures to your list. It can be very difficult to come up with a physical response to new content on the spot, and

it might result in inconsistencies. The most effective TPR is consistent TPR.

- **Partial TPR:** TPR (Total Physical Response) in online classes means upper body movements, gestures, and mime as both the teacher and the learner sit during the class. Therefore, TPR becomes PPR (Partial Physical Response). This requires the communication and understanding of the commonly used gestures and upper body movements between the teacher and the learner. Teachers should realize the limitations and try to teach the meaning of those gestures when they are used for the first time so that the learner will follow instructions more easily and react or respond more effectively.

Reflection

- What is your current approach to teaching online? How can you better incorporate TPR?
- Consider one of the courses you currently teach. Which strategies above could you apply to improve your use of TPR?

12 | SKILLS TRANSFER

How can I help my learner transfer skills from our online classroom back to their regular classroom?

Keywords
#skills #transfer #online classroom #public school

▶ The Situation

Some of my learners' parents report that although their child seems to be able to perform certain skills or demonstrate certain English knowledge online, that learning does not seem to transfer well to their English classes in public school. *How can I help my learner transfer skills from our online classroom back to their regular classroom?*

Analyzing the Situation

- Just as it takes some time to build rapport with a child to overcome shyness or a fear of making mistakes in your online lessons, it may take time for a learner to overcome those obstacles in their English classes in public school.
- The curriculum of a Chinese public school likely does not align exactly with the curriculum you are using. Thus, we should try to teach learners "soft skills" such as confidence and willingness to take risks; teachers should also give them a strong background in a wide variety of language skills.

Suggested Strategies

You cannot guarantee results outside your own online classroom. You can encourage learners to show their confidence and abilities outside of your lessons and be more successful in their English classes at school. Here's how.

- **Balance Academic and Casual Language:** Academic language that can transfer to school settings is incredibly useful and often included in a curriculum, but it is important to experiment with more casual language as well. Casual language enables learners to "show off" what they learned with their online teacher once they are back at school. Even simple greetings like, "What's up?" and, "How's it going?" are high-utility phrases that learners are often eager to share with peers.
- **Introduce New Contexts:** To prepare learners for the wide variety of situations, they will encounter outside of your classroom, make sure you provide opportunities in class to rehearse the language they might need in those contexts. This can even be posed as a role play in order to be more engaging for your learner. Consider swapping roles and having your learner play the role of their teacher at public school.
- **Encourage English at Home:** Encourage pre- and post-class activities so that learners have as much English exposure while outside your actual lesson as possible. Not only does this help to reinforce the child's learning, but it also keeps them ready to interact in English at any time. Set aside time at the beginning of class to ask learners how they prepared for class and set aside time at the end of class to have learners describe their post-class and enrichment plans.

- **Gather Information:** Find out from parents if there are certain areas of their child's public school performance that seem weaker than other areas. For example, does the learner struggle with listening, speaking, reading, or writing, or certain subskills such as phonics, spelling, or pronunciation? Then adjust your teaching to put more emphasis on any weak areas the learner may have in order to boost their confidence with that skill and better prepare them for their public school classes. For example, a learner who struggles with asking questions will benefit from engaging in a practice game like Twenty Questions.

- **Review:** Regularly review your learner's knowledge of previously learned language so that when they do encounter a topic in public school that they have learned with you, they are ready to be actively involved.

Reflection

- Consider one of your recent lessons. How could you encourage learners to use the language they learned outside of class?
- How often do you make an effort to review or refresh previously learned content? How can you do this more intentionally to make sure learners are prepared to use that language outside of class?

13 | FLIPPED CLASSROOM

How can I help my learner benefit from the flipped classroom model?

Keywords
#**flipped classroom** #**pre-class** #**post-class** #**active learning**
#**synchronous**

▶ The Situation

Online learning is a unique way to bring learners and teachers together over a certain platform. I've heard of "flipped classrooms" and enjoy the format of the interaction with my learners, but I'm not really sure what a "flipped classroom" actually means or how to best capitalize on this model while teaching online. *How can I help my learner benefit from the flipped classroom model?*

Analyzing the Situation

- A **flipped classroom** introduces topics and input outside of the classroom. Some online companies do this by using pre-class videos and post-class extension activities. Learners are expected to engage with these materials independently. This model allows for more time in class dedicated to active learning and practice.
- The teacher's role in a flipped classroom is to help guide learners by answering questions they have as they study the out-of-class materials. This allows the teacher to tailor the learning experience to a learner's specific learning style and the lesson's learning objectives.
- A good online learning company offers multiple out-of-class materials, including pre-class videos, post-class extension activities ("homework"), a digital library, etc.

Suggested Strategies

You don't have to try to monitor every move your learner makes when they are not in your lesson. You do need to try to make sure your learners are getting the most in and outside class. Here's how.

- **Focus on Interaction:** Use class time for meaningful engagement and interaction. Talk about content, the learner's life, and yours. Ask questions and actively listen. For example, for a slide with animal vocabulary, tell a story about your feelings about that animal (e.g., "Do you like dogs or cats?") using the **target language**. Remember that learners can access class materials once the class has completed, so they have multiple opportunities to interact with the content. However, their interaction with you is limited to when they see you in class.
- **Build Relationships:** Class time should be used to build rapport with your learner and interact in ways that are not possible outside your time together. Ask your learner about their likes and dislikes, how they feel about the class materials, and if there is any input about how they could learn better. Keep these notes and return to them if you have the learner again. For repeat learners, use your notes to reconnect quickly and deepen your relationship with that learner.
- **Walk Through Problems:** If your learner struggles to complete in-class activities, work through the process together with

them step-by-step. Have your learner describe the task and their process. For example, when selecting an answer in a multiple-choice question, ask, "How did you select your answer? How confident are you? What was the hardest part?" A flipped classroom model gives the learner the one-to-one, synchronous class time to ask questions about the content in class, enabling them to more successfully complete pre- and post-class work independently.

- **Share Resources:** Remind your learners about the other materials they have available on the platform you are using. Encourage the learner to watch any pre-

class videos and complete post-class enrichment activities. Also, tell learners to practice with flashcards or by accessing the content in a digital library.

Reflection

- Watch the recording of one of your recent lessons. How much time is spent in active engagement with the material versus reviewing externally introduced materials?
- Consider one of your upcoming lessons. Using the strategies above, how could you make better use of classroom time?

PRE- & POST-CLASS

How can I help my learner understand the value and importance of pre- and post-class activities (e.g., pre-class videos, homework, self-study)?

Keywords
#pre-class #post-class #exposure #routine #practice

▶ The Situation

I have a learner who I teach regularly, but she isn't making much progress. I know my company offers pre-class videos and homework, but learners are not required to complete them. I ask my learner if she does this work, and she says she doesn't have time. I think that if she came to class more prepared, she would progress much more quickly. *How can I help my learner understand the value and importance of pre- and post-class activities (e.g., pre-class videos, homework, self-study)?*

Analyzing the Situation

- When a learner is prepared for class, it increases their ability to engage meaningfully. Ideally, in a **flipped classroom model**, learners are familiar with new language before the lesson starts. However, when learners do not commit to this work, it becomes difficult to make progress because learners are not familiar with the new concepts and vocabulary. The teacher may have to move more slowly and spend extra time explaining some of the content the learner could have reviewed ahead of time.
- Reviewing after class is also vital to language learning. Regular, ongoing review helps learners reinforce content learned in class. If learners do not do homework or post-class practice, it is difficult to make

progress.
- Teachers have a responsibility to encourage pre- and post-class work. Parents put their trust in you to find a way to reach and teach their child, and learners need to know their teacher can be counted on to motivate and inspire them to continue their learning outside of class.

Suggested Strategies

You cannot control what a learner does outside of class, but here are some methods for encouraging them to develop a healthy habit of doing the pre- and post-class tasks.

- **Bring It Up:** Talk with your learners about the importance of attempting the pre- and post-class tasks. Connect with them about where they are now and how these tasks can help them get to where they or their parents want them to be.
- **Connect in Class:** At the end of a lesson, you can set a routine to help learners plan for their next class. You can help generate ideas for practice, and they can choose the tasks they want to do before the next class. This helps get learners to buy into a practice schedule.
- **Lower the Stakes:** Besides the regular requirement of homework on the platform, you can do your best to provide options with even lower stakes. Encourage learners to access resources like a digital library

with a simple but specific task such as finding three books in a digital library about animals or choosing their favorite book cover.

- **Encourage Exposure:** Teachers should remind learners and parents that exposure to English and English practice before and after class is invaluable to the learner's success and might even help them reach their language learning goals quicker.
- **Reinforce It:** Once you establish a routine, and your regulars expect you to ask about homework and pre-class activities, provide positive reinforcement and

encouragement. Give a reward at the beginning of class for those learners who show off the work they have done.

Reflection

- How do you currently encourage learners to complete pre- and post-class tasks?
- Consider one of your upcoming lessons. Using the strategies above, how could you encourage homework and post-class review?

BENEFITS OF AI

How can I help my learner and their parents benefit from AI components in courses?

Keywords
#**AI** #**customer experience**

▶ **The Situation**

I've heard that some of the new technology features being rolled out on the platform I'm using use artificial intelligence (AI), but I don't understand what that means or how best to use them in my teaching. I am sure that learners and parents have questions too. I want to be able to use my role as a teacher to demonstrate the benefits of this kind of technology. *How can I help my learner and their parents benefit from AI components in courses?*

Analyzing the Situation

- **Artificial Intelligence (AI)**, also referred to as machine learning, involves training machines to learn from experience and adjust to new input.
- Much of the AI in use online is used to improve customer experience and reduce administrative work. This includes reducing turnaround time for customer support and improving sales calls.
- AI is also used to supplement learning by providing in-class lesson support, a judgment-free speaking partner for the learner, and improved personalized learning.

Suggested Strategies

You don't need to be afraid that the robots are taking over. You do need to think about how AI

can enhance the experience of your learners. Here's how.

- **Let the System Help:** Many platforms have some form of AI assistance that can be a very useful tool for both learner and teacher during a lesson. Such functions are developed to help teachers better explain activities to learners who struggle to understand what they are supposed to do. When a learner has difficulty following task instructions or understanding a platform feature, an AI assistant is a useful tool to supplement and personalize the learner's classroom experience.

- **Encourage Practice with Other AI Functions:** Other AI-based features may be available so that learners can use them to practice their speaking with a non-judgmental partner. This lowers a learner's anxiety levels and increases confidence. The feedback a learner receives can then help them practice sounds and words with which they struggle.

- **Understand Placement:** A computer placement test (CT) uses computerized adaptive testing to provide learners with a personalized testing experience. Learners who take a CT receive questions that fit their ability and are placed into the curriculum at an appropriate level.

- **Share Highlights:** Some platforms use AI to discover clips of exemplary learner behavior. Companies can create lesson reports using these clips to demonstrate to parents and learners the gains they achieve while studying online. Parents can share these reports with pride.

- Reflect on your current learners. How could you use one of the strategies to encourage this learner?

16 | DIGITAL LIBRARY

How can I help my learner benefit from digital library resources?

Keywords
#activities #digital library #extensive reading #intensive reading
#practice #reading comprehension #reading strategies #resource
#self-access

▶ The Situation

I often feel that my learners would benefit from additional exposure to English outside their actual lessons. I do my best to expose them to good input and practice during our lessons, but some of my learners could really use further practice once the lesson has ended. While there are many opportunities for learners to engage with the platform I'm using, a digital library seems like a great resource for this kind of practice. ***How can I help my learner benefit from digital library resources?***

Analyzing the Situation

- A good digital library includes enrichment activities, vocabulary flashcards, English educational games, and many electronic books for children. It also includes searchable filters to help a teacher or learner look for a resource more specifically (e.g., genre, Lexile, etc.)
- Many learners do not leverage digital library resources and use them outside of the fixed lesson time.
- It is possible that some teachers are unaware that a digital library exists or have forgotten about it.

Suggested Strategies

You don't have to be a master librarian in order to help your learners benefit from a digital library. You do need to promote the idea of your learners extending their language learning by exploring **self-access** tools available to them.

- **Encourage Outside Exposure:** EFL learners (i.e., those learning English in non-English speaking environments) may only be exposed to what they study in their English lessons or encounter while doing homework assignments. Resources like a digital library can provide valuable input that is not as easily accessible for them as they are for ESL learners (i.e., those learning English in English-speaking environments).
- **Become Familiar:** Spend some time becoming familiar with the tools and resources available to learners through a digital library and recommend certain books by name.
- **Follow Up:** After recommending a digital library to your learner, ask them to share how they used the digital library and what they read that was particularly engaging or useful.
- **Keep Other Teachers Informed:** If you recommend a learner try a certain asset from a digital library, make a note that this recommendation was made (then if the learner's next lesson is with another teacher, that teacher can follow up with the learner).

• **Keep a Log:** Teachers can recommend readings to their learners at a given level and ask them to keep a log of what and when they have read. You could also decide to discuss and compare these logs with learners to promote healthy competition and growth.

Reflection

• Do you do a lot of reading? If so, how do you feel extensive reading helps your vocabulary and other language skills?

COURSEWARE INTERACTIONS

How can I help learners better understand the language needed to interact with our courseware?

Keywords
#**classroom language** #**classroom management** #**courseware**
#**grading language** #**instructions**

▶ The Situation

I recently taught a learner who was still learning to use courseware. She had difficulty understanding my directions like "read," "circle," "trace," "drag and drop," etc. I tried to explain, but she still did not seem to get it. I want to be able to help her; even if she is familiar with traditional classroom language and instructions, it is different when learners are in an online classroom. *How can I help learners better understand the language needed to interact with our courseware?*

Analyzing the Situation

- Online environments can pose significant obstacles for young learners without the proper instruction (especially for learners new to online learning). Our youngest learners may be especially challenged by the combination of technology and language skills involved.
- Teachers must use language appropriate for an online learning environment and the language of online instruction in addition to the content language. Some of this may be supported through resources like pre-class videos, but it is important to reinforce this language in class.

Suggested Strategies

You don't have to get into the nuts and bolts of how the courseware you are using specifically works or try to make that kind of explanation understandable to young learners. You do need to help your learners take full advantage of online learning by getting them familiar with new technology and new tasks quickly. Here's how.

- **Get Visual:** Use props and gestures to accompany oral instructions. A tag board or foam core cursor and flashcard can go a long way to helping a learner understand the concept of "dragging" an object with the mouse and "dropping" the object. A flashcard can act as a stand-in for whatever the learner might drag on the screen.
- **Model Onscreen:** You may need to repeatedly demonstrate a certain action on screen while saying the words *circle* or *underline* to help a learner understand the relationship between what they hear, what they are being asked to do, and what kind of action actually takes place on the screen.
- **Think of Utility:** Before you start your unit or learning cycle, look over the materials and consider how the learner will need to interact with the courseware. Next, decide which online classroom language is going to be the most supportive of these interactions as learners encounter new features or activities.
- **Practice It:** It may be worthwhile, at least

initially, to start each lesson with a series of classroom language-related tasks to hammer home the language related to our courseware. This can be a series of tasks that require the learner to underline, circle, drag and drop, etc.

- **Give Clear Instructions:** Giving clear and precise instructions to learners can ensure that they fully comprehend what they need to in the courseware. Pause frequently and repeat your instruction sometimes to give learners time to understand and follow your instruction.

Reflection

- What is your current approach to introducing the courseware?
- Consider your learners. Which strategies above could you apply to improve your learners' understanding?

OVERCOMING TECHNICAL ISSUES

How can the teacher and learner respond to and overcome unexpected technical issues?

Keywords
#**online courseware** #**interference** #**technical issues** #**wifi**

▶ The Situation

Sometimes when I teach my lessons, the screen will freeze or I will run into some other technical glitch that interrupts the lesson. I know that I should expect technology to fail sometimes. In a traditional classroom, I could have a backup plan for when the computer decides not to work or a video does not want to play. When both teachers and learners rely on technology to connect them for class, it becomes a little more difficult to think on our feet. ***How can the teacher and learner respond to and overcome unexpected technical issues?***

Analyzing the Situation

- While we are aware that technical issues invariably occur, this does not change the fact that they can derail a lesson. It is important that, as the teacher, you are calm throughout any technical outage or interference to the online courseware.

Suggested Strategies

First and foremost, be ready to reach out to your company's technical support team in case an issue pops up that you are unable to diagnose or recover from. Continue teaching as best as you can until you hear back from the company. It can be frustrating when technology becomes an obstacle to an effective class. Being prepared to think on your feet will help you effectively navigate classes in the event of an issue. Here's how.

- **Use Approved Hardware:** Most online companies list their system requirements; be sure that your device and physical classroom setup are in compliance with these requirements.
- **WIFI vs. Ethernet:** A hardline connection (e.g., Ethernet) will ensure a more stable and consistent experience for yourself and your learner. Using WIFI can be spotty. You can check your connection speed by pinging the server. You want your number to be below 200.
- **Refresh the Page:** If something is not working, try refreshing your page. A refresh button is located on many online platforms, typically near the top of the screen.
- **Switch Lines:** At times, many classes are in session at the same time, and this can create a lag for users. Depending on the classroom you teach in, how to switch lines varies.
- **Be Near Your Router:** Using WIFI? Try to be nearby as this will increase your connection's strength. If you notice your connection dipping during class, be prepared to physically move yourself closer to your router.
- **Backup Sources:** Sometimes, connection issues persist with your main connection source. Having a backup source, you can switch to (like a different WIFI source, a phone hotspot, or an ethernet connection) can fix an IT issue.
- **Know How to Screenshot:** Depending on your computer or tablet, the process to

screenshot an issue can vary. Know how to complete a screenshot in order to provide the company with more information should they request it.

Reflection

- What is your current approach if you encounter technical issues? How can you better prepare in case of a technology emergency?

ONE-TO-MANY METHODS

How can I adjust my teaching methods when teaching a one-to-many class online?

Keywords
#**classroom environment** #**ICQ** #**nominate** #**one-to-many** #**one-to-one** #**rapport** #**relationship-building** #**TTT** #**teaching methods**

▶ The Situation

I have been teaching multiple learners online at once, and it is a lot harder than I thought. It is difficult to monitor everyone equally, and because learners are more familiar with one-to-one classes, they do not always seem to understand that there are other learners in the class. I, too, find myself falling into old habits of extended interactions with one learner. *How can I adjust my teaching methods when teaching a one-to-many class online?*

Analyzing the Situation

- Online classes that are one-to-many are likely new for both you and your learners. Do not expect learners to understand how or why things are different from their one-to-one classes.
- Just as in your one-to-one classes, you are responsible for maintaining a positive classroom environment. This includes learner teacher relations, rapport-building, setting expectations, and establishing classroom norms.
- One-to-many classes offer opportunities for authentic interactions between learners as well as an opportunity to hear other learners and their language choices. This can benefit learners who may see positive role models in other learners. It can also be validating to hear other learners make similar errors.

Suggested Strategies

Teaching one-to-many does not have to be stressful for you or your learners. You can use some simple strategies to get started. Here's how.

- **Set Even Clearer Expectations:** When teaching one-to-many, clear expectations are critical. Teachers do not have the time to explain every activity to every learner individually. This makes it even more important to make expectations clear the first time. Demonstrate activities in a way that involves all learners and have one of your learners help you model tasks for the group. Do not forget to ask **instruction checking questions (ICQs)** and be sure to ask ICQs of more than one learner.
- **Call On Everyone:** Avoid one learner dominating the conversation by nominating learners you would like to speak and use their names to make sure they know that it is their turn. Set the expectation that everyone will get called on. Then, be sure to give enough wait time for learners to respond and step in as needed to model responses for the rest of the group.
- **Give Space to Communicate:** More learners mean more opportunities to communicate. This also means that if **teacher talk time (TTT)** is not adjusted, each learner ends up with fewer opportunities to practice. Facilitate opportunities for peer-to-peer interaction and monitor TTT. For example, put learners

in pairs, use a timer, and have learners ask and answer three basic icebreaker questions. (What's your name? How old are you? How are you?) Do this regularly, and learners will anticipate it as part of their one-to-many routine in your classes.

- **Make Turn-Taking Easy:** Consider visual or prop-supported cues for turn-taking. Stop signs and props indicating time remaining (1 minute, 30 seconds, etc.) can help with things like letting learners know their turn is almost over without having to interrupt learners.

- **Have Them Pass the Ball:** Once the first learner responds to your question or prompt, have them give the prompt to another learner who has not yet responded. In this way, you can make sure that each learner responds and have each learner both answer and ask the prompt language. (If you always ask the questions and your learners always respond, you are only teaching half the language.) Motion to the last learner who has answered to toss the ball back to you by asking you the target question.

Reflection

- Consider your current one-to-one classroom strategies. Which of the suggested strategies will be most meaningful as you transition to teaching one-to-many?
- Consider a lesson you taught recently. How could you have taught that lesson one-to-many? What would have changed about how you taught the lesson?

20 | EQUAL PARTICIPATION

How can I make sure that all learners participate equally in a one-to-many class?

Keywords
#**one-to-many** #**anxiety** #**comprehensible output** #**participation** #**risk-taking**

▶ The Situation

In my one-to-many classes, some learners talk a lot, and some do not talk very much. I want to encourage learner participation as much as possible, but I also want to make sure all learners have the opportunity to learn through interacting with me and the other learners. *How can I make sure that all learners participate equally in a one-to-many class?*

Analyzing the Situation

- Interacting with a teacher in front of other learners can cause a lot of anxiety for learners. It is also likely that this type of participation is unfamiliar for many Chinese learners, especially in an online environment or on the company's platform.
- Be aware that learners may be more familiar with participating passively through listening and notetaking. It is OK to praise this type of participation as learners become more comfortable with participating actively in class.

Suggested Strategies

Making sure learner voices are heard is important, but in one-to-many classes, it can be a challenge. You don't have to portion out every class to ensure that each learner gets the exact same number of seconds to be heard, but you should use these strategies to provide more equal opportunities.

- **Say Their Name:** In a one-to-many class, learners may not always feel like you are paying attention to them as much as during a one-to-one class. Be sure to learn and use learner names as a way of reminding them that you are indeed paying attention. Encourage classmates to use each other's names as well.

- **Name Dropping:** If you are practicing a sentence structure, etc. that includes personal pronouns or names and you notice one of your learners losing attention, replace the name in the example with theirs. As soon as you make their name part of the activity, they will become much more focused.

- **Set Expectations:** Your learners may not know how one-to-many classes are different from their one-to-one experiences. Participating actively might not be as obvious an expectation as it would be if the individual is the only learner (and even then, it is not always obvious). Consider setting clear expectations at the beginning of class with an activity that is entirely focused on modeling equal participation and establishing ground rules, especially with lower levels. Provide visual support when explaining how participation will work.

- **Assign and Change Roles:** If learners are unfamiliar with working in groups, be sure to give them something to try it and stay focused and actively involved even when they are not speaking. There are several roles that could be appropriate for learners: notetaker, timekeeper, and reporter. However, make sure that these roles do not distract from learning or interfere with their ability to participate meaningfully.

- **Keep Track:** It can be difficult to monitor four webcams at once when teaching a lesson. Keep track of learner participation with a simple tally. Every time a learner participates, add to their tally. There is no need to share this with the learners, but it can help you know when one or more learners need to be more actively encouraged and engaged.
- **Praise Passive Participation:** Initially, it is

important to acknowledge that learners may be fully engaged without speaking in class. Be patient with learners who may still be processing but not yet ready to take the risk of independent production.

Reflection

- How do you encourage learners to participate in one-to-one classes? How could you use those successful strategies to support learners in one-to-many classes?
- Consider your next one-to-many class. Which of the suggested strategies could you use to support balanced participation in class?

References

Aydin, H. (2013). Interaction between teachers and students in online learning. *Journal of Environmental Protection and Ecology, 14*(3A), 1337-1352.

Bui, G. (2018) Total physical response. In J. I. Liontas, T. International Association, & M. DelliCarpini (Eds.), *The TESOL encyclopedia of English language teaching.*

Buskist, W., & Saville, B. (2001). Creating positive emotional contexts for enhancing teaching and learning. *APS Observer*, 12-13.

Cameron, L. (2001). *Teaching languages to young learners*. Cambridge: Cambridge University Press.

Gonzalez, D., & St. Louis, R. (2018). Online learning. In J. I. Liontas, T. International Association, & M. DelliCarpini (Eds.), *The TESOL encyclopedia of English language teaching.* doi:10.1002/9781118784235.eelt0423

Harmer, J. (1998). *How to teach English: An introduction to the practice of English language teaching*. Harlow: Longman.

Harmer, J. (2007). *How to teach English*. London: Pearson Longman.

Kim, N. Y. (2017). Effects of voice-chat conditions on Korean EFL learners'

affective factors. 외국어교육, *24*(1), 43-66.

Larsen-Freeman, D. (2013). Transfer of learning transformed. *Language Learning, 63*, 107-129.

McClelland, E.R. (2018). Exploration of positive teacher-student relationships in the online context of VIPKid. *Graduate Education Student Scholarship, 14.*

Mackkay, R., Barkham, R., & Jordan, R. R. (Eds.), (1979). *Reading in a second language*. Rowley: Newbury House.

Promoting effective classroom participation. (n.d.) Retrieved from https://uwaterloo.ca/centre-for-teaching-excellence/teaching-resources/teaching-tips/assessing-learner-work/grading-and-feedback/promoting-effective-participation

Moore, M.G. (1997). Theory of transactional distance. In Keegan, D. (Ed.), *Theoretical Principles of Distance Education* (pp.22-38). London: Routledge.

Moon, J. (2000). *Children learning English*. Oxford: Macmillan Heinemann.

Reeves, J. (2018). Teacher identity. In J. I. Liontas, T. International Association, & M. DelliCarpini (Eds.), *The TESOL encyclopedia*

of English language teaching. doi:10.1002/9781118784235.eelt0268

Rubesch, T. (2013). Interactive competence in student use of a conversational agent. *Studies in Linguistics and Language Teaching, 24*, 157-172.

Safargalina, A. (2018). Teaching speaking in EFL environments. In J. I. Liontas, T. International Association, & M. DelliCarpini (Eds.), *The TESOL encyclopedia of English language teaching.* doi:10.1002/9781118784235.eelt0699

Senior, R. (2010). Connectivity: A framework for understanding effective language teaching in face-to-face and online learning communities. *RELC journal, 41*(2), 137-147.

Scott, W. A., & Ytreberg, L. H. (2004). *Teaching English to children*. Harlow: Longman, Pearson Education.

Sousa, D. (2002). *How the brain learns*. New York: Corwin Press.

TESOL International. (2008). TESOL technology standards framework. Retrieved from https://www.tesol.org/docs/default-source/books/bk_technologystandards_framework_721.pdf?sfvrsn=4bd0bee6_2

Part 4

Case Analyses in the Role of Learner Factors in Teaching Children Online

▶ Introduction

Teaching English to young learners or children is a totally different thing than teaching English to adults, let alone the specific strategies needed in teaching children English online. Cases in this part are centered around a few themes. One is teaching English to young learners whose unique characteristics in learning English online call for special strategies. The other involves the social and cultural dimensions and implications of Chinese children learning English online. English language teachers should not only understand learner factors but also how these factors affect learners learning English as a second language with regard to language-learning processes and achievements.

As we know, some learners acquire a new language faster than others. They seem to have an easier time of it. Others can, through sheer determination and hard work, achieve a high level of success. Many factors can hinder or help learners in acquiring a second language. Apart from language aptitude or innate ability to acquire a language as some scholars believe, learner factors, both internal and external, impact language-learning processes and results. Factors that impact second language-learning from within the individual learner are considered internal factors. These include the learner's age, aptitude and intelligence, attitudes and motivation,

personality, anxiety, willingness to take risks, wait time, and willingness to communicate, among others. Factors that come from circumstances beyond the controll of learners are called external factors. Examples are parental expectations of the learner, societal pressures, teacher-learner rapport, and cultural pressures.

Let us take two examples for illustration. One is attitude and motivation as learner factors, and the other is Chinese parental expectations for children's education as a social cultural factor.

Example 1: Attitude & Motivation as Learner Factors

As we know, attitudes are beliefs an individual holds, and motivations are reasons or desires to engage in a behavior. Attitudes can be both positive and negative and develop with time and circumstances. They are sometimes shaped by parents and role models, local culture, and upbringing but can be reshaped by a learner's experiences. Teachers have the opportunity to help bring learners who have a negative attitude towards learning the **target language** to the point of desiring to succeed in their language development.

Attitudes and motivations are closely related. Positive attitudes can foster an increase in the learner's motivation, resulting in a successful language-learning experience while a negative attitude can hinder or even kill a learner's motivation and result in language-learning failure. Motivation is usually interpreted as the drive to learn; it could be both intrinsic and extrinsic. When a person is interested in or fascinated with a task or area of learning and engages in it for its own sake (rather than being driven by rewards or punishment), we say they have **intrinsic motivation**. Young learners' natural curiosity and innate love of learning are **intrinsic motivators**. Parents and teachers can encourage these traits in a young learner. On the contrary, **extrinsic motivators** are generally associated with incentives or punishments. Good grades or praise as well as a gold star on a paper, stickers, or candy, are positive external motivators. Negative motivators include knowing that poor learning will mean a poor grade, a physical punishment, a scolding from a parent or teacher, failing a class, or, as a last resort, peer pressure and "losing face" in society.

Therefore, motivation is paramount in learning English. Language instructors have the responsibility to motivate the learner. However, to what extent does the motivation lead to learning outcome? Will highly motivated learners perform better than less motivated ones? These are the questions we try to explain in this part of the book.

Example 2: Parental Expectations as an External Factor

It is commonly understood that parents play an important role in their children's education. In particular, because of the one-child-per-family policy that lasted for a few decades in China, Chinese parents are obsessed with their children's education. Among middle-class parents, the expectation is that a good education will be directly linked to good jobs, higher income, and a better lifestyle. Chinese parents connect university education with employment, face-saving, and a sure income that will support them in their retirement years. Children are both the social and financial security net and a source of family pride. Parents want their child to attend a top university and earn an advanced professional degree, preferably becoming a doctor, lawyer, scientist, or engineer. To ensure this will happen, parents monitor the child's grades in school and activities at home. They will enroll them in extracurricular activities and courses. When parents sign up for an online English course, they assume their child and teacher will work hard toward a shared goal.

Often, there are cultural factors at play when Chinese children enter an English learning environment. Some cultural norms may impact the dynamics of lessons taught by those who are not familiar with Chinese culture. For instance, Chinese parents typically expect teachers to strictly follow the curriculum and textbook. With an online curriculum, they will expect teachers to adhere to teaching the targets they have been notified of prior to every lesson. Teachers should prioritize their teaching time to make sure that their learners have fully acquired the new language targets called for and review any similar structures from earlier in the curriculum before they vary from the curriculum in any way.

It is also worth mentioning that Chinese parents are accustomed to their children's mistakes in language learning being overtly corrected by the teacher. It is common to hear Chinese parents tell the teacher that they want more **overt correction** of mistakes their children make. In fact, overt correction (where a teacher tells the child they have made a mistake and has the learner repeat the utterance accurately) is less effective than **recasting** (when a teacher simply repeats the statement back to the learner using the grammatically correct language.) In this part of the book, you will find cases in error correction such as pronunciation errors or grammar errors, and we will make recommendations regarding what you should do to maximize learning results. You will also find cases related to parents' obsession with children's examination results, parental involvement, and parental interference. Because parents play a significant role in the child's online language learning, it is important to know their perspectives, their expectations, and their needs so that teachers will teach more tactfully and strategically without compromising academic integrity or being totally driven by parental obsession in dictating what the teacher does.

Learning a second language is not a simple endeavor. Some learners are more inclined to acquiring a second language, while others must work hard to learn basic vocabulary and concepts. While an innate gift to learn languages is wonderful, at some point, there are habits and practices that every language learner needs to draw upon. Here are four characteristics we selected that successful **L2** (second language) learners exhibit. These are learned habits that any teacher can impart to their young learner.

- Willingness to take risks, which translates into being relatively unafraid to try new things, making mistakes, and having the confidence to try again.

- Active participation. Learners use class time to take in as much as possible and also grab chances to use what they know outside of class. Any chance to use their new language is an adventure they jump into.
- Realization that learning a language is not easy, that it takes consistency and hard work. The learners understand that culture is part of language and seek to understand that culture.
- Successful learners use methods and strategies that work for them. If the trick of creating mnemonics helps, they use them. Music or chants? They make them up and use them frequently. Maybe flashcards, drills, or extensive reading helps; maybe copying your notes helps more. Successful language learners use a variety of methods.

Good language learners are not born. They are developed by skilled teachers providing good learning opportunities. There is the desire to learn a new language and a willingness to work hard on their part. As language teachers, we should try our best to bring a wide range of strategies and suggestions to assist them on their journey to success in their new language.

Question	Sub-Topic
1. How does motivation influence learning?	**Motivation and Learning**
2. How can I keep my young learner focused during the 25-minute lesson?	**Keeping YLs Focused**
3. How can I better communicate or demonstrate the benefits of starting foreign language learning at different ages?	**Critical Periods**
4. How can I help my learner unlock skills they might not realize they have?	**Unlocking Skills**
5. How can I support a learner who wants to give up or lacks the confidence to keep trying?	**Giving Up**
6. How can I better understand why a learner is struggling or unable to participate, and what can I do to help?	**Struggling or Unable Learners**
7. How can I better understand cultural differences in a way that will help me successfully teach, rather than distract, my learner?	**Understanding Cultural Differences**
8. How can I help parents understand the benefit of a language learner having exposure to various accents?	**Teacher Accents**
9. How do Chinese parents typically select foreign teachers for their child?	**Selecting Foreign Teachers**
10. How can I make the material relatable for my Chinese young learner?	**Relatable Material**
11. How can I help my older learner understand the value of multilingualism and English education?	**Valuing Multilingualism**
12. What opportunities does my learner have outside of class to interact in English, and what can I do to prepare them for those interactions?	**Interacting in English**
13. How can I accommodate the typical pronunciation errors made by Chinese young learners?	**Pronunciation Errors**
14. How can I help my learner feel more comfortable speaking independently to their foreign teacher?	**Speaking Independently**

Question	Sub-Topic
15. How can I accommodate the typical grammar errors made by Chinese young learners?	**Grammar Errors**
16. How can I help my learner build the metacognitive strategies he needs to be successful and strategic in class and beyond?	**Metacognitive Strategies**
17. How do family planning policies affect educational experiences in China?	**Understanding the One-Child Policy**
18. How can I appropriately use rewards and incentives during class?	**Using Rewards and Incentives**
19. How can I support a learner who is primarily focused on competition and grades?	**Competition and Grades**
20. How can I better communicate with Chinese parents seemingly obsessed with exams?	**Parents and Exams**
21. How can I help parents be more appropriately involved outside class (even if they don't speak English)?	**Parental Involvement**
22. How can I navigate a class if a parent is too involved and impeding a learner from participating?	**Parental Interference**
23. How should I respond when my learner brings up inappropriate language or asks me to teach words that are questionable?	**Responding to Inappropriate Language**

MOTIVATION AND LEARNING

How does motivation influence learning?

Keywords
#affective filter #extrinsic #interest #intrinsic #learning styles #motivation #negative cognitive feedback #positive affective feedback #risk taker

▶ The Situation

I have taught English to many learners for almost two years. One thing that bothers me is that some learners seem highly motivated in learning, but their learning outcome is not that obvious. Sometimes, some quiet children who do not show much enthusiasm for learning, or who are less motivated, seem to have mastered content well. *How does motivation influence learning?*

Analyzing the Situation

- The first step of learning starts with motivation or interest, especially with children. However, motivation is only the condition for learning rather than the factor that guarantees the outcome of learning.
- **Extrinsic motivation** is often caused by external factors such as the teacher, the teaching method, or the content. Often, extrinsic motivation is built up through rewards like stars and tokens. **Intrinsic motivation** usually occurs when actual learning takes place, and the learner feels gratified by the ability to use the language when they have learned in a meaningful way. Teachers should focus on how to turn extrinsic motivation into intrinsic motivation.
- Motivated learners tend to produce language more quickly, practice language more intensively, and retain language learning more easily.

Suggested Strategies

Teachers should not expect to be the only motivating factor in their learner's life. After all, every learner has so much going on outside of their lessons. Teachers should focus on motivating their learner within their limited class time and encouraging motivation outside the classroom. Here's how.

- **Gear Content to Age:** Present your lesson in a meaningful and engaging way geared towards your learner's age. For younger children, songs, games, animation, gamification, or short video clips may be more effective. For children who have learned English for longer periods of time, tapping into what they have already learned and creating some interesting scenarios for interaction might be a good way to engage them. In general, children respond well to storytelling or interesting questions.
- **Focus on Meaningful Repetition:** Due to the fact that learners in China learn English in an environment where English is not necessarily used outside class, your learner needs constant repetition to reinforce what they have been taught. Therefore, meaningful repetition and interaction are very important. Teachers may use questions and answers, role play, stories, and jigsaw puzzles to engage a learner.
- **Have Fun:** Learn what particular learners enjoy doing the most, find ways to imbed intensive language practice into those

activities, and use them in class. Smile. Laugh. Use funny actions and physical modeling. Your learners will need to keep improving their English for their whole life, so the most important lesson you can teach them is that learning English is fun.

- **Provide Rewards and Incentives:** Teachers should always be encouraging and patient whenever a learner makes progress and use positive reinforcement to support interaction and risk-taking. Using symbols like stars or diamonds will lower the **affective filter** of your learner as well.

- **Use a Token Economy:** Have learners collect their reward symbols such as stars or diamonds towards a goal. The goal could be as simple as moving one step at a time towards the end of a pathway terminating at a desired destination such as an illustration of an amusement park, or it could be to be rewarded by playing their favorite vocabulary game or doing a language-learning activity they particularly enjoy.

- **The Power of Praise:** Do not forget to praise your learner very often. Praise them for taking risks and making attempts, even if the language they produce is not entirely accurate. Praise them for being able to produce at least part of a response. Praise them for producing accurate responses and also praise them for doing something correctly that they may have struggled with in the past. Praise can be simple verbal cues or (especially for younger learners)

physical praise such as a high five, a thumbs up, or applause.

- **Use Feedback:** When your learner makes errors, you should point them out without discouraging them. Teachers should provide **positive affective feedback** and **negative cognitive feedback**. That means when positive reinforcement does not work, or when a learner repeatedly makes an error no matter how hard the teacher tries to imply the correct forms, the teacher should pause and point out the errors until the learner gets it followed by reinforcement. Once the learner gets it, the **intrinsic motivation** kicks in.

- **Be a "Positive Tattle-Tale":** When a learner does particularly well at certain things, be sure to notify their parents of their successes so their parents can continue giving praise or other rewards outside of class time. This will motivate not only the child but also their parents.

Reflection

- Which strategies do you currently use to support motivation? Which strategies would be new for you?
- Consider one of your most motivated learners. What seems to be motivating them? How can you apply those lessons to less motivated learners?

KEEPING YLs FOCUSED

How can I keep my young learner focused during the 25-minute lesson?

Keywords
#attention span #classroom management #competition #early learners (EL) #engagement #focus #gamification

▶ The Situation

It is difficult for one of my learners to stay focused during our 25-minute lessons, especially because she is very young. We have so much content to get through, and I do not want to let the next teacher down because I know they depend on me to get through our lesson objectives. *How can I keep my young learner focused during the 25-minute lesson?*

Analyzing the Situation

- **Early learners** (**ELs**) have short attention spans that gradually increase with age. Young children require constant stimulus, especially when interacting through a digital platform.
- Using good **classroom management** to maintain focus is essential for successful learning; once a learner is no longer mentally engaged in the lesson, their learning potential will dramatically decrease.
- Teachers should take every measure possible to keep their learner engaged, but they should also know how to regain their learner's attention if they lose focus.

Suggested Strategies

New teachers often struggle to keep their learner focused, but it is simpler to maintain focus in a one-to-one or small group learning environment than in a large class. You need to establish certain practices from the beginning and help your learner become familiar with them. Here's how.

- **Change Activities Frequently:** A good rule of thumb is that a child's attention span is roughly equivalent in minutes to their age in years. Thus, if your learner is a four-year-old, markedly change activities at least once every four minutes. If teaching a seven-year-old, change activities at least every seven minutes.
- **Keep Their Attention:** The easiest way to get your learner to focus is never to lose their focus in the first place. This may seem obvious, but you should watch for signs of the child losing focus: wandering eyes, turning their head away, lowering their head slightly. These are all hints that a learner is losing focus.
- **Use Their Name:** If you notice a learner losing focus, consider "name dropping," or intentionally using a learner's name as the subject of a practice sentence. Hearing their own name being used in practice will help maintain your learner's attention.
- **Use Sounds:** Sounds can be used both to retain and to regain focus. Keep something on hand that makes an attention-getting sound, whether this is a triangle instrument you can ring, a hotel check-in desk bell, a slide whistle, etc. You can use this sound every time your learner is expected to

respond. You may even want to establish certain sounds that will regain the learner's focus.

- **Use Your Voice:** In public speaking, many of the most important tools used to keep an audience's attention depend on your use of your voice. Speak slightly louder when you are trying to emphasize something. Pause to let your learner know when to respond (and to allow them time to formulate a response). Speak more quickly as practice continues to increase language exposure and to pass on a sense of urgency to the child. You can also try to speak quietly, which encourages your learner to lean in and focus; then gradually build your volume up to a normal speaking voice.

- **Use Corrective Measures:** Even the best teachers may sometimes lose a learner's focus. In such cases, try to regain it. For

example, start clapping your hands rhythmically and count backward from three. The important thing to remember about corrective measures and refocusing techniques is to be consistent. You want to get to a point where your learner recognizes your cue and its purpose.

Reflection

- What do you do to help your learner regain focus? How does your learner typically respond?
- Which strategies from above do you want to try? How could you tweak your approach to fit the needs of your learner?

CRITICAL PERIODS

How can I better communicate or demonstrate the benefits of starting foreign language learning at different ages?

Keywords
#**ability** #**affective filter** #**age** #**critical period** #**deductive learning**
#**inductive learning**

▶ **The Situation**

I had a parent express concern about starting her child in an English learning program when he was still at preschool age. I have always heard that starting young is helpful, but is this true? Are there real-life examples I can mention that support starting early? *How can I better communicate or demonstrate the benefits of starting foreign language learning at different ages?*

Analyzing the Situation

- Parents, especially Chinese parents, want to be certain they are making the best educational decisions for their child. Parents may be concerned that introducing their child to a second language could interfere with the child learning their first language.
- The **Critical Period Hypothesis** is supported by extensive research and suggests that young children have a natural propensity for language learning. It is believed that this heightened ability to acquire languages starts to diminish after puberty, possibly because this is when the brain reaches full maturation, so the earlier,the better for learners to start learning languages.

Suggested Strategies

You do not need to anticipate that you will start teaching a bunch of toddlers. You do need to make sure you have a thorough understanding of why it is beneficial to start learning English at a young age. Here's how.

- **Understand Childhood Bilingualism:** Children who begin learning a second language prior to the age of six find it easier to learn to pronounce sounds that do not exist in their native language, resulting in more native-like pronunciation versus children who start learning English later. Research also shows that very early learners can easily learn two languages simultaneously, keep the two separated, and not have their native language development impeded or disrupted by the second language.
- **Think About Public School:** Chinese public schools are very competitive. Suppose a child starts learning English prior to entering primary school. In that case, early starters will likely have more confidence in their school English lessons and generally perform better than children who start learning English later.
- **Understand the Affective Filter:** If a child is stressed, shy, or distracted, their affective filter is raised, impeding their ability to take in new language learning. Younger children tend to have a lower affective filter. If they do struggle with their affective filter, it is usually easier for the teacher to lower it

using patience, an encouraging voice, verbal praise, and rewards.

- **Know Different Ways of Learning:** Young children learn language well through **inductive learning** or through exposure to multiple examples of language structures being used and practiced. **Deductive learning** is more commonly used with older children and adults and requires consciously learning and applying grammar rules and a great deal of **rote memorization**. Inductive learning results in greater fluency than deductive learning.

- **Activity Variety and Motivation:** Explain to parents that there are many, many ways to get very young and young learners motivated and practicing English intensively, including playing language-learning games, teaching through language-learning songs, teaching through drama (and dramatic play), construction activities in which children must follow simple instructions, etc. Older learners start to lose interest in such activities.

- **Language is a Skill:** Explain that language is more of a skill than a science. Like almost any skill from sports, to playing an instrument, to dancing, to drawing, starting exposure and practice from an early age is nearly essential to future success.

Reflection

- How has your learner's affective filter presented itself in your lessons?

UNLOCKING SKILLS

How can I help my learner unlock skills they might not realize they have?

Keywords
#learner autonomy #multiple intelligences

▶ The Situation

One of my learners sometimes struggles with tasks. Recently he told me he felt he would never be "good at English." He was feeling very pessimistic about his future as an English speaker and wanted to give up. I see so much potential in him, but I am unsure how to help him discover this potential or see himself as a successful language learner. ***How can I help my learner unlock skills they might not realize they have?***

Analyzing the Situation

- It is very common for learners to feel pessimistic or negative when they struggle to complete a new language task.
- Help your learner recognize their strengths in other areas, According to Dr. Howard Gardner, everyone seems to possess **multiple intelligences** to a greater or lesser degree. Gardner initially included the following intelligences: linguistic, bodily-kinesthetic, spatial, musical, logical-mathematical, intrapersonal, interpersonal, and naturalistic intelligences. It is important to remember that these intelligences are not labels and that learners' intelligences may evolve and adapt over time.
- Knowing your own strengths and weaknesses will help you reach your learner. Be prepared to be outside of your own comfort zone in order to help your learner recognize that they are smarter than they realize!

Suggested Strategies

You do not have to completely overhaul your lesson in order to see what fits for your learner. You do need to pepper in strategies here and there that allow your learner to feel comfortable taking risks and discovering more about their language capabilities. Here's how.

- **Switch It up:** If your learner struggles with the language, you should try to approach the language from a different angle. For example, if your learner struggles with grammar or spelling, try to code the sentences numerically. Set 1 as the letter *a*, 2 as the letter *b*, 3 as the letter *c*, etc. and turn a seemingly simple activity into a brain teaser warmer, transition task, or end of lesson cooler activity.
- **Introduce Multiple Intelligences (MI) Theory:** Your learner may believe that being "smart" comes one-size-fits-all. Help them recognize that there are multiple types of intelligence and that we are all strong in some and weak in others. Raise your learner's understanding by asking them questions to uncover their strengths and praise their abilities. If they struggle to remember a spoken sentence structure, can they sing it, rap it, draw it, create a dance for it, etc.?
- **Understand Your Own Intelligences:** As a language teacher, you likely have a strong linguistic intelligence. Recognize that your ability to describe concepts may not be connecting with your learner's specific intelligence strengths. Uncovering your MI strengths will help you also address other

intelligences outside of your personal set. An additional resource is the **Styles and Strategies Based Instruction (SSBI)** developed by the Center for Advanced Research on Language Acquisition (CARLA).

- **Provide Time:** Let your learner take more time to figure things out and make mistakes. Break tasks down into smaller chunks so that your learner can understand each step. This will allow them several opportunities to feel successful instead of just one.

- **Be Careful with Correction:** If you use too much correction, a learner may shut down. If you use too little correction, the learner may not have enough guidance. Versus the "providing time" strategy above, consider

providing feedback only after completing an activity to encourage risk-taking.

Reflection

- Have you studied a second language? What was your preferred method of study and instruction? What did you struggle with? If you haven't studied a second language, have you ever been faced with other learning tasks where you struggled to understand the concept?

- Consider one of the learners you currently teach. Which strategies above could you apply to improve your learner's recognition of their multiple intelligences?

GIVING UP

How can I support a learner who wants to give up or lacks the confidence to keep trying?

Keywords
#competition #confidence #giving up #grades #meaningful interaction #mistakes #one child policy #praise #stamina

▶ The Situation

One of my learners seems to lack stamina in class. He gives up on an activity so easily, even after only one or two attempts. I try to tell him that making mistakes is OK and that it's just part of the process, but it does not seem to work. Sometimes, he does not have the confidence that he can succeed, so he just relies on me to provide the answers. *How can I support a learner who wants to give up or lacks the confidence to keep trying?*

Analyzing the Situation

- Chinese schools are designed to facilitate a different style of learning—one focused on one-way transmission of knowledge. In this type of system, each learner is responsible for listening, memorizing, and repeating what they have learned. Language learning requires a different mode of learning that may be unfamiliar to many of your learners.
- This may not be your learner's first language class. Previous experiences at school with English or other teachers may impact a learner's feelings of confidence in your class: confidence both in content understanding and in familiarity with the way content is delivered.
- Every learner has an active life outside of their time in class. If a learner is not immediately showing a desire to keep trying at something difficult, it may or may not have anything to do with the content itself. Getting to know your learner can help you better understand the origin of this behavior.

Suggested Strategies

Watching a learner struggle in class can be hard, but you can feel confident to jump in and support your learner and help them find the confidence they need to succeed. Here's how.

- **Make Every Step Matter:** Find ways to make each step in the learning process seem like an accomplishment or "product" of learning.
- **Praise Partial Success:** Find small but meaningful opportunities to praise progress. Do not wait for complete responses to provide positive feedback and encouragement. Sometimes, especially with a younger learner, you may have to help your learner build a response one word or even one sound at a time. You may also have to settle for them just repeating everything you say at first. Good repetition, too, is worthy of praise.
- **Switch It Up:** Do not dwell on an activity that may be overwhelming your learner. Try using props, whiteboards, or other resources to get your learner out of the slides or simply try the next activity and

gauge your learner's response. "Skipping" an activity and returning later in class can sometimes allow your learner to reset, gain confidence, and perform better the second time around.

- **Pre-Teach:** If you know a learner will struggle with a new concept, structure, etc. it may be a good idea to spend a few moments pre-teaching it in small incremental steps before challenging them with the full task. After all, it is not easy to go from one level of a building to the next without using a staircase, is it?

- **Provide Opportunities:** Build in multiple opportunities for a learner to succeed at a task. Instead of getting something right the first time, consider giving your learner three times to get it right. Then the next time you work on a difficult task, you can consider challenging your learner to get it right after two attempts, etc. If this practice becomes part of your regular routine, your learner will feel less stressed to take the time they need or make the mistakes that are required in order to demonstrate progress.

- **Empathize:** It is often helpful to study a new language yourself, whether it is Chinese or another language. This will allow you to empathize with your learner, and you can tell them that you are going through the same experience.

- **Use Examples:** Sometimes, examples speak better than words. Refer to a learner in a similar situation before and how this learner made adjustments, such as learning new words in context, and caught up with the study. Sometimes it is even better to communicate with parents who can help encourage their children to continue learning and praise their children when efforts are made and progress seen.

Reflection

- How do you currently support a learner who seems to give up or struggle with confidence? What is working? What is not?
- Consider learners in different levels. How could you use the suggested strategies to support younger learners and older learners?

STRUGGLING OR UNABLE LEARNERS

How can I better understand why a learner is struggling or unable to participate, and what can I do to help?

Keywords
#behavior #motivation #participation

▶ The Situation

For the last several months, I have had a regular learner who never really participates in class and often seems tired, sick, or upset. Sometimes, he goes through a few activities with me, but then suddenly, he shuts down again. I am not always sure what is going on, but there is always something that seems to make him struggle. I have tried to be upbeat and engaging to keep things moving, but it doesn't seem to work. ***How can I better understand why a learner is struggling or unable to participate, and what can I do to help?***

Analyzing the Situation

- Learners face the same physical and emotional struggles we all do. As children, their ability to control their feelings about these struggles is still developing. Keep this factor in mind when trying to understand and address a learner's behavior.
- Helping a learner find and connect with motivation can also greatly impact their willingness to participate.
- Remember that regardless of these struggles, teachers have a responsibility to keep trying. Parents are putting their trust in you to find a way to reach and teach their child, and learners need to know their teacher can be counted on to encourage them.

Suggested Strategies

You do not need to have all the answers, but some patience and flexibility can go a long way. Give yourself some confidence in interacting with a learner who doubts themselves. Here's how.

- **Adapt Activities:** Find opportunities for a learner to be successful by adapting activities. For example, if a learner is struggling or unable to respond orally during an activity, provide the option of responding nonverbally. Use these responses as opportunities to give praise and rewards and as a bridge to full responses. You can also adapt activities by breaking them down into smaller chunks.
- **Skip It:** Don't be afraid to give the learner an opportunity to skip a problem or activity and return to it later. This gives your learner some control but returns the focus to learning.
- **Get on Their Level:** Be aware of your learner's energy and emotions and adjust your teaching as appropriate. It is not about matching their level; rather, it is about acknowledging that there is an issue by changing up your class. If a learner is very upset and unable to participate, you may want to pull back on some of the normal pressures of feedback and simply focus on production. Learners and parents will appreciate your willingness to adjust.

- **Bring Up Successes:** By reminding a learner of a time when they were successful in the past, you can encourage them to participate in the present. This can be especially effective when a learner is reminded of a similar situation in which they overcame a challenging task.
- **Ask the Parents:** Ask the parents if there may be a reason the child is tired or unmotivated during their lesson. Perhaps their lesson is right after they get home from school, and they need a short break before starting to study again. Perhaps eating a bit of fruit or drinking some juice before starting the lesson would help. Perhaps the parents would be willing to try a couple of other lesson times to see if they work better.

- **Ask the Learner:** If you are working with an older learner at an intermediate level, try asking them directly if they are feeling tired, if they are not motivated, if another time would be better for them, etc. Consider asking them what would make the lessons more engaging for them. Language-learning games? Certain types of content?

Reflection

- How do you currently handle a learner who struggles or is unable to participate? What is working and what is not?
- Reflect on a recent situation with one of your learners. How could you have applied a strategy from above to reengage that learner?

 **UNDERSTANDING CULTURAL DIFFERENCES**

How can I better understand cultural differences in a way that will help me successfully teach, rather than distract, my learner?

Keywords
#cultural differences #culture #exams #feedback #gaokao
#meaningful interaction #parents #parent expectations

▶ **The Situation**

Teaching online is my first experience teaching Chinese learners. I know there are obvious cultural differences beyond just language. I'm nervous about doing something that will offend my learner, being offended by something they say to me, or just trying to anticipate how cultural differences might affect our lessons. *How can I better understand cultural differences in a way that will help me successfully teach, rather than distract, my learner?*

Analyzing the Situation

- It is important to acknowledge any relevant cultural differences that might affect the relationship between you as a teacher and your learner. These differences might not show up right away in your lessons, but they could appear in other places like in feedback.
- You may have heard about Chinese test culture. Chinese parents push their children to work hard and demonstrate results, and they start thinking about the *gaokao*, the test that determines from a very young age which university learners attend. Understand that the Chinese approach to teaching and learning is different from a Western approach.

Suggested Strategies

You do not need to understand every cultural difference between you and your learner, but you should have a game plan to help you navigate any awkwardness. Here's how.

- **Trust the Materials:** Part of the reason online teaching is attractive to teachers is that the materials for lessons are typically developed ahead of time. These materials are usually created by a team of curriculum developers who have extensive experience in the field of EFL; they often include material appropriate for each Chinese learner throughout the levels and across the curriculum so that you do not have to stress about the content.
- **Be Yourself:** If you get to the point where you actually start teaching online, it is because you have done everything right up to that point! This means you should feel confident going into your lessons and injecting your own personality. Part of the reason it can shock your Chinese learner to have a new foreign teacher is that, depending on the city they live in, they are simply not used to seeing foreigners. This does not mean you need to change who you are; it just means you need to mentally prepare yourself for a curious learner.
- **Know Your Learner:** Find out what kinds of clubs your learner is involved in or what hobbies they enjoy. What do they do on the

weekends? Understanding just a bit more about your learner can help you tailor your lessons, where possible, to fit their needs and respond to cultural differences. If you demonstrate a willingness to know more about them, your learner might reciprocate.

- **Personalize Your Lessons:** Once you find out more about your learner, think of ways you can inject a bit of their personality (or your own) into your lessons. This could mean learning the name of a friend or pet and including that name in dialogues or sharing pictures or stories about your own family. Opening up a bit about yourself can help you find common ground rather than just highlighting differences.

- **Be Open-Minded:** You may experience behavior from your learners that surprises you, but before taking offense, always tell yourself that it could very likely just be a "cultural thing." After all, your learner is likely having to do the same thing regarding some of your behaviors that they may not be used to seeing in Chinese culture. In fact, that is one reason Chinese parents want their children to have exposure to foreign teachers. They want them to understand both the language and the culture and be comfortable with both.

- **Go to the Boards:** Your company may provide teacher discussion boards online, and there are a number of public discussion boards available. If you feel offended by something your learner says or does or want to be sure you are not doing something offensive or off-putting, some of the more experienced teachers, Chinese English teachers, or native English-speaking teachers on these discussion boards may have some useful advice. (Of course, a company-run board is usually your best bet to avoid some of the disgruntled "trolls" who may be haunting the public boards!)

- **Check or Ask for Feedback:** You will receive feedback from your students and/or parents. Try to see what goes well and what does not go well and try different things to see the changes in the feedback. Sometimes when you try something new, you can also ask for learners' feedback or notice their reactions. Constant and immediate feedback can always help you make a proper adjustment and improve your teaching.

Reflection

- Which adjectives would you want a learner to use if they described you? How do you present this side of yourself in your lessons?
- Which strategies from above have you tried? How could you tweak your approach?

TEACHER ACCENTS

How can I help parents understand the benefit of a language learner having exposure to various accents?

Keywords
#accent(s) #diversity #L1 #scaffold #teacher talk time (TTT)
#teacher variety

► **The Situation**

My learner has two different teachers that she meets with each week, and we both have very different accents. I'm from the Southern part of the United States, and the other teacher is from the Northeast. My learner's parents have given feedback that they notice the different accents or that we say things slightly differently. I think they are worried about our accents affecting their child's pronunciation. ***How can I help parents understand the benefit of a language learner having exposure to a variety of accents?***

Analyzing the Situation

- One of the main reasons parents are so drawn to online learning is because of the opportunity for their child to have one-to-one interaction with a native or near-native speaker. Parents are eager to help their children gain more exposure and speaking opportunities than they might have at their regular schools.
- Accents are not necessarily the markers of one teacher's English being "better" or more effective than another teacher's. After all, the teachers in this situation are both fluent speakers of English. Both would likely acknowledge that they sound different, but neither should argue that their accent is better or worse (or that their different accents make them better or worse teachers).

Suggested Strategies

You do not need to sound like every other teacher. You should not feel self-conscious or concerned about your accent as long as you connect with your learner and deliver quality lessons. Here's how.

- **Share and Understand Diversity:** A company like VIPKid prides itself on delivering a very large number of classes each month with various teachers. With these numbers and this sort of teacher variety, of course, we are all going to sound and look different and connect with each learner in unique ways. This is just one way big online companies offer opportunities that learners might not otherwise get. Our Chinese learners are diverse, too, and have different accents and dialects. What better way to help your learner feel comfortable in their own skin than demonstrating that we are comfortable in ours?
- **Listen to Yourself:** If you have any fears about how you sound to a learner, go back and watch your videos. There is a difference between accidentally mispronouncing a word and including regional colloquialisms that are not a critical piece of the lesson or are grammatically incorrect, like *pop*

instead of *soda* or *ain't* instead of *isn't*. You might ask yourself how, when, and if it hurts or helps your learner to hear this language. (E.g. *Gonna* is a feature of connected speech, which is a fluency marker in oral English, but that does not necessarily mean it should show up in a formal writing assignment.)

- **Provide Context:** If you are worried about your accent, especially with a new learner, consider using props like a whiteboard you have written on or even words on the screen so that your learner can follow along while you talk. You can think of this as **scaffolding** for your learner to help them more easily understand you. This will also help you raise awareness of your own **teacher talk time** (**TTT**) as well.

- **You Are in the Same Boat:** Tell parents that you also have to understand English speakers with various accents. A person's accent is not relevant as long as those they are communicating with can understand them. After all, language is about communication. As long as effective communication occurs, even if sometimes you have to ask someone to repeat or rephrase something, the language interaction has been successful.

- **Think Ahead:** Suggest to parents that, in the future, it will be helpful for their child to be able to comprehend multiple English accents because they want their child to be successful English communicators as adults. They may sometimes be communicating with a native speaker from Atlanta, sometimes from New York, sometimes from London, Cape Town, Sydney, etc. Likely, they will communicate in English with people who have a Korean accent, Japanese accent, Russian accent, etc.

- **Listening is Not Speaking:** In real life, you cannot control what you hear, but you can control what you say. Exposure to communication with different people and with different accents will help learners adjust better and communicate better. We should not worry about our learners' accents as a result of being exposed to a variety of them. You can tell parents that it is beneficial for learners to understand different accents so learners can have the ability to understand English better in the real world. You can also use the example of the benefits of having Chinese children understand different dialects and accents rather than understanding the Beijing Dialect or Putonghua only, which will disadvantage them in real communication in China when people they communicate with do not speak Putonghua or the Beijing Dialect.

Reflection

- How would you describe your accent? When and how does it appear in your lessons?

09 | SELECTING FOREIGN TEACHERS

How do Chinese parents typically select foreign teachers for their child?

Keywords
#**Chinese parents** #**profile** #**teacher selection**

▶ The Situation

I have been an online teacher for a few weeks. Except for a few learners that I met while teaching their trial classes, I have only been booked a handful of times by new learners. Unfortunately, most parents of these new learners did not choose to rebook me for more sessions. *How do Chinese parents typically select foreign teachers for their child?*

Analyzing the Situation

- When Chinese parents select foreign teachers for their children on a company's platform, the following information is usually available to them:
  - teacher's profile where teachers generally include their pictures, information on teaching experience, education background, and personal interests;
  - other parental feedback on the teacher;
  - the teacher's absence rate; and
  - the number of parents who added the teacher as a favorite.
- In terms of rebooking, it depends on whether parents are satisfied with the lesson, as well as the match of a teacher's available time slots and learner availability.
- Like parents in other countries and regions, Chinese parents also have varied personal preferences in selecting teachers for their children

Suggested Strategies

Although parents have individual preferences in selecting teachers, popular teachers do share some of the commonalities on the profile information they provide online as well as their teaching practices. You can learn from these popular teachers. Here's how.

- **Work on Your Profile:**
  - A profile picture leaves the first impression on parents. Choose a high-resolution image that conveys your friendliness and professionalism as a teacher.
  - If you do not have multiple years of teaching experience, emphasize your previous experience interacting with children, including your own children. Remember, Also, remember ESL/EFL teaching experience (in any capacity) is always a plus to Chinese parents.
  - Emphasize your educational background. Although Chinese parents usually value elite universities, you can point out how your educational background and training areis related to good online teaching. A degree or certificate in teaching and/or language is also a plus.
  - Include personal interests in your profile that demonstrate you are child-friendly, positive, patient, humorous, and have other interests besides language teaching (e.g. music, Chinese culture, sports).

○ Try not to miss your classes. The absence rate information may be available to parents and impact their choices.

• **Be Consistent:** As there are so many teachers available for parents to choose from, be sure to be consistent as you deliver pleasant and successful learning experiences. Chinese parents often favor friendly, patient, and knowledgeable teachers who pay particular attention to the learning outcomes of each lesson. If a learner is able to make noticeable improvements over the course of a lesson, parents feel like their time and money are well-spent. This impacts the feedback that parents leave about your teaching.

• **Be Available:** Sometimes, the reason you are not selected by parents is that your time slots do not match. Try to keep as many times slots open as you can and consider the time difference. The best study times for Chinese learners are from 6 pm to 9 pm on weekdays, and 8 am-9 pm (all day) on weekends.

• **Provide Quality Feedback:** Many teachers rush through writing feedback on learner performance to be sent to parents. Parents very much value quality feedback from teachers, so spend some time on it so they will book future lessons with you. Always start with a greeting, then some positive feedback followed by notes on what you are trying to help their child improve, and finally close with additional positive feedback and/or encouragement. Sometimes it is a good idea to mention that you have made a note to help a learner work on something they were struggling with in future lessons. This will indicate to parents that you are invested in their child's success and will keep helping with those areas if given the opportunity.

• **Smile:** It is universal that your students and their parents will welcome friendly smiles, which can help relax the learners and shorten the distance between the teacher and the learner. Whether you are introverted or extroverted, your smile will send a signal that you are willing, open, friendly, and approachable, especially in online scenarios where personal contact is limited to the screen. Your smiles will go a long way, and your smile will get you rebooked more easily.

• **First Three Minutes:** To leave a deep impression on your learner or impress your learner, your first few minutes are crucial. Since you might not follow a particular learner for a period of time, you should build your rapport with your learner immediately by not only smiling, but also using friendly questions, prompt praise, encouragement, and showing familiarity with what the learner has done previously. This requires the teacher to be familiar with the curriculum, lessons, and challenges a learner might have for each lesson. It requires practice to get the first three.

Reflection

• Take a look at your teacher profile. Is your profile child-friendly, strong, and inviting enough to attract Chinese parents?
• How can you use the strategies above to ensure that parents continue to choose you as their child's teacher?

RELATABLE MATERIAL

How can I make the material relatable for my Chinese young learner?

Keywords
#application #culture #personalize #relatable

▶ The Situation

With some of my learners, I don't feel like they are really connecting well to the topics and material. They will go through what's provided to them by the curriculum, but don't seem to think about how it may relate to anything beyond study within the lesson. *How can I make the material relatable for my Chinese young learner?*

Analyzing the Situation

- It is very common for children who attend Chinese public schools to have huge classes with little personalized attention. This means your learner may tend to focus only on the materials with which they are presented. They simply are not accustomed to considering how material may apply to their own lives and experiences other than the fact that it will likely show up on a test.
- When you teach one-to-one with children on a platform, you have plenty of opportunities to personalize lesson content and make it more relatable to the learner.
- It is always helpful if the teacher knows a bit about Chinese culture and life in general in China. It will be easier for you to personalize lessons if you do as much as you can to learn more about China, keeping in mind there may be variation from one region of the country to another.

Suggested Strategies

Helping your learner connect language learning to their personal lives is one of the most significant benefits of small group or one-to-one lessons. You can help your learner get used to connecting what they are learning in the curriculum to their everyday lives. Here is how.

- **Demonstrate Knowledge Application:** It often helps your learner relate content to their own life if you do so yourself as the teacher. If doing a lesson on foods, tell the learner what your favorite foods are. If talking about pets, speak to the learner about any pets you may have or even show pictures of your pets or describe the type of pet you would like to have.
- **Ask Direct Questions:** Directly ask your learner questions that relate the content to their lives or personalities. Ask them what their favorite foods are. Ask them if they have any pets. Ask what pet they might like to have.
- **Become Familiar:** Of course, it would be great if every teacher could spend a decade or so living in China, but that certainly is not usually the case, nor is it an expectation or requirement to be an online teacher. You can do things like watch documentaries or historically factual movies about China, especially about modern China. However, that is a slow way to learn about a specific topic area such as foods or pets. You may find it helpful to do

a couple of searches online such as "most popular foods in China" or "most common pets in China."

- **Involve Parents:** In messages or feedback to the parents, ask them to have their child apply what they are learning in their English lessons to real life. Parents can encourage their children to name favorite foods or pets using English vocabulary. Depending on the child's English level, they might have their child identify or say things in English outside class (e.g. at restaurants, supermarkets, the bank, at a shopping mall, etc.)

- **Think Ahead:** Look ahead at the topics for future lessons. Ask the parents to have their child attend class with any pictures, toys, etc. that reflect how they have experienced those topics in their lives and share them with you during the appropriate lessons.

- **"What About...?":** Try to go beyond the content you cover, always ask the leaner,

"What about this or that?" to relate the content with their own familiar situations, topics, or something they want to share. It depends on the language proficiency level of the learner. Usually when a learner is at an intermediate or high intermediate level, they can do much better to apply or relate to similar topics or situations that they have experienced, observed, or heard about. This is also a way to extend the content to real circumstances.

Reflection

- How much information do you get about your learner before teaching them the first time?
- Which strategies from above have you tried? How could you tweak your approach?

11 | VALUING MULTILINGUALISM

How can I help my older learner understand the value of multilingualism and English education?

Keywords
#**English as a Lingua Franca** #**globalization** #**interaction** #**study abroad** #**work abroad**

▶ The Situation

My older learners do not seem interested in learning English. I feel like they don't think they will need it outside of school, especially if they do not plan on studying or living abroad. I know that learning another language can help them later in life, but I'm not sure how to bring it up in class. *How can I help my older learner understand the value of multilingualism and English education?*

Analyzing the Situation

- English is used not only within countries where English is an official language but also as a de facto global lingua franca for millions, allowing those who speak less-commonly-learned languages to communicate with each other.
- In recent years, many major US corporations have established a presence in China. Many of the same restaurant brands, retail chains, and technology companies you find in the West can be found in cities across China. Increasingly, Chinese brands have also expanded their presence around the world. The result of this is a growing need for Chinese-English bilingualism.
- Although the share of internet users who speak languages other than English has dramatically increased in recent years, English is still the most common language of web content, with over half of all websites displaying English content.

Suggested Strategies

Helping your older learners maintain an interest in English is just as important as kickstarting the interest of younger learners. Here's how to keep your learner interested and on track.

- **Highlight Local Evidence of English:** Send learners on a mission to collect examples of English and other languages in their city. Advertisements, storefronts, and grocery stores can be great places to start. This awareness of their city's linguistic language can have a positive impact on motivation and encourage interaction.
- **Discuss 21st Century Skills:** The development of critical thinking, communication, collaboration, and creativity can all be supported by multilingualism. Although communication and collaboration may seem to have the most obvious connection to English language learning, the increased exposure that multilingualism enables can similarly support a learner's development of critical thinking and creativity.
- **Explore School and Work Opportunities:** Regardless of a learner's desire to study or work abroad, there are many ways to explore how English can support their academic or career goals. For example, even in China, some exciting and lucrative opportunities are increasingly available only to those who can demonstrate proficiency in English and collaborate with partners worldwide.
- **Encourage Online Learning:** There are

hundreds of learning opportunities and resources available to learners online in addition to those that may be provided by your company, and many of those are presented in English. Help your learner identify online resources related to topics of interest (e.g., technology, design, music) and support them as they become more autonomous in language learning and learning more broadly.

- **Model Multilingualism:** Even minimal efforts to demonstrate your own interest or study of another language can help learners view multilingualism as a new norm. Share a new word or phrase you learned this week or empathize with a learner's challenge by sharing your own language-learning experiences.

- **Connect It to Their Current Interests:** Find out what your learner's current interests are. Chances are many of them can be made more enjoyable if the learner improves their English. They can look up online tips on how to better play their favorite video games.

They can understand the meaning of lyrics of Western pop music. They can watch many Western movies or other media without always depending on subtitles or voice-overs. They can find and understand a lot of information online about almost any hobby they may have.

- **Use Anecdotes or Problems:** Anecdotes or problems can be used to encourage learners' thinking and brainstorming to show how important English is as an international language and how English can help resolve some problems in daily communication. The teacher can use their own anecdotes or stories that have happened in their own lives or those of others to make the activity more meaningful, relevant, and engaging.

Reflection

- Consider one of your current learners. Which of the suggested strategies could you use to support that learner and encourage their study of English?

12 INTERACTING IN ENGLISH

What opportunities does my learner have outside of class to interact in English, and what can I do to prepare them for those interactions?

Keywords
#active listening #authentic practice #fluency #native speaker
#oral English #productive skills #role play

► The Situation

The number of people who speak English in China seems to have grown pretty rapidly in recent years, both in terms of foreigners who live there and Chinese people who speak English. This presents a unique opportunity for our learners to transfer their English from school and online lessons to the outside world. *What opportunities does my learner have outside of class to interact in English, and what can I do to prepare them for those interactions?*

Analyzing the Situation

- Your learner is in a unique position to use an online platform to support their English language learning with an online provider as well as regular school. This real-time, **authentic practice** removes the constraints of a classroom. It provides a valuable opportunity for an online learner to think on their feet and become more confident using language and building **fluency.**
- Your learner does not need to seek out native English speakers or foreigners in their community to practice oral English. There are more and more people in China who have spent time learning English; they present good opportunities to use English for communication.

Suggested Strategies

You do not need to move your classroom outside to prepare your learner for authentic language experiences that might exist outside the view of a webcam. You do need to set your learner up to be confident if they find themselves in a position to speak English to someone besides their teacher or a fellow online learner. Here's how.

- **Venture Out:** Encourage your learner to go outside if they can. If your learner can go outside when class is not in session, make sure they know that they do not need to go looking for English-speaking foreigners to talk to. This could potentially be very intimidating. That being said, it is a good idea to look for places where foreigners might spend time. The people who work in these places might be able to speak some English. If they are also Chinese, they might be better able to relate to your learner's English language learning experience. This could be an accessible way to get valuable practice.
- **Rely on Extensive Reading and Listening:** In the absence of communication in English, your learner should build the habit of extensive reading and listening to maximize exposure to English. Over time, sufficient input and exposure will prepare your learner to communicate when opportunities occur.
- **Role Play:** While in class, be sure to role-play

activities that mimic real-world experiences your learner might have. This can include ordering at a restaurant or coffee shop where you know the staff speaks English or basic small talk and conversation starters.

- **Extend Language:** Try to find opportunities to extend the language your learner uses and interacts with. Beyond just the provided extension opportunities and free talk slides, encourage your learner to add their own sentence after the last one in a reading passage or predict what comes next in a text. After a listening task, ask them what they would like or expect to hear next. Create opportunities for your learner to think beyond what is provided. This will help prepare them for real-world speaking opportunities.

- **Practice Asking Questions:** One of the easiest ways to do this is to engage in a simple role play, where your learner plays the teacher's role. This can be funny if you and your learner really get into character. Questions are great conversation starters for real-world interaction.

- **Teach Others:** One of the best ways to solidify learning a language (or nearly anything) is to teach it to others who may be at a lower level. Try to interest your learner in helping to tutor their less-skilled

friends or classmates, younger children in their community, etc.

- **Get Clubbed!:** Schools and communities all over China have English speaking clubs where people can get together and practice speaking English. Encourage your learner to get involved in any such clubs organized by their school or to go to community "English salons" (English-speaking clubs) with family members.

- **Pen Pals:** Find another learner at the same level or around the same age and practice using English only for communication via email or WeChat. The teacher may help introduce learners to each other if needed. But usually, the teacher can encourage parents to find their pen pals for children.

- **Online Chat Buddies:** This is the same concept, but it can be done more easily via talking online in English. The teacher can suggest digital readings or readers for children to share their thoughts about with each other.

Reflection

- Which strategies from above do you want your learner to try? How can you prepare your learner in class for these experiences outside the class?

13 | PRONUNCIATION ERRORS

How can I accommodate the typical pronunciation errors made by Chinese young learners?

Keywords
#accuracy #Chinese #errors #fluency #intonation #phonological system #pronunciation #rhythm #stress

▶ The Situation

I know that pronunciation is a challenge for many of my learners, but because I teach different levels and lessons, I do not see all of the issues all of the time. This makes it hard for me to keep track, so I am often unprepared when problems arise. I feel like if I knew the most common types of errors, I could help more. *How can I accommodate the typical pronunciation errors made by Chinese young learners?*

Analyzing the Situation

- There are a number of differences between the **phonological** (sound) **systems** of English and Chinese. Some sounds that exist in Chinese do not exist in English and vice-versa. Here are three examples, but there are many more:
  ○ The /θ/ and /ð/ sounds do not occur in Chinese. Your learner may replace them with other consonant sounds like /t/ or /d/ or another approximation of what sounds the most familiar to their **L1** (first language). For example, *think* /θɪŋk/ might become *sink* /sɪŋk/.
  ○ There are more vowel contrasts in English. For example, because the /i/ versus /ɪ/ contrast does not exist, pearners may have difficulty noticing and producing these contrasting sounds in words like *seat* and *sit*.

- Because Chinese words do not often end in final consonants, this can challenge your learner. They may add an extra vowel (often a schwa sound) at the end of the word or drop the consonant entirely. For example, *book* /bʊk/ might sound like "book-uh" /bʊkə/.
- There are also differences in **rhythm**, **stress**, and **intonation**:
  ○ In Chinese, changes to pitch are used to differentiate words, not for sentence intonation. Your learner may struggle to produce sentence-level intonation, including rising and falling intonation.
  ○ Chinese is very monosyllabic, so your learner may have a hard time joining or linking words.

Suggested Strategies

You do not have to be an expert linguist to help your Chinese-speaking learners. You do need to feel prepared to address specific pronunciation issues with confidence. Here's how.

- **Use Examples:** As you review slides before class, notice activities that might involve some of the pronunciation issues mentioned above. For example, if there are vocabulary words with the /θ/ and /ð/ sounds, be prepared to provide some additional visual explanation and support for your learner, including plenty of examples.

- **Get Creative:** Props and gestures can be a great way of supporting noticing of specific sounds or to illustrating intonation. Use arrows to indicate rising and falling intonation or a "slow down" sign to encourage your learner to focus on final consonant clusters.
- **Drill:** Because pronunciation involves a physical process, developing muscle memory is critical. Drilling can be an effective way to train these muscles, but as with everything, remember that balance is key.
- **Minimal Pairs: Minimal pairs** are pairs of English words that differ only in one letter sound. If your learner is struggling with differentiating two English **phonemes** (sounds), you can try to think of lists of these words on your own or find lists online (search for "minimal pairs" or "minimal pairs for English RP"). Once you have a list, share it with your learner, then randomly say one of the words or the other and have your learner mark which word they thought they heard. After a few attempts to distinguish the sounds, switch rolls and see if you can correctly discern which word your learner is saying.
- **Establish Pronunciation Routines:** If you notice that your learner struggles with particular sounds or words, build a routine into your lessons to address these pronunciation issues in a fun and low-stress way. For example, consider some simple tongue twisters or words that share the same tricky sounds that you can practice at the start of every class. Have your learner practice saying these tongue twisters and tricky words alternating between saying them slowly and saying them quickly.
- **Be Persistent:** Learning new sounds that do not exist in one's native language after the age of six can be extremely difficult. It takes a lot of practice over time for a learner to be able to distinguish these sounds. Do not practice too long at once. It is better to practice a little bit each time you meet with the learner and share what you are doing with them with other teachers they may have so they can also practice the sounds with them. Keep in mind that there are 44 sounds in English, not just 26. Learning them all is no easy task.
- **You Try It:** If you do not speak Chinese, take up learning it so you can relate to how hard it is for your learners and discover what works for you. The same techniques may work well for your learners. Even if you do not want to learn the entire language, at least try to learn all the sounds of Chinese and the four tones that are applied to vowels. In that way, you will have a good idea of which sounds a Chinese learner may struggle with in learning English.

Reflection

- What is your current approach to helping learners improve their pronunciation?
- Consider one of your learners who struggles with pronunciation. Which of the suggested strategies could you use to support this learner?

SPEAKING INDEPENDENTLY

How can I help my learner feel more comfortable speaking independently to their foreign teacher?

Keywords
#language production #productive skills #speaking #young learners (YL)

► The Situation

I have a learner who is very capable and consistently keeps up with slides as we go through our lessons; she always does her homework and is prepared. However, when I try to facilitate free talk or extension, she shuts down and does not want to talk to me. It is almost like she is two different learners. *How can I help my learner feel more comfortable speaking independently to their foreign teacher?*

Analyzing the Situation

- Children may be quiet for a number of different reasons on any given day. These reasons may or may not have to do with the class itself.
- If your learner thinks they are going to be judged for mistakes they make while communicating or demonstrating **productive skills**, they may be less likely to speak up.
- Sometimes it can be difficult for a learner to relate to the content (the launching off point for particular language you hope they produce) or to relate to the teacher.

Suggested Strategies

You do not have to know all about the latest trends that Chinese children think are cool or be your learner's best friend. You do need to be creative in your approach in order to get them talking. Here's how.

- **Set Clear Expectations:** Make sure your learner knows that accuracy is not the focus of every task. If your learner is used to doing more accuracy-based tasks and getting feedback in the form of error correction, it may be difficult for them to transition to a task that allows them to speak freely. This may require some more handholding and modeling at first.

- **Build Up to More Language:** If your learner is not used to speaking freely in your lesson or others (online or at their regular school), you need to consider building up free talk incrementally. For a learner with limited language, even a minute or two of free talk can be quite challenging. Use a timer as a motivator; in the first month, encourage your learner to speak uninterrupted for 30 seconds. Then the following month, you could try again for 35 seconds and build up from there.

- **The Big Question Mark:** Make a large, brightly colored card or sign on a stake with nothing on it but a big question mark. Ask your learner a free-talk type of question they should easily know how to answer, then hold up the question mark, lean forward, and cup your ear to indicate you are waiting for them to ask you a question. It could be the same question you just asked them or something different.

- **Use Scaffolds:** Asking a learner to speak freely can be intimidating (the same way a teacher asking you to "write about anything you want" might be intimidating). Consider using sentence frames shown on the screen to help them get started (e.g., My name is _____. My favorite color is _____. My favorite _____ is _____.) You can also include parameters that do not have anything to do with accuracy in the form of prompts and clear instructions. (E.g., Tell me three things you will do this weekend.)

- **Put Yourself Out There:** A learner who is unsure of what to do or what the point of a task is might be hesitant to put themselves out there (especially an older, more self-conscious learner). If you can demonstrate a silly side or speak more freely, you may be able to establish a judgment-free speaking zone in which your learner feels more comfortable participating.

- **Be Patient:** Free talk is incredibly intimidating to learners, especially learners who are only used to structured drill-type practice of the language, which is the case with most Chinese learners. If you're a foreigner, that's more intimidating. Be very patient and take baby steps with your learner. Eventually, they will reach a comfort level and want to nothing in class but free talk!

Reflection

- How do you usually try to structure free talk or extension opportunities with your learner?
- Which strategy from above are you eager to try in your lesson?

15 | GRAMMAR ERRORS

How can I accommodate the typical grammar errors made by Chinese young learners?

Keywords
#accuracy #comprehensible input #errors #fluency #grammar #L1 influence #noticing

▶ The Situation

After teaching online for a while, I am starting to notice that a lot of my learners make similar types of grammatical errors. Even if I can keep track of these errors, I am not always sure how to address them, especially because I know some are influenced by their native language. *How can I accommodate the typical grammar errors made by Chinese young learners?*

Analyzing the Situation

- The grammatical systems of English and Mandarin are very different. Nothing should be considered obvious to your learners.
- Mandarin can also influence your learner's grammar in different ways. For example, certain categories of words, like the articles *a*, *an*, and *the* exist in English but not in Mandarin. The same goes for gendered pronouns like *he*, *she*, *him*, and *her*. This means your learner may commonly leave these articles out or confuse pronouns.
- Certain categories of words are also modified differently. For example, verbs in Mandarin do not get conjugated to express time (e.g., present, past, etc.) as they do in English, meaning errors involving verb endings are also common.

Suggested Strategies

You do not have to speak Chinese or be an expert linguist to support your Chinese young learner. You do have to help your learner build grammar intentionally. Here's how.

- **Be Prepared:** By understanding the typical grammar errors made by your learner, you can have the appropriate props, resources, and explanations at the ready. Think about these as you plan for each lesson.
- **Target the Issue:** Think about specific strategies relevant to the common errors above. For teaching and reinforcing verb tenses, timelines can help your learner visualize the differences. For differences like those related to pronouns, consider other visuals to prompt your learner.
- **Allow for Extra Time:** Your learner may need time when expected to produce new grammatical structures, especially at the sentence level. Even if they are only required to fill in a single missing word in an exercise, your learner may need more time than you might think to consider their choices and make a decision. For example, choices regarding word forms (*difficult* (adj.) versus *difficulty* (n.) can be challenging because Mandarin does not distinguish between word forms in this way.
- **Support Input and Noticing:** Because of the distance between the two languages, **comprehensible input** is critical. Use the stories that are part of the curriculum and other relevant resources to provide enough examples of the target grammar in order for your learner to **notice** how and when to use the new structure.

- **Turn the Table:** Once you have made notes regarding what grammatical mistakes your learner habitually makes and have gotten them to notice their own mistakes, have them play the role of the teacher and you a learner. Do a practice activity in which you intentionally make the mistakes you have been trying to teach your learner to notice and have them correct you for a change. (Kids love to correct their teacher!)

- **Focus on One at a Time:** Do not attempt to address all of these common issues at once. Identify issues that affect your learner's communication and meaning first and address other issues as needed.

- **Know Where the Traps Are:** Do an online search for "most common English mistakes made by Chinese." You will find many lists of common mistakes Chinese English learners make (typically due to **linguistic interference**). If you are familiar with what is likely to be problematic, you can prepare for it in your delivery, lesson time allocation, supplemental materials, etc.

- **Put Yourself in Their Shoes:** If you can make the time, consider studying Chinese. It may come in handy someday, and it will very quickly help you anticipate where your learner is going to struggle.

- **Corrective Feedback:** It is always a good idea not to repeat learners' errors, but to provide the correct sentences by confirmation likes, "Do you mean your dad went to the hospital yesterday to visit your grandma?" when the learner said, "My dad goes to the hospital yesterday to visit my grandma." Such **corrective feedback** can provide **noticing** of errors and an opportunity to repeat the correct one, "Yes, my dad went to the hospital to see my grandma yesterday."

Reflection

- Reflect on your own experiences with other languages. What were some challenging grammatical differences between English and the other language(s) you were learning?

- Watch the recording of a few of your recent lessons. What are the most common learner errors your notice? Which of the suggested strategies could you use in your next lesson to support your learner?

METACOGNITIVE STRATEGIES

How can I help my learner build the metacognitive strategies he/she needs to be successful and strategic in class and beyond?

Keywords
#autonomous #challenges #metacognitive strategies

▶ The Situation

My intermediate learner can be very focused on the content he is learning, but he does not seem very interested in learning about how he is learning or how to strategically deal with challenges; he just wants to know whether something is right or wrong. I want my learner to think more about how he learns and become more autonomous. *How can I help my learner build the metacognitive strategies he needs to be successful and strategic in class and beyond?*

Analyzing the Situation

- Cognitive strategies involve how learners build and apply knowledge (e.g., reading and visualizing content). Metacognitive strategies support cognitive ones and involve how learners prepare for learning, respond to challenges, and appraise their language learning outcomes (e.g., using a dictionary with a challenging text or visualizing success on an exam).
- Metacognitive strategies require learners to know about themselves and their tasks as well as specific strategies.

Suggested Strategies

Your learner is in control of their learning. You can help them build strategies to learn strategically and autonomously. Here's how.

- **Gather Info:** A learner may come to your class with a variety of strategies. Make sure you spend time observing and discussing what strategies have already been taught and how successful they have been for the learner.
- **Support Awareness-Raising:** Help your learner identify moments in which they can apply metacognitive strategies. If a learner dives straight into a task, ask them what might be useful to do first. You might encourage goal setting, planning, or prediction strategies then make sure to connect these strategies to the situation in which they are needed: Before I start reading a challenging task, I should set a goal for this reading (e.g., identify the main idea).
- **Build and Review Task Knowledge:** As your intermediate learner encounters an increasing variety and complexity of tasks, it is important that they understand these tasks'goals and purposes. This knowledge helps your learner apply appropriate strategies for the task at hand. One common behavior you might see is your learner applying the same strategies to every situation they encounter. Instead, especially in high-pressure testing situations, your learner needs to be strategic in how they apply their energy and efforts.
- **Introduce a Range of Strategies:** There are many metacognitive strategies that

should be introduced. Depending on your learner, some of these strategies may seem obvious, but for others, they need to be taught explicitly. Take time before a task to discuss strategies like using appropriate resources, preparing their environment, and planning an approach. During a task, take time to discuss strategies like making and checking guesses, monitoring how they feel (e.g., overwhelmed, confused), and looking for mistakes before moving on. After a task, take time to discuss strategies like comparing their performance to the goals they set before the task, rating their comfort with what they had to do in the task, and looking back on progress your learner has made across this and previous tasks.

- **Metacognitive Strategies Start with Reading:** If a learner can build and use metacognitive strategies in their reading, the learner is said to be able to use it well for other skills such as listening, speaking, and writing. For example, when reading, the teacher can help learners to pay attention to the following metacognitive strategies: making connections, making predictions, making inferences, using context clues, using text features, identifying text structures, using graphic organizers to identify particular types of text information, and raising questions before, while, or after

reading. The teacher can demonstrate these strategies in class and encourage learners to apply them to other readings on their own.

- **Learning Strategies are Individualized:** Try to encourage learners to utilize whatever strategies they find useful to them. The teacher can ask the learner *how* questions. For example, after telling a segment of the story, the teacher asks, "How do you think the story will end?" For another example, a teacher can ask a few questions at the beginning of a lesson before a text is read and discussed in class. Different learners might use different strategies to get the answers, and that individualized learning should be encouraged and supported.

Reflection

- Watch a few of your recorded lessons (if available) with intermediate learners and identify any of the suggested strategies. How do you currently encourage learners to be strategic with their learning?
- Watch a few of your recorded lessons with intermediate learners and identify any challenges your learner was having with the lesson. Which of the suggested strategies could you use to support your learner?

UNDERSTANDING THE ONE-CHILD POLICY

How do family planning policies affect educational experiences in China?

Keywords
#educational experience #family planning #gaokao #little emperor #one child policy

► The Situation

I am a little familiar with the one-child family policy implemented in China, and I have taught many learners who are the single child of their family. As someone who grew up with brothers and sisters, it is sometimes difficult for me to consider what this might be like for Chinese children and, of course, how that experience plays out in a classroom or learning environment. *How do family planning policies affect educational experiences in China?*

Analyzing the Situation

- In January 1979, the Chinese government implemented the "one-child" policy to control the size of its rapidly-growing population. The policy allowed for many exceptions and exemptions. In 2015, the policy began to be formally phased out, and beginning in early 2016, all families were allowed to have two children.
- Though the policy has been phased out, it has still shaped how parents, teachers, and learners view their role in education.

Suggested Strategies

Family planning policies have impacted Chinese children's educational experiences in many ways. While you are not expected to be a Chinese policy expert, you should have an understanding of this part of Chinese culture so you have realistic expectations in your classroom. Here's how.

- **Understand Chinese Parents:** Chinese parents are more willing to invest in their children's education. The single child in the family is often viewed as the one to sustain or improve the family's socioeconomic status. As teachers, we want to ensure that parents trust us to deliver quality education for this investment. This pressure on parents, coupled with the cultural considerations below, means that parents might try to involve themselves too much or inappropriately in lessons.

- **Learn About Chinese Test Culture:** The *gaokao* entrance examination determines which university learners can go to and, to some extent, socioeconomic status later in a learner's life. This means that from a very young age, children have to accept competition because families expect their child to excel at everything. Your learner already faces intense pressure from their parents to succeed in a competitive educational system and later in the job market. As teachers, we want to help our learners achieve great academic success while avoiding imposing unnecessary additional pressure on them.

- **Understand Other Cultural Implications:** As most Chinese families only have one child raised under the shelter of six adults (parents and grandparents on both sides), children are often used to excessive amounts of attention from their parents and grandparents. Therefore, Chinese children are frequently labeled as spoiled "little emperors" in private and public settings. It is important to know what this might look like in a classroom. It might mean that your learner craves immediate feedback on tasks. Your learner may also be too hard on themselves if they make mistakes, or they might take more time to put themselves in a position to make mistakes in the first place.

- **The "Family" Lessons:** Of course, the curriculum you are teaching will have one or more units on family members using family member vocabulary terms. When you teach such lessons, keep in mind that your learner probably does not have any brothers, sisters, aunts, uncles, or cousins. Perhaps use photos of your own family or an imaginary family when teaching this content.

- **Generational Responsibility:** When communicating with parents or even learners, keep in mind that in Chinese culture the younger generation is expected to care for their elders late in life. Your learner's parents are responsible for caring for their parents and grandparents. They expect to depend on their one child (or perhaps two) to care for them and their parents as they grow old. You can easily see why parents are so heavily invested in their child's education, sometimes resulting in that child (and the parents for that matter) being under a great deal of pressure to succeed.

- **Encourage Peer Learning:** Knowing that many families in China have only one child, the teacher should encourage parents to find an English-learning peer or buddy to learn with their child. The teacher can also purposefully assign some tasks that can only be completed by more than one learner. Peer learning or collaborative learning is missing in one-to-one teaching scenarios, but the teacher can make assignments to bridge the gap.

Reflection

- Based on the explanations above, how might these policies account for some of your learner's behavior during class?
- How can an understanding of the Chinese culture pieces discussed above help you successfully adapt the way you teach?

USING REWARDS AND INCENTIVES

How can I appropriately use rewards and incentives during class?

Keywords
#augmented reality #AR #incentive #praise #token #motivate #reward

▶ The Situation

Most of my learners seem to respond very positively to rewards and incentives. I wonder, however, if it is possible to give too many rewards. Also, some learners do not respond as positively to this type of incentive. I wonder how I can motivate these learners during my lessons. *How can I appropriately use rewards and incentives during class?*

Analyzing the Situation

- Most learners, especially younger learners, respond quite well to rewards and incentives. However, some learners, especially older learners, are more motivated by different rewards or incentives.
- If you give out too many rewards, they tend to lose their value to your learner. There are other ways to motivate your learner that are not what you may typically think of when you hear the terms reward or incentive.

Suggested Strategies

It is essential to keep your young learner motivated to learn English. Here's how.

- **Use Verbal Phrase and Gestures:** Don't forget to use a great deal of simple verbal praise such as, "Good," "Great," or "Right." Often teachers combine verbal praise with something like a thumbs-up sign or a virtual high-five. It is unlikely that your learner will tire of pure verbal praise, but some may not be as willing to participate in something like a virtual high five.

- **Use Physical or Digital Rewards:** Your younger learner may enjoy having their teacher give them a star or some other sort of point or reward token. You can do this by using physical stars and so on that you post up on your online classroom background or by using digital stars or **augmented reality (AR)** stickers, either those available on the platform you are using or those available from external vendors.

- **Use Intentionally:** It is possible to overdo it when giving out either physical or digital stars, points, stickers, and so on as they may lose their importance or value. Make sure to reward your learner's especially good performance or behavior, but for many things, simple verbal praise will suffice. Decide ahead of time what you will reward, explain it to your learner, and consistently follow through.

- **Consider Activity Rewards:** Your learner may be more motivated by earning points or tokens toward being able to engage in a favorite activity late in the lesson. If your learner loves songs, they can gain points towards being able to sing along with one of their language learning songs. If they love a particular type of game, promise to play with them if they collect enough points by a certain point in time during the lesson.

- **Use a Token Economy:** A token economy is a system in which learners must collect many small tokens in order to earn a larger reward, such as playing a language-learning game they like. Let the learner name the reward they want, then set a number of digital stars or diamonds, etc. they must receive during the lesson to earn that prize.

- **Raise the Price:** If you are using a token economy, think about your lesson plan. How often will you want to give a token to your learner for positive responses? If you are going to need to give out a lot of tokens, set the token "price" to win the big prize higher.

- **Collude with Parents and Go Long Term:** Consider taking a token economy long term. As a child, did you at home or at school work with siblings or classmates to fill a jar with beans or something to win a pizza party or something? You can work with the learner's parents to do the same thing. If their kid fills a jar with beans, each one representing positive behavior or performance, they will treat the learner to an ice cream, a toy they really want, etc. (We know this sounds difficult to set up, but you can pretty much guarantee that you will be the teacher of choice for every lesson if you can get it arranged!)

- **Go Charitable:** If you take a token economy long term, perhaps the child could choose a charitable act that they are working towards. Fill a jar with beans, and your parents will plant a tree for a reforestation project. Fill a jar with beans, and your parents will donate to an animal rescue organization. Fill a BIG jar with beans and you can adopt an abandoned puppy?

Reflection

- Consider your own learning experiences as a child. What was the best way to motivate you? Why do you feel you were motivated by these things? Can you use your personal experience with motivating factors, perhaps with some modification, to motivate your learner?

- What is your current approach to rewards and incentives?

COMPETITION AND GRADES

How can I support a learner who is primarily focused on competition and grades?

Keywords
#competition #feedback #grades #tests #parental involvement #process #score

▶ The Situation

My learner always seems so concerned with whether they got something right or wrong. It seems like they are more interested in the score or feedback they get than they are in actually learning English. I want them to care more about the process and not worry so much about the end result. *How can I support a learner who is primarily focused on competition and grades?*

Analyzing the Situation

- Chinese schools have traditionally been designed for one-way transmission of knowledge. Assessment of this knowledge has been in the form of high-stakes tests in a very competitive system. While there are increasingly more reforms aimed at different types of learning experiences, your learner will likely be most familiar with one where scores greatly impact their lives.
- Parents instill the importance of performing well as measured by these tests and may regularly monitor their child's performance focusing on these assessments.
- Your learner's experiences with the Chinese language also affect the way they perceive progress and success. Since learning Chinese involves memorizing a large amount of individual characters, learners and parents may transfer this view to English and be concerned with how many words they have learned.

Suggested Strategies

Consider some additional strategies to support your learner. While it should not be the goal to dismiss the value your learner may place on grades, you can be responsive and redirect your learner's attention. Here's how.

- **Don't Ignore:** If you notice a learner who seems more distracted than helped by attention to scores, make an effort to address the issue. Not only will you be supporting other teachers who will have this learner in the future, but you are also helping your learner understand the varying expectations they may encounter in future learning online.
- **Focus on Process:** It is often the case that your learner will not be as interested in the intermediate steps of a task as they are in the final answer. Make the process fun by strategically giving out rewards and making each step seem meaningful and important to the learner.
- **Connect Process and Product:** Make sure you draw connections between your learner's effort in particular parts of the process and the final product. For example, you can highlight all the new words learned in early activities that were used in a final assessment. Praise your learner for their earlier effort. For an older learner, you can discuss how an outline improved the quality of their final project.
- **"Test" Communicative Competence:** Although it is not likely required by the

curriculum you are teaching or the assessment rubrics provided, it may also be helpful for you to follow up on the established test with a brief (albeit very subjective) test of free talk. You can have your learner engage in a short conversation with you and give them a scaled score on free talk (although this, of course, will not become part of their recorded assessment results).

- **Be Sensitive:** Regardless of your own attitude about the importance of competition and grades, understand that these issues are very serious for some families. Keep this in mind as you deliver feedback during class. Remember that high-stakes formal written exams were invented in China in the form of the "imperial examination."
- **Communicate with Parents:** Inform parents (and the child if their English is advanced

enough), that international testing such as the TOEFL exam is becoming more and more sophisticated and requires learners to perform in unpredictable English communication rather than on the types of questions used in traditional written exams. Chinese testing is also becoming more sophisticated and will likely soon be testing just as much on communication ability as on language forms.

Reflection

- How does a current learner respond to getting negative feedback or missing a question? Which of the suggested strategies could help this learner respond more positively?

PARENTS AND EXAMS

How can I better communicate with Chinese parents seemingly obsessed with exams?

Keywords
#**Chinese parents** #**exam** #**gaokao** #**parent teacher communication**
#**testing**

► **The Situation**

I have been an online teacher for a while, and I have noticed that many of my learners' parents pay particular attention to exams. They worry about their children not getting perfect scores on the unit assessments. Some even ask me to teach and help their children improve test scores on their exams at school. *How can I better communicate with Chinese parents seemingly obsessed with exams?*

Analyzing the Situation

- There is a strong testing culture in China. The *gaokao* entrance examination determines which universities a learner can go to, and to some extent, socioeconomic status later in a learner's life. Because of that, Chinese parents care a lot about their children's test scores and may put intense pressure on them to succeed in the competitive educational system.
- Many offline English language training programs in China emphasize enhancing a learner's test scores at school. Chinese parents may have similar expectations of online courses.
- Think about the population of China, which includes more than 1.3 billion people. Considering the sheer number of people, think about why standardized tests are so important. If standardized tests are not used, there is no way to differentiate one learner from another. This means that Chinese people are driven by societal pressures to take testing very seriously down to every point in a test.

Suggested Strategies

As a teacher of Chinese learners, it is important to understand Chinese testing culture. Here's how.

- **Understand Chinese Parents:** Due to the pressure of the *gaokao* Chinese parents can be obsessed with exams. Test scores play a critical role in determining a learner's future life. This pressure on parents, coupled with the one-child policy and cultural considerations, means that parents might try to involve themselves too much or inappropriately in lessons.
- **Help Parents Understand Language Learning:** Parents need to understand that communication is not only the goal, but also the means to learn a new language. Through continuous learning online, a learner can practice native-like pronunciation skills, fluent communication skills in English, and global competence. These skills can make your learner go far beyond what test scores can promise in language learning.
- **The Test is Meant to Measure Communication:** Explain that the tests are meant to measure communication, but that

formal testing cannot measure all aspects of good communication. However, if a learner can communicate well in English, they will perform better on the formal exams than those learners who cannot communicate well.

- **Think Long-Term:** Although what we teach online may not directly link to a learner's exams at school, in the long run, this experience will enhance language proficiency. As a result, there will be an improvement in overall test performance, especially listening, speaking, and reading. The score on a single test (e.g., the unit assessment) does not provide a full picture of a learner's performance. Teachers, parents, and learners need to be patient as learners work to develop full competence in English.
- **Focus on Components:** Components like vocabulary, grammar, and sentence structures are more closely related to what a Chinese learner focuses on at their regular school. You can encourage parents to monitor their learner to review these components of each lesson. Also, encourage your learner to complete their homework because the homework item types often resemble their test items at school.
- **Empathize:** Explain to parents that you understand the importance of learners performing well, especially on the *gaokao*. Explain, however, that while the *gaokao* can help their child get into a good university, it cannot fully assess a learner's communicative competence in the language. **Communicative competence** will be more important once their child

graduates from their university and embarks on their career. Explain that you will do your best to help their child perform well on formal exams as well as to prepare them for true international communication in English.
- **Do What They Want, but Point Out the Strategic Emphasis:** It won't work if you spend time and effort telling parents that exams are not important. In Chinese contexts, exams are important. However, you can explain to parents that in order to do better in exams, a solid foundation in language and constant practice at the beginning levels is more important. We should deemphasize the exams when students are forming their learning habits, accumulating core vocabulary, and formulating grammar rules. Children will be far better off if they do not focus on exams for the beginning stages. Help parents understand that output is not possible without input first, and output is meaningless without interaction, which is the very purpose of learning English.

Reflection

- Have you communicated with parents or Chinese colleagues about exams and test scores? Was your communication appropriate and effective?
- How can an understanding of the Chinese test culture and strategies discussed above help you better communicate with Chinese language-learning colleagues or Chinese parents? How can these strategies help you interact more appropriately with your learner?

PARENTAL INVOLVEMENT

How can I help parents be more appropriately involved outside class (even if they don't speak English)?

Keywords
#expectations #feedback #gaokao #parent #parental involvement

▶ **The Situation**

Some of my learners' parents speak English and will reach out to me about their child, asking how they can help them outside of class. I feel very lucky to be able to communicate with these parents. Still, I have other learners whose parents do not speak English. I want all parents to feel like they can be a part of their child's success as a language learner. *How can I help parents be more appropriately involved outside class (even if they don't speak English)?*

Analyzing the Situation

- You may have heard about Chinese test culture—Chinese parents push their children to work hard and demonstrate results. They start thinking about the **gaokao** (the test that determines which university learners attend) from a very young age.
- Parents might not fully understand how they can help their learner practice English, but they are often quite eager to help. We may as well steer them in the right direction.

Suggested Strategies

You do not need a parent to have perfect English in order for them to help their child be a successful language learner. There are some simple ways parents can promote language learning, regardless of a parent's level of English. While online teachers are not usually encouraged to interact directly with parents, it is important to understand the strategies parents may want to use at home in order to help their learners be more successful with language.

- **Set Aside Time:** One of the most significant ways a parent can help a learner is by carving out time and checking in. Think about particularly difficult courses in your middle or high school experience. Even if a parent or adult figure could not do every single math problem or speak French or Spanish as well as you, that does not mean they did not expect you to study or that they did not check in with you on your progress.
- **Show Interest:** Even if a parent knows little about English, it is incredibly important that they act like they are interested in the fact that their child is learning it and provide space for a child to practice (even if this just means talking at them).
- **Play Teacher:** Children love to role-play. The same way that a learner may love to correct their teachers when they make mistakes, they also like to demonstrate that they know more than their parents or elder family members. Tell parents to pretend they are a learner while their child pretends to be the teacher. Ask the child to teach the parent English. (Using their first language to do this is fine.)
- **Learn Two English Words:** If a parent is

willing to learn the two words, "What's this?" it can open up many opportunities for them to engage with their child. They can ask their child, "What's this?" repeatedly and promote language recall.

- **Go with What You Know:** It is common for Chinese parents to ask how many new English words their child learned as **rote memorization** is familiar to Chinese families. Instead of promoting the idea of a list of new words, try having parents ask for just one new word after each lesson.

- **Ask the Parents:** If you have a successful learner whose parents seem to be involved in their child's language learning journey, find out how these parents help their child. Then see about sharing any good techniques with other parents.

- **Put It in Writing:** Write bullet-pointed or numbered tips in very simple English when you send suggestions to parents. If your English is clear and straightforward, parents can use an electronic translation tool to translate and at least roughly understand your tips on how they can help at home.

Reflection

- Which strategy from above are you eager to suggest to your learner's parents?

22 | PARENTAL INTERFERENCE

How can I navigate a class if a parent is too involved and impeding a learner from participating?

Keywords
#affective filter #disrupt #interference #involvement #parent #scaffold

▶ The Situation

I have a fairly low-level learner whose mom always hovers over or near him during lessons. She even provides him answers or responses (some of which are incorrect). If left alone, I feel my learner can do what is suspected, possibly with a bit of support and coaxing. I don't believe it does him any good to have his mom constantly telling him how to respond. ***How can I navigate a class if a parent is too involved and impeding a learner from participating?***

Analyzing the Situation

- Most Chinese parents will do anything they can to help their child learn English, even if their actions are actually disruptive to the learning process.
- Parents mean well, but they may need some guidance as to how best to support their child's learning process.
- Sometimes teaching English as a foreign language is almost as much about educating parents (in a constructive, non-critical way) as it is about educating the child.

Suggested Strategies

It is very beneficial to have parents who are invested in their child's language education; sometimes, they just need help in knowing the best way to do so. While online teachers are not often encouraged to interact directly with parents, it is important to understand the strategies parents may use to leverage their enthusiasm for their child's learning in more positive and constructive ways.

- **Address Parent and Child Separately:** If you are already in a class and encounter a parent telling your learner what to say, treat them both like learners and encourage the parent to provide examples. If talking about hobbies, first ask, "Mom, what are your hobbies?" Then ask the learner, "[Name], what are your hobbies?" and maybe even look towards Mom and put your fingers across your lips to encourage her to let the child try to answer on his or her own. In this way, the parent has an active role in the lesson. However, the learner must still produce the required language individually.

- **Use Scaffolds:** If the learner struggles to answer a question, you can provide **scaffolding** (non-intrusive hints) to help them produce a sentence of their own. This will help show the parent how the child can produce the expected language without being told exactly how to answer. For example, if you want your learner to speak about hobbies, consider providing a word bank for them to choose from instead of assuming they can come up with hobbies off the top of their head or recall the hobbies you have already discussed. Your learner may not actually need to use the word bank, but the beauty of scaffolding is that it is there just in case your learner needs it.

- **Follow Up:** Communicate with parents after the lesson to explain why scaffolding is superior to just telling a learner what to say. Explain the concept, which was first introduced by Russian educational researcher Lev Vygotsky in 1934, and how it works. It is much like putting training wheels on a child's bicycle, then slowly rasing them in increments as the child learns to ride.

- **Encourage Appropriate Engagement:** Encourage parents to step back and maybe even just listen in from a neighboring room. In messages to the parents or with the help of a Chinese-speaking colleague, explain that having a parent actively involved in the lesson can increase a learner's stress levels, thus raising their **affective filter** (which inhibits language acquisition).

- **Talk with Parents:** You can ask the learner's parents to sit aside and observe rather than sit together and learn. Parents can play a very important role as long as they do not interfere with the teacher. They can suggest, inform, or talk with the teacher before or after class or in writing if they wish. Usually those parents who can communicate in English will interfere with the class more than those who do not have adequate proficiency in English communication. The teacher should play the teacher's role unless parents are invited to role-play with their child.

- **Set Up Rules with Parents:** The teacher can proactively make clear to the parents what the basic rules for parent involvement are to avoid future conflicts. The teacher can also be flexible and only set the rules when such rules are necessary. In brief, you are the teacher, and you have the say regarding what facilitates learning in your lessons.

Reflection

- Which strategy from above are you eager to suggest to your learner's parents?

RESPONDING TO INAPPROPRIATE LANGUAGE

How should I respond when my learner brings up inappropriate language or asks me to teach words that are questionable?

Keywords
#attention-seeking behavior #disruption #classroom management

▶ **The Situation**

I have had the occasional learner who wants to share some colorful English or offensive language or gestures with me. I have also had learners who want me to teach them language I do not feel comfortable with (or that they probably should not know in English). *How should I respond when my learner brings up inappropriate language or asks me to teach words that are questionable?*

Analyzing the Situation

- A learner who purposefully demonstrates these attention-seeking behaviors might not seem any different from a learner who is well-intentioned. Sometimes learners try to get a rise out of their teachers. Still, they do not understand how offensive their language or gestures might actually be. Other times learners are just eager to show off language or gestures they learned outside of your class, so, as teachers, we have to be careful about interpreting intentions.

Suggested Strategies

You don't need to be afraid that your learner is out to get you, and you certainly should not lose your cool or blow up in class. You do need to have backup plans to help you get through a potentially awkward lesson. Here are some ideas.

- **Reach Out for Support:** If your learner consistently uses offensive or threatening language, reach out to a Chinese-speaking colleague, whose job it may be to act as a liaison in what can be seen as particularly tricky or difficult situations. If you find yourself in a particularly distressing moment, be sure to reach out to your company for support.

- **Tell Them It's Wrong:** It is up to you, in the moment, to decide if you want to use one of these strategies OR if you want to simply say, "That's a bad word in English that we don't want to use in our class." Not every learner intentionally wants to distress their teacher (sometimes a learner gets excited because they hear something at school and want to share it with you!) You have an opportunity to help them avoid future awkward situations by making sure they know when language or gestures are inappropriate.

- **Take Away a Reward or Token:** If you have been giving the learner digital rewards or tokens in a token economy system, take a reward or token away each time the learner uses the word. You could also give "negative" tokens; then at the end of the lesson, each negative token removes one of their positive tokens.

- **Stay Calm and Move On:** If a learner is using

language or gestures intentionally because they want to distress or get a rise out of you, do not let them have the satisfaction of seeing you sweat. Move on quickly to the next slide or change the topic.

- **Play Dumb or Ignore:** If a learner has a specific word that they want to know or use in English, and you don't feel comfortable responding (e.g., a curse or slang word or something else offensive), tell them you don't know the word or phrase and move on (see above).

- **Refocus:** If a learner is relentless with their choice of colorful language or inappropriate gestures, consider revisiting a song or video that draws their attention back to the screen (and any appropriate physical modeling or gestures) and away from you in an effort to get them refocused.

- **Communicate with Parents:** Let the parents know that their child used an offensive

English word in class and how you handled it. Explain that kids often do that when learning a new language, either out of curiosity or trying to rile the teacher, but in any case, it shouldn't be encouraged (or allowed). Don't make a big deal out of it with parents; a child intentionally trying to agitate a teacher is a very big deal in Chinese culture.

Reflection

- Consider a learner who has used inappropriate language in class. Which of the suggested strategies would you use next time to approach the situation? If you have not had an experience like this yet, what might make you feel uncomfortable in class? Which of these strategies might be your new go-to in that situation?

References

Behavioral Intervention Guide. (2013). Retrieved from https://www.vtnea.org/uploads/files/Behavior%20Intervention%20Guide-9.13.pdf

Chen, J. F., Warden, C. A., & Chang, H. T. (2005). Motivators that do not motivate: The case of Chinese EFL learners and the influence of culture on motivation. *TESOL Quarterly, 39*(4), 609-633. doi: 10.2307/3588524

Cohen, A. D., & Dörnyei, Z. (2002). Focus on the language learner: Motivation, styles, and strategies. In N. Schmitt (Ed.), *An introduction to applied linguistics* (pp. 170-190). London: Arnold.

Dewey, J. (1938). Experience and education. New York: Kappa Delta Pi.

HE, D. (2017), The use of English in the professional world in China. *World Englishes, 36*: 571-590. doi:10.1111/weng.12284

Hoffmann, K. F., Huff, J. D., Patterson, A. S., & Nietfeld, J. L. (2009). Elementary teachers' use and perception of rewards in the classroom. *Teaching and Teacher Education, 25*(6), 843-849.

Hurford, J. (1991). The evolution of the critical period for language acquisition. *Cognition, 40,* 159-201.

Hymes, D. (1964) *Language and culture in society.* New York: Harper and Row.

Kosier, K. (2002). *Discipline checklist: Advice from 60 successful teachers.* Annapolis Junction. MD: National Education Association of the United States.

Iwashita, N. (2018). Grammar and language proficiency. In J. I. Liontas, T. International Association, & M. DelliCarpini (Eds.), *The TESOL encyclopedia of English language teaching.* doi:10.1002/9781118784235.eelt0069

Lang, G. (2007). Speaking up, regardless of your accent - At Home Abroad - International Herald

Tribune. Retrieved from https://www.nytimes.com/2007/01/26/style/26iht-avoice.4360664.html

Lin, X. (2019). "Purchasing hope": the consumption of children's education in urban China. *The Journal of Chinese Sociology,* 2-26. Retrieved from https://journalofchinesesociology.springeropen.com/articles/10.1186/s40711-019-0099-8

Luo, M. N., & Huang, M. (2019). ESL teachers' multiple intelligences and teaching strategies: Is there a linkage? *TESOL.* doi: 10.1002/tesj.379

Marlina, R., & Xu, Z. (2018). English as a Lingua Franca. In J. I. Liontas, T. International Association, & M. DelliCarpini (Eds.), *The TESOL encyclopedia of English language teaching.* doi:10.1002/9781118784235.eelt0667

Montessori, M. (1964). *The montessori method* (A. E. George, Trans.). New York: Schocken Books.

National Education Association. (2012). Preparing 21st century students for a global society: An educator's guide to the "Four Cs". Retrieved from: http://www.nea.org/assets/docs/A-Guide-to-Four-Cs.pdf

OECD. (2016). Education in China: A snapshot. Retrieved from https://www.oecd.org/china/Education-in-China-a-snapshot.pdf

Oxford, R. L. (2001). Language learning styles and strategies. In M. Celce-Murcia (Ed.), *Teaching English as a second or foreign language* (3rd ed.) (pp. 359-366). Boston: Heinle & Heinle/Thompson International.

Oxford, R. L. (2016). *Teaching and researching language learning strategies: Self-regulation in context.* London: Routledge.

Prabhu, N. S. (1987). Second language pedagogy. New York, Toronto: Oxford University Press.

Practising speaking outside the classroom. Retrieved from https://www.cambridgeenglish.org/

learning-english/parents-and-children/information-for-parents/tips-and-advice/practising-speaking-outside-the-classroom/

Rogers, J. (2018). Teaching/developing vocabulary through metacognition. In J. I. Liontas, T. International Association, & M. DelliCarpini (Eds.), *The TESOL encyclopedia of English language teaching.* doi:10.1002/9781118784235.eelt0737

Rublik, N. (2018). Chinese cultural beliefs: Implications for the Chinese learner of English. *Sino-US English Teaching, 15*(4), 173-184. doi: 10.17265/1539-8072/2018.04.001

Schütz, R. (2000). Vygotsky and language acquisition. In *English Made in Brazil.* Retrieved from http://www.sk.com.br/sk-vygot. html

Smith, B. (2001). Learner English: A teacher's guide to interference and other problems. Cambridge, UK: Cambridge University Press.

Social and Affective Strategies. 2012-2013. UGC ICOSA Project, Hong Kong. Retrieved from http://elss.elc.cityu.edu.hk/ELSS/Resource/Social%20and%20Affective%20Strategies/

Swan, M., & Smith, B. (1987). Learner English: A teacher's guide to interference and other problems. Cambridge UK: Cambridge University Press.

Thakkar, D. (2011). Social and cultural contexts of chinese learners: Teaching strategies for American educators. *Multicultural Education, 19*(1), 51-54.

Tyner, A. (2017). Can test-obsessed China change? A look at three paths for Chinese education reform. Retrieved from: https://thediplomat.com/2017/09/can-test-obsessed-china-change/

Usage statistics of content languages for websites. (2020). Retrieved from: https://w3techs.com/technologies/overview/content_language

Vigil, N. A., & Oller, J. (1976). Rule

fossilization: A tentative model. *Language Learning, 26*(2), 281-295.

Wen, X. H. (2008). Motivation and language learning with students of Chinese. *Foreign Language*

Annals. doi: 10.1111/j.1944-9720.1997. tb02345.x

Zhang, L. J., & Zhang, D. (2018). Metacognition in TESOL: Theory and practice. In J. I. Liontas,

T. International Association, & M. DelliCarpini (Eds.), *The TESOL encyclopedia of English language teaching.* doi:10.1002/9781118784235.eelt0803

► Epilogue

As we have seen, teachers have many exceptionally good questions about how best to teach English to young learners online, especially when it comes to teaching children in China through this rather new medium of instruction. We, as authors of this book who work in various capacities for a very large online English teaching company, have unique access to questions asked by the Company's nearly 100,000 online English teachers. We also each have decades of experience in teaching English as a foreign language in traditional classrooms and now in online classrooms. It has always been a bit of a rollercoaster ride. Here, we have done our very best to identify the most commonly-asked teacher questions and make informed suggestions as to how online teachers can tackle some of the challenges beset by online, face-to-face language education.

We started by addressing in Part 1 questions that relate to concepts which have been heavily studied by researchers in the field of applied linguistics. This research field has a history of well over 100 years. We now know that some of what has been suggested in the past does not work well towards teaching English as a foreign language to children (especially in modern times). Yet, in each period of historical research, there usually remains something valuable that can still be used very effectively while teaching certain aspects of the language or in certain situations. Thus, we encourage our readers not to "throw the baby out with the bathwater" as they learn about these historical theories and approaches to language education (and general education, for that matter). Rather, know those theories and approaches and glean from them the good ideas that work for you and your learners in general or in specific types of learning situations. Use those "diamonds in the rough" that have survived the filtration of twists and turns of theory applied through practice to create what we and other practitioners in the field now refer to as Principled Eclecticism.

Part II discusses how more specific classroom delivery methods could be used to answer teacher questions. Many of these methods come rather directly from those proven in brick-and-mortar classrooms but needed to be adapted to apply more directly to online teaching situations. Without that sort of adaptation, it can feel like the bottom has just dropped out of what you knew would work in your physical classrooms. Other methods suggested are rather new due to certain capabilities enabled by modern online technologies. As the field continues to climb this hill, we are sure to see more and more new methods largely made feasible by modern technology.

In Part III, we focused on the medium of online instruction and how to work with that medium. In many cases, traditional techniques or strategies have simply been borrowed and adapted. That said, we must make sure our technology allows us to deliver a good online lesson, that our online classroom backgrounds are well-designed for learning, and that we have easy access to physical tools and props to make sure our lessons are as productive as possible. We also have new tools we can use, including easy access to videos, songs, digital reward systems, learning management systems, and even artificial intelligence (AI) and augmented reality (AR) tools. These are new and exciting elements we can leverage towards better helping our young learners to acquire the language.

Part IV is tailored to teaching children of Chinese culture, but you can be sure that children in any location on Earth are influenced by certain cultural expectations and that their native language may affect the English learning process. **Extrinsic motivations** for learners tend to be rather universal, but their **intrinsic motivations** (and those of their parents) are often specific to their culture. Different children may have different intrinsic motivations. Their parents may have different motivations. As a teacher, you need to try to understand such cultural differences, accept them, and possibly explain why you are using certain methods and techniques your learners and their parents may not be used to. This can help them to become comfortable with the process.

As a final note, we hope you will follow in our footsteps because the field is now changing and progressing incredibly quickly. Each of us has actively evolved with and leveraged the kind of technology use we have begun to see today. In fact, we have pushed for it. Those who were unwilling to embrace new ideas and technologies have been left in the dust. Together, we won't always get it right, but that is all part of the process of advancing the field. Just as your learners learn best by trying new things, taking risks, and learning from those risks, errors, and mistakes, so should we. Make sure you clearly understand your current approach when making future-minded changes. When you hear about new ideas, always think about how to apply them to your lessons. The children's English teaching field is rapidly changing, and you need to change with it, contribute to the advancement of the field, and see the benefits of those changes (if not for you, then for the children.)

This is an incredibly exciting time in the children's English learning field. We are still riding roller-coasters, but this ride is going to be beyond those we have experienced before. Thus, as they announce when you seat yourself in a very modern roller coaster, "Sit down firmly in your seat. Place your valuable possessions in the zipper pocket on the back of the seat in front of you. Lower your safety bar down firmly against your shoulders and waste, and hold on for the ride!"

"The greatest advantage of Teaching English Online to Young Learners: 100 FAQs is its accessible format. Your questions can direct your reading and increase your competence to teach English online to young learners."

Neil J Anderson. Ph.D.
Professor, Brigham Young University–Hawaii
past President, TESOL International

"This book addresses questions arising from online foreign language instruction to young learners, a timely contribution to understanding a new and fast-growing mode of delivery of foreign language instruction. Grounded in observations of online lessons, the book strives to bring relevant second language acquisition research to bear on practical issues that teachers of young learners have encountered, thereby offering a refreshing synergy of theory and practice."

ZhaoHong Han, Ph.D.
Professor of Applied Linguistics; Chair, Department of Arts and Humanities; Director, Center for International Foreign Language Teacher Education (CIFLTE); Teachers College, Columbia University

"Lying at the heart of student success in learning English online is our teachers who have to quickly adapt to an online teaching mode and transfer their skills to enhance digital learning. This book by Professor Liu and his team, grounded in the field work and close observations and interviews with teachers teaching English to young learners online could not be more timely to empower them with analyses of problems and challenges and practical recommendations. This should be a desk copy for all online English teachers."

Cindy Mi
CEO and Founder, VIPKid International

"Live online language learning is exploding. Children are quick to pick up a language, and technology now affords them the chance to learn anywhere in the world with a qualified teacher. Teaching English Online to Young Learners: 100 FAQs by Dr. Jun Liu and his team of experts, is a timely and accessible read for new online language teachers. Based on years of research in

applied linguistics, this book empowers teachers to analyze their own teaching situations, engage students, and act on a specific set of strategies to best help their students to learn English. The future is online, and this book adds remarkable value to the teacher's repertoire for success."

Suzanne Panferov Reese, Ph.D.
Chair and Professor, Second Language Acquisition and Teaching; University of Arizona
past President, TESOL International

"Teaching all subjects of a typical school curricula online has become the norm in today's world, but perhaps none are more challenging to teach long-distance than language, literacy and culture. Based on over 100 case study analyses, Teaching English Online to Young Learners focuses on keeping young learners focused and motivated throughout the learning process and ultimately becoming confident speakers of the language. This book is an indispensable resource to language educators, school administrators, parents, and other stakeholders interested in supporting young learners to become plurilingual and successfully carrying out their academic and career goals in the world marketplace."

Duarte M. Silva, Ed.D.
Executive Director Emeritus,California World Language Project, Stanford University Graduate School of Education

"As an online ESL teacher, I am truly excited about this new book by Professor Jun Liu! Having been honored to host Professor Liu in my own classroom, I have seen firsthand how deeply he cares about and values both the ESL teacher and the online language learner. In his book, Teaching English Online for Young Learners: 100 FAQs, Professor Liu brilliantly identifies hurdles faced by teachers and students alike, analyzes each situation individually, and aptly suggests strategies for overcoming obstacles while maximizing learning in the online classroom. The indexed key word search makes this book incredibly user-friendly, and it is with great enthusiasm that I recommend all of my online ESL teacher colleagues procure a copy."

Amy White
VIPKid Teacher